Relearning History

A Question-Driven Approach to the Study of the Past

Joe Regenbogen

Vernon Series in Education

Copyright © 2018 Vernon Press, an imprint of Vernon Art and Science Inc, on behalf of the author.

All rights reserved. No part of this publication may be reproduced, stored in a retrieval system, or transmitted in any form or by any means, electronic, mechanical, photocopying, recording, or otherwise, without the prior permission of Vernon Art and Science Inc.

www.vernonpress.com

In the Americas:
Vernon Press
1000 N West Street,
Suite 1200, Wilmington,
Delaware 19801
United States

In the rest of the world:
Vernon Press
C/Sancti Espiritu 17,
Malaga, 29006
Spain

Vernon Series in Education

Library of Congress Control Number: 2017950244

ISBN: 978-1-62273-254-8

Product and company names mentioned in this work are the trademarks of their respective owners. While every care has been taken in preparing this work, neither the authors nor Vernon Art and Science Inc. may be held responsible for any loss or damage caused or alleged to be caused directly or indirectly by the information contained in it.

Cover design by Vernon Press, using elements selected by freepik.

*To Jack and Julie,
a father has never been so proud...*

Table of Contents

"The most effective way to destroy people is to deny and obliterate their own understanding of their history."

George Orwell

Preface — vii

Introduction

| Chapter 1 | Why do many people need to relearn history? | 1 |

Politics and Government

Chapter 2	Why is the Constitution important and why is it so difficult to change?	13
Chapter 3	Why does the two-party system dominate American politics?	23
Chapter 4	Why is there such diversity in the way nations govern themselves?	37

Business and Economics

Chapter 5	Why is wealth so unevenly distributed?	51
Chapter 6	Why has the United States become such a global economic force?	67
Chapter 7	Why is capitalism increasingly prevalent around the world?	79

People and Demographics

Chapter 8	Why has the world population exploded and why is it so unevenly distributed?	91
Chapter 9	Why does race and gender still play such a large role in modern society?	105
Chapter 10	Why has the prison population in the United States grown so large?	121

Culture and Religion

Chapter 11 Why has the role of popular culture
            expanded in modern society?   137

Chapter 12 Why is organized religion at the center of so
            many world conflicts?   149

War and Peace

Chapter 13 Why has there never been a World War
            Three?   165

Chapter 14 Why has terrorism become increasingly
            prevalent in the modern world?   179

Science and Technology

Chapter 15 Why has the pace of technological change
            grown so fast in recent times?   193

Chapter 16 Why does industrial progress threaten the
            future of our planet?   205

Conclusion   221

Acknowledgements   223

Index   225

Preface

The author and his little sister Debby play in a sandbox, 1959.
Courtesy of Al Regenbogen (PD-self)

My sister, Debby, was born on New Year's Eve. I was born ten months earlier on March 3 of the same year. It might have been easier on my mom if she had just carried twins since the entire experience could have concluded in nine months. Be that as it may, Debby is my only sibling and except for the typical high school rivalry years, we have always been close.

There was a period during my sister's adolescence when she talked about finishing high school and then attending a junior college to develop some sort of trade. Her aspirations changed, however, after she moved to a new city during her senior year. A biology teacher saw Debby's intellectual potential and provided the encouragement that only great teachers can bestow. Debby enrolled in Illinois State University the following year, and nine years later, she was walking across the stage to accept her diploma for a doctoral degree in social work. Presently, my sister is a valued faculty member in the school of social work at Case Western Reserve University. She has taught research courses, organized annual trips to other countries as the director of international education and served on academic committees. In addition, she has raised three bright children who have pursued impressive academic careers of their own. As her big brother, I could not be more proud.

However, Debby would be the first to admit that there is something missing in her remarkable academic record. Like so many other adults I have met, she learned very little history in school. Part of the problem emanates from lackluster history classes built around boring textbooks. Of course, if her high school teachers could be consulted on the matter, they might say that much of the problem resided in Debby's lack of interest or motivation.

My sister's story reminds me of the many students who have walked through the doors of my own classroom on the first day of school asking why they needed to study history. *"I plan to be an accountant, why do I need to know about the past?" "After college, I plan to work for my dad, and one day, I will take over his business. Why do I need to learn American history?"* I usually responded that school was intended to prepare them for life, not just a career. Part of that preparation involved molding them to be effective citizens in a democratic society. Often this rationale fell on deaf teenage ears, and only after teaching an engaging class that defied most of their expectations did many come around to appreciate the value of learning history.

In Debby's case, she managed to succeed in life despite her mediocre social studies education. Yet she would openly admit that she has not always been a model citizen when it comes to her participation in our democratic processes. Even now, if a political issue comes up in conversation, she often prefers to change the subject or leave the room.

Therefore, it should probably not come as a surprise that my sister was the individual who suggested the focus of this book. In one of our Sunday afternoon telephone conversations (Debby lives in Cleveland while I make my home in St. Louis), she asked an intriguing question: how many adults are like herself? People who may be well educated, at least in a particular career field, but who are largely ignorant of the past when it comes to understanding the world today. When she raised the question, I immediately thought of other family members, friends or even the person who cuts my hair. Time after time, when I have told people that I teach history for a living, I hear the same sentiment. *"Oh, I hated history in school, it was so boring. Though I wish I could have a better understanding of it now."*

As I reflected on Debby's question, I realized she was right. There are probably millions of educated adults who struggle to make sense of the current headlines. The planet we live on has become an enormously complicated place, and without a solid understanding of the past, making sense of the present or future is an insurmountable undertaking. I have always loved teaching history, and now my sister was presenting me with a new challenge.

When I was a child, my parents gave Debby and myself an astonishing amount of freedom every summer. We could play with our friends, ride our bikes all over the city or relax in a backyard swimming pool. The only requirement was that we had to read for an hour every day. Within reasonable limits, we could choose whatever we wanted to read, and I always chose history books. Ever since, I have had a burning desire to learn about the past, and for the last 37 years, this has manifested itself in a career where I could pursue my passion for teaching history to others.

Properly taught, history is a collection of amazing stories that could rival the richest literature or fiction. It is also a necessary component for building effective citizenship skills that will enable our democracy to flourish and endure. Students should ideally study their history while in school. For those people like Debby, however, who did not, it is never too late to relearn history. Thank you, little sister, for suggesting and inspiring the writing of this book.

manifested itself in a career where I could pursue my passion for teaching history to others.

Properly taught, history is a collection of amazing stories that could rival the richest literature or fiction. It is also a necessary component for building effective citizenship skills that will enable our democracy to flourish and endure. Students should ideally study their history while in school. For those people like Debby, however, who did not, it is never too late to relearn history. Thank you, little sister, for suggesting and inspiring the writing of this book.

Chapter 1

Introduction:
Why do many people need to relearn history?

David Cameron
(CC-BY-2.0)
https://www.flickr.com/photos/lensicle/16318316691/

"I think it's important in life to speak as it is, and the fact is that we are a very effective partner of the U.S., but we are the junior partner. We were the junior partner in 1940 when we were fighting the Nazis."

Prime Minister David Cameron, July 21, 2010

When Mr. Cameron spoke these words during an interview with Sky News on his first visit to the United States as Prime Minister, he incited a furious backlash. Most Americans did not pay much attention, but in the United Kingdom, he was widely accused of forgetting the sacrifices made in 1940 by those who fought in the Battle of Britain, the heroes of Dunkirk and the Londoners bombed in the Blitz. In fact, Britain stood alone in 1940 against the behemoth of Nazi Germany. America did not actually enter the war until December of 1941 and only after the Japanese bombing of Pearl Harbor. In the early years of the war, Britain had an army of 2.4 million men in the field when the Americans had just 240,000, one tenth of the fighting force. It was not until 1944, one year before the war's conclusion, that the Americans had more men on the ground than the UK. By the end of the war, Britain had lost a total of 449,800 men compared with 418,500 Americans. One former veteran, Special Air Service hero Andy McNab said, *"It's very important to get this history right because people are still living who fought in 1940. There are still survivors of Dunkirk and fighter pilots from the Battle of Britain. For them, it is very, very important to recognize the role they played. This is living history."*

Cameron's blunder is just one of many examples when an elected politician has allowed ignorance of the past to hurt feelings and generate controversy. Prime Minister David Cameron arguably made a simple gaffe of historical details and did not intend to insult British veterans. After stating the insulting remark, Downing Street immediately claimed that Cameron had meant to refer to the 1940s in general. In addition, he issued an ambiguous apology upon his return to Great Britain. In contrast, the situation was far more serious in the case of former U.S. President George W. Bush.

On May 1, 2003, President Bush stood on the deck of the aircraft carrier, the USS *Abraham Lincoln*, and proclaimed that America's military mission in Iraq had been accomplished. He stated that because of the U.S. military, *"the tyrant has fallen and Iraq is free."* He went on to say, *"in the images of fallen statues we have witnessed the arrival of a new era,"* and that *"our coalition will stay until our work is done and then we will leave and we will leave behind a free Iraq."* The reality is that 13 years after President Bush made this speech, the United States still had 5,000 troops stationed in Iraq. They are there because much of the country is still plagued by violence, instability and chaos. By 2016, Iraq was effectively divided. The government in Baghdad controlled the central and southern parts, the Kurdistan Regional Government governed the northwest and the Islamic State of Iraq and Syria (ISIS) occupied the western part. This hardly constitutes the *"new era"* promised by President Bush.

American involvement in Iraq was originally justified out of concerns that Saddam Hussein, Iraq's dictator, had supported terrorism and was building weapons of mass destruction. The available evidence has never proved these assertions. More important, the removal of Saddam Hussein as Iraq's leader unleashed a bloody civil war involving Shiites, Sunnis and ethnic Kurds. Close to 5000 American military personnel have given their lives in the cause of ushering in this *"new era,"* and nearly half a million people have died from war-related causes in Iraq since the US-led invasion in 2003.

When President Bush and his advisors made the decision to invade Iraq and overthrow Saddam Hussein, did they take into account the following historical facts?

1. Since the 16th Century, the land of Iraq, which included the famous "Fertile Crescent" considered to be the birthplace of modern civilization, was under the control of the Ottoman Empire. This remained the case until the Ottoman Turks joined the losing side of World War One.

2. After the First World War, Iraq was handed over as a "mandate" to be controlled by the British. When drawing its boundaries, the Europeans did not take into account that rival religious and ethnic groups would populate the area.

3. Saddam Hussein came to power in July of 1979 and set up a brutal but stable government. Until 2003, he proved to be the "glue" that generally held the country together.

4. Throughout history, whenever a strong ruler is removed, it has often created a vacuum of power that has resulted in civil war. Thousands of years ago, the Greek empire under Alexander the Great quickly fell apart upon his untimely death. The overthrow of Norodom Sihanouk in Cambodia in 1970 paved the way for civil war and the repressive rule of the Khmer Rouge that cost the lives of up to two million people. When Marshall Tito, the ruler of Yugoslavia, died in 1980, the stability that held that nation together dissolved, unleashing the disintegration of the country into several new republics, including Slovenia, Croatia, Bosnia and Serbia. The ensuing civil war and "ethnic cleansing" that accompanied the breakup took the lives of up to 140,000 people.

If President Bush had given stronger consideration to these historical trends, he might have made a much different decision. Even the former president has stated that he regrets using the phrase *"mission accomplished"* in his speech because it conveyed the erroneous message that America's involvement in Iraq would soon wind to an end. Considering the long-term consequences of his actions, President Bush made a choice that cost the lives of thousands and created a volatile disaster in much of the Middle East. All of this might have been prevented if he had possessed a deeper understanding of the region's history.

David Cameron and George W. Bush are not the only leaders to speak or act out of historical ignorance. Furthermore, there are also millions of voters who lack the same knowledge and understanding. Clearly, the world would be a better place if historical ignorance could be replaced by historical enlightenment. Why does ignorance seem to prevail? The fact that so many people do not possess this understanding reflects largely on the failures of our social studies educational system.

The purpose of social studies education

Despite some of the more popular misconceptions, the purpose of history classes is not to provide a nap period during the school day, nor is it to afford high school football coaches a place to hang out while they are not on the gridiron. Unlike academic areas such as math or science, social studies is not as concerned with the preparation of students for future careers, since only a tiny fraction will ever grow up to become historians or history teachers. The primary purpose of history classes is to produce effective citizens who will participate in a vibrant democracy.

Americans take great pride in the belief that the ultimate political power in our nation rests with the people. Counting every level of government from Congress down to the most localized boards and commissions, there are just over 500,000 elected representatives in a nation of almost 324 million people. Almost every citizen of the United States is eligible to run for one of those elected positions, and all adult Americans should participate in the electoral process whenever possible. While casting a ballot usually takes little effort and just a few minutes, voting intelligently requires a comprehensive understanding of the candidates, the issues and the overall state of affairs. This is virtually impossible to achieve without at least some historical knowledge.

In addition, an effective democracy requires active participation from the citizenry in the form of taking part in political campaigns, regularly communicating with elected representatives and joining movements when warranted by the circumstances. During the 1930s, when the nation was suffering through the longest and most severe economic trial in its history, more than two-dozen pieces of New Deal legislation were enacted to help Americans survive the Great Depression. Our democracy thrived even as other nations turned to communism or fascism. Twenty years later, when Rosa Parks was arrested for refusing to give up her seat on a bus because of the color of her skin, tens of thousands joined a boycott of the busses in Montgomery, Alabama, and this soon turned into a movement that involved millions. The result was civil rights legislation that abolished barriers to voting, jobs and public accommodations. In the 1980s, millions of Americans voted to support the "*Reagan Revolution*" that limited the role of the federal government in our nation's economy and helped to bring an end to the terrifying Cold War.

There have obviously been failures as well as successes. Over 600,000 Americans lost their lives in the Civil War, and even though it brought an end to slavery, bigotry and segregation continued to thrive for over another century. Women did not gain the right to vote until 1920. Indigenous tribes have endured massacres, broken treaties and debilitating heartbreak. Even today, more than 45 million Americans live below the poverty line. However, for 240 years, democracy has continued to flourish within the United States, and the only hope for its future lies in the education of its citizens. This is why social studies education deserves its status along with English, mathematics and science in the *"big four"* of the secondary curriculum.

The problem

Unfortunately, too many history classes have been fraught with teacher-centered instruction built around mind-numbing textbooks. The curriculum has often focused on the requirement that students memorize lists of chronological facts and details. Rather than engage students in the compelling stories that can potentially make history the most interesting subject, the past is presented as lacking any connection or relevance to the present. Consequently, a majority of students find history to be boring. They avoid taking any history classes beyond the required high school subjects and remember very little of what is taught in those courses. The end result is that we have largely become a democratically illiterate society. A study by the McCormick Tribune Freedom Museum found that while 22 per cent of Americans could name all five *Simpson* family members, just one in 1000 could name all of the five freedoms in the First Amendment.

For years, political pundits and late-night talk show hosts have derived considerable pleasure from citing the results of the latest polls that show the extent of American ignorance in the field of history. What happened in 1066? Just ten per cent know it is the date of the Norman Conquest of England. Who said the *"world must be made safe for democracy?"* Just 14 per cent knew it was Woodrow Wilson. Which nation dropped the atomic bomb? Only 49 per cent of Americans knew it was their own country.

The solution

If this is the current state of our democracy, what is the solution? First, there remains a dire need to continue improving the delivery of social studies curriculum in our schools. There are still too many students who endure the same mind-numbing experience of text readings, lectures and fill-in-the-blank assessments that confronted their parents and grandparents. An entire new generation of historically inept citizens is being churned out by our educational assembly lines, and in many school districts, the situation is going from bad to worse. Many history teachers are currently complaining that they are disfavored compared to their peers in the English, Math and Science departments, particularly when it comes to budgets, supplies, room assignments and staffing.

Some have admirably sought to improve the discipline of social studies, and efforts to reform the social studies curriculum date back over one hundred years. In 1916, John Dewey published his seminal book, *Democracy and Education*, where he wrote, *"Were all instructors to realize that the quality of mental process, not the production of correct answers, is the measure of educative growth, something hardly less than a revolution in teaching would be worked."* Dewey's emphasis on student-centered learning and active engagement echoed other great thinkers from the more distant past. More than 2300 years ago, Plato wrote, *"Do not train a child to learn by force or harshness; direct them to it by what amuses their minds, so that you may be better able to discover with accuracy the peculiar bent of the genius of each."* In the 18th century, Jean-Jacques Rousseau admonished the educator to, *"Teach your scholar to observe the phenomena of nature; you will soon rouse his curiosity, but if you would have it grow, do not be in too great a hurry to satisfy this curiosity. Put the problems before him and let him solve them himself."*

This historical background laid the foundation for the New Social Studies Movement in the 1960s. Many school reformers in this decade took a different approach to teaching and learning, emphasizing inquiry, discovery and depth in pursuit of meaningful learning. A wide assortment of new projects emerged that attempted to reorganize curriculum according to higher-level skills and concepts, require students to engage in problem-solving activities and make connections within and across the curriculum. The emphasis was placed on issues, themes and ideas.

In 1977, a book was published that had a profound impact on my own teaching. *Defining the Social Studies* by Robert D. Barr, James L. Barth and S. Samuel Shermis divided social studies education into three traditions: *"citizen transmission," "social science"* and *"reflective inquiry."* All three traditions attempted to produce good citizenship skills, but they were distinguished by how they defined a good citizen. The first tradition assumed that a good citizen must possess a prescribed body of knowledge and a disposition that lent itself towards the value of patriotism. The second was based on the thinking that good citizenship required skills similar to those used by historians, economists, sociologists and other social scientists. The third, reflective inquiry was built around the idea that the heart of the social studies, and therefore good citizenship was effective decision-making. This tradition, the one clearly advocated by the three authors, emphasized the need to teach students how to research and investigate answers to questions that stemmed from their own curiosity. Then, through the critical examination and analysis of different answers to these questions, students can be taught to develop the decision-making skills necessary to be good citizens in a democracy.

Seven years later, Theodore Sizer, a leader of educational reform at Brown University, came out with *Horace's Compromise*. In this highly influential book, Sizer described the frustrations of a fictional English teacher attempting to survive in the traditional high school that operated more like a bureaucratic factory than an effective place of learning. By the book's end, Sizer prescribed ten common principles by which schools should operate. Among these were *"learning to use one's mind well,"* emphasizing *"depth over coverage,"* increased *"personalization," "student as worker," "teacher as coach"* and *"demonstration of mastery."* Sizer's principles swept the nation as secondary schools from coast to coast joined his Coalition of Essential Schools.

Despite this long record of reform, there is still much to be done. A greater stress needs to be placed on social studies instruction in our schools, and more importantly, teachers of history and the other social studies need to come to a consensus that student-centered engagement must take priority over the tradition of textbooks, lectures and passive learning. But even if this change came to fruition in the near future, there would still be millions of adults for whom it would appear to be too late. The rebuttal to this assertion is that it is **never too late**.

The solution for the non-student

The prescription for grown adults must not involve textbooks. Since the traditional rendering of the past in the form of irrelevant details presented in a chronological sequence did not work well when used in school, it is doubtful that these types of textbooks would be any more effective today. Even if presented as compelling story telling, much of the information would bear little relevance to the lives of these people. They might enjoy reading the stories as they would good fiction, but it still would not necessarily transfer into better decisions being made on Election Day.

Therefore, a new paradigm is necessary. Borrowing from the intellectual foundation established by Plato, Rousseau, Dewey, Barr, Barth, Shermis and Sizer, this new approach to learning history must be based on inquiry. The first step calls for generating questions that originate from a person's curiosity of the current state of the world. The second step involves delving into the past to find answers to these questions. This should enable people to satisfy their curiosity, gain valuable background information and expand their field of understanding. Third, and most critically, the adult should practice a routine where this knowledge and understanding is applied to current events and issues. Rational thought processes should be developed and exercised the same way an athlete learns to hone the muscle memory needed to effectively swing a baseball bat or consistently sink a basketball foul shot. This combination of knowledge, understanding, public concern and decision-making process is the recipe for a more-informed citizenry.

A relevant example

At this point, an example of this approach might prove useful. In preliminary discussions with my daughter about the purpose of writing this book, the question was raised as to why the gender pay gap still exists. The presidential election campaign in 2016 brought this issue back into the regular news, and as a young woman with a law degree, my daughter saw the relevancy of this question with respect to her budding career. Women earn only 79 per cent of men's average hourly wages, as the media has repeatedly informed us. Why does this inequity from the past continue to plague American society today?

Like all of the questions in this book, my daughter's query does not have a simple answer. History is the study of the past, but unlike the hard sciences, experiments cannot be performed to prove or disprove a hypothesis. Instead, the study of the past is messy. The evidentiary record is often incomplete and frequently generates more debate than consensus. Liberal historians often interpret the past differently from their more conservative counterparts. Each new generation of historians regularly uncover new *"truths"* about the past that their parents and grandparents failed to understand. Therefore, how should this question be answered so that my daughter might be able to gain credible information she can apply to the current political setting?

There is no perfect solution, but the approach that will be employed in this book is to break the past down into manageable blocks. Smaller, more specific chunks of knowledge are less subject to conflicting interpretations than larger conclusions. Once these blocks are combined, readers can then apply reason to draw their own conclusions. What should be the building blocks to answer the question about gender equality? Different history educators might possibly arrange different blocks, but in the end, they all should help my daughter make sense of this phenomenon. Here is what I assembled:

Building block #1 – The United States is still reeling from a long history of sexism. Most American women did not gain the right to own property until the middle of the 19th century, and it was not until 1920, less than 100 years ago, that women finally acquired the right to vote. The Equal Rights Amendment, which simply stated *"Equality of rights under the law shall not be denied or abridged by the United States or by any state on account of sex,"* was first introduced into Congress in 1923, where it did not get passed for almost 50 years. Then, when it was sent to the states for ratification, it failed to gain the final three states that would have inserted this amendment into the Constitution. As for jobs, despite the enormous gains made by the *"Rosie the Riveters"* during the war years between 1941 and 1945, by 1947, women's labor-force participation was only 32 per cent.

As of 2013, there had been stark improvement. The women's labor-force participation rate had nearly doubled to 57 per cent. In 2011, women had earned 57 per cent of the bachelor's degrees and half of the PhDs and professional degrees. By 2014, women made up 34 per cent of the lawyers in this country, 37 per cent of the doctors and 61 per cent of the market analysts. Why the transformation? There are several reasons: the spread of household appliances, which saved time; the advent of the birth control pill, which made it easier to plan pregnancies; the availability of college to more women, which expanded job opportunities; and the rise of feminism, which challenged dominant stereotypes. Nevertheless, the wage gap is still a reality, and many of the prevailing sexist attitudes that dominated the 1950s have not entirely disappeared. This leads to the next building block.

Building block #2 – There has been continuing resistance from several male-dominated job bastions. According to a study by Francine D. Blau and Lawrence M. Kahn, two Cornell University economists, the wage gap is at least partially explained by ongoing discrimination. They cited one study showing that when five symphony orchestras shifted to blind auditions with the candidate's identities unknown, women's success rates climbed dramatically. In another study, men and women with similar resumes applied for restaurant positions with high-priced eating establishments; the women's job offers were 50 per cent lower than the men's. The degree of the role played by discrimination is open to discussion, but there is no question that at least some of the employment barriers facing women in the past still exist in the present.

Building block #3 – The pay gap is simply the ratio of women's average hourly pay to men's hourly pay. Many people cite the 79 per cent figure to demand, *"equal pay for equal work,"* but the jobs in comparison are not necessarily the same. According to Blau and Kahn, when these differences are taken into account, the ratio of women's pay to that of men rises to almost 92 per cent. Despite the advances, women remain more likely to work in lower-paying jobs, such as health-care aides, receptionists, cashiers and food servers. In addition, women on the whole still have slightly less on-the-job experience than men. All of this helps to explain their lower wages.

Building block #4 – Finally, there is *"the motherhood wage penalty."* Throughout history, a common assumption was that the woman was the more important parent, particularly in the early formative years of the child. Even the most modern woman still has biological reasons for taking some time off after giving birth. As a result, many careers are interrupted. Even when employers allow greater job flexibility, promotions and incomes often suffer, and many end up slamming into the *"glass ceiling."* According to Blau and Kahn, this is the reason why wage gaps between men and women are the greatest among the best-paid workers. Of the chief executive officers of Fortune 500 companies, only 4 per cent are women.

In the late 19th century, many Americans accepted the premise that there were separate *"spheres of influence."* Men were expected to work, support their families and play the political role in the larger world. Women were the masters of the household, with the primary task of tending to their children and maintaining the home. In fact, one sign that a family had successfully climbed into the ranks of the middle class was when a married woman could confine her work to within the home. This viewpoint dates back to prehistoric times when men tended to be the hunters while women were the gatherers. Both men and women inhabited separate worlds, but while different, most at the time considered them to be equal.

The Woman's Suffrage Movement at the turn of the century and the modern feminist movement in the 1960s shattered these roles and expectations, and the wage gap is at least partially explained by the fact that the dust has yet to settle from these relatively recent social advances.

When the information contained in these building blocks is presented to my daughter, she must then assemble them into a meaningful answer to her question. In addition, she should not rely only on her dad as a source for this information, because despite my best intentions, there is bound to be a degree of inaccuracy, incompleteness and bias contained within the blocks I have assembled for her. As stated before, history does not hold the precision of math or science. All historical sources, primary or secondary, come from the perception of a human being. Since no one is perfect, there is bound to be imperfections contained within every historical artifact and treatise.

Following her curiosity and employing her intellect, my daughter, like any other citizen in a democratic society, bears the ultimate responsibility for relearning the history not mastered during her years of secondary education. It is best to begin the process with a question focused on the contemporary world. Blocks of information can then be gathered from a wide array of sources and considered collectively in order to gain a better understanding of the present.

Relearning history

The traditional pattern has been to learn history from a book written by a historian who chooses what to include, the order it is presented and the language that shapes its meaning. In classrooms across the nation, social studies educators strive to reinforce this knowledge through lectures, teacher-centered activities, worksheets and quizzes. Students study primarily through memorization and attempt to provide evidence of what they have learned on pencil-and-paper assessments. This pattern may have worked for some, but many others have been left dumbfounded and overwhelmed when attempting to make sense of the complicated planet we inhabit.

Another option for these adults might involve beginning with questions like those explored in the remainder of this book. After reviewing the building blocks suggested within each chapter, the reader is encouraged to seek other sources that address the question from other angles, and then synthesize these perspectives into a meaningful answer. If this is done habitually with a wide spectrum of questions, the end result will be the civic education that may have evaded the reader back in school.

The questions in the table of contents are by no means a fully comprehensive list, but they do explore a wide range of current issues that are of concern to many people. It should be noted that many of these questions are enshrouded in controversy. This selection was deliberate. Questions with consensual answers generate little interest, while those that stir up passionate debate will incite a learner's curiosity. The danger is that no matter how the question is answered, there will be some who will disagree with at least some of the points raised. This is a risk worth taking.

By reading the review and analysis of the history provided in each chapter of this book, the reader will be able to begin the process of relearning history. Each person will gain a greater understanding to a host of problems and issues that dominate the evening news. What happens after reading this, however, will be up to the individual learner. While this book is a start, it should be understood that the process never ends.

Sources and further reading:

Barr, Robert D., James L. Barth, and S. Samuel Shermis. *Defining the Social Studies*. Silver Spring: National Council for the Social Studies, 1977.

Blau, Francine D., and Lawrence M. Kahn. "The Gender Wage Gap: Extent, Trends, and Explanations." *IZA.org*. January 2016. http://ftp.iza.org/dp9656.pdf.

"Bush Makes Historic Speech Aboard Warship." *CNN.com*. May 1, 2003. http://cnn.com/2003/US/05/01/bush.transcript/.

Byford, Jeffrey, and William Russell. "The New Social Studies: A Historical Examination of Curriculum Reform." *Social Studies Research and Practice 2*, no.1(2007): 38-48. Accessed May 23, 2016. http://www.socstrpr.org/files/Vol%202/Issue%201%20-%20Spring%202007/Research/2.1.3.pdf.

"Common Principles." *Coalition of Essential Schools*. Accessed May 25, 2016. http://www.essentialschools.org/common-principles/.

Dewey, John. *Democracy and Education*. New York: The Free Press, 1944.

Gongloff, Mark. "45 Million Americans Still Stuck Below Poverty Line: Census." *HuffingtonPost.com* September 16, 2014. http://www.huffingtonpost.com/2014/09/16/poverty-household-income_n_5828974.html.

Loewen, James W. *Lies My Teacher Told Me: Everything Your American History Textbook Got Wrong*. New York: Touchstone, 2007.

Nir, David. "Just How Many Elected Officials Are There in the United States?" *Daily Kos.com*. March 29, 2015. http://www.dailyKos.com/story/2015/3/29/1372225/-Just-how-many-elected-officials-are-there-in-the-United-States-The-answer-is-mind-blowing

Plato. *Proverbia.net. Accessed* May 23, 2016. http://en.proverbia.net/citasautor.asp?author=15744.

Rousseau, Jacques. *Goodreads.com*. Accessed May 23, 2016. https://www.goodreads.com/quotes/215598-teach-your-scholar-to-observe-the-phenomena-of-nature-you.

Samuelson, Robert J. "What's the Real Gender Pay Gap?" *WashingtonPost.com* April 24, 2016. https://www.washingtonpost.com/opinions/what's-the-real-gender-pay-gap/2016/04/24/314a90ee-08a1-11e6-bdcb-0133da18418d_story.html.

Shenkman, Rick. "Ignorant America: Just How Stupid Are We?" *Alternet.org*. July 1, 2008. https://www.alternet.org/story/90161/ignorant_america%3A_just_how_stupid_are_we.

Sheridan, Kerry. "Iraq Death Toll Reaches 500,000 Since Start of U.S.-Led Invasion, New Study Says." *The World Post*. October 15, 2013. http://www.huffingtonpost.com/2013/10/15/iraq-death-toll_n_4102855.html.

Shipman, Tim. "Cameron's Historic Blunder: Fury as PM Says We Were 'Junior Partner' to Americans in 1940." *DailyMail.com*. July 22, 2010. http://www.dailymail.co.uk/news/article-1296551/David-Cameron-describes-Britain-junior-Partner-Americans-1940.html.

Sizer, Theodore R. *Horace's Compromise: The Dilemma of the American High School*. New York: Houghton Mifflin Company, 1984.

"29 of the Most Outrageous Donald Trump Quotes." *MarieClaire.com*. May 11, 2016. http://www.marieclaire.co.uk/blogs/550112/donald-trump-quotes.html.

Chapter 2

Why is the Constitution important and why is it so difficult to change?

"March for Life" in Knoxville, Tennessee January 20, 2013
Courtesy of Brian Stansberry (CC-BY-3.0)
https://commons.wikimedia.org/wiki/File:Knoxville-march-for-life-2013-3.jpg

"This right of privacy... is broad enough to encompass a woman's decision whether or not to terminate her pregnancy."

Justice Harry Blackmun, Roe v. Wade, January 22, 1973

The United States Supreme Court handed down the *Roe v. Wade* decision on January 22, 1973. At the time, the assumption was that the contentious issue of abortion had been resolved and could be placed on a back burner. Since then, the issue has continued to simmer in an emotional cauldron. According to a Gallup Poll in 2015, Americans are divided between 50 per cent who consider themselves *"pro-choice,"* while 44 per cent call themselves *"pro-life."* Three years earlier, the pro-life side led by 50 per cent to 41 per cent. The matter has remained one of the closest and most contested issues over the last half century. With roughly 50 million abortions performed in the United States since 1973, few issues have also had such widespread impact.

A woman's decision to terminate her pregnancy is gut-wrenching and emotionally charged. What does a rather dull document written way back in 1787 have to do with this subject? To many, the United States Constitution was probably the focus of a unit taught in a civics, government or U.S. history class in high school. Whatever lessons were learned probably withered away over the years. Many people are familiar with the *Roe v. Wade* case and understand that in the Supreme Court's 7-2 decision, the Constitution was being interpreted in such a way as to legalize abortions throughout the nation. States would no longer have the power to prevent a woman from having an abortion, at least in the first trimester. Nonetheless, without a deeper understanding of how the Constitution was construed to structure government powers such as the regulation of abortion, this vital document remains fixed in their minds as a musty piece of parchment lodged somewhere in the National Archives building.

The powers of the government

John Locke, the great English political philosopher that dominated much of the 18th century Enlightenment, wrote that *"the only way whereby anyone divests himself of his natural liberty, and puts on the bonds of civil society, is by agreeing with other men to join and unite into a community."* He argued that we are all born into a state of nature possessing three natural rights: life, liberty and property. In order to ensure the defense of these rights, we create a government and endow it with just enough power to protect these fundamental freedoms. This was the famous *"social contract"* that has become the basis of the limited government that dominates political ideology throughout the free world.

In other words, if we are to have a government, it must have a specified amount of power. To protect life, governments typically create criminal laws concerning homicide. They provide the police to enforce these laws as well as a system of courts to assure that justice is fairly dispensed. Therefore, if anyone threatens to take your life, the government will help to protect this basic natural right with which we are all born. Laws and courts, both civil and criminal, play a similar role in the protection of property. Anyone who threatens to take the property of another without consent, be it land, personal belongings or intellectual property (patents, copyrights, and trademarks) will have to contend with the powers of government.

It is the third natural right specified by John Locke that has proven to be the most problematic. One person can certainly threaten the liberty of another, and once again, the victim can turn to the government for protection. However, potentially the greatest threat to liberty, including the liberty to enjoy our lives and own property, comes from the government itself. What happens if a government violates the terms of the social contract, and rather than simply protecting our natural rights, infringes upon them? At that point, John Locke stated that people *"have a right to resume their original liberty."* In other words, the usurping government can be overthrown and replaced by another that will agree to honor the social contract.

In order to minimize the risk of a bloody revolution, however, most democratic governments have developed peaceful methods to maintain the social contract. Political leaders can be recalled, impeached or simply voted out of office if they are oppressing the liberties of the people. People can circulate petitions and conduct referendums that transfer power directly to the voters. Then there are also the courts. The highest court in the United States has been empowered with judicial review, which means it can examine a law passed by a majority of the elected legislators and signed by the chief executive, and if it deems the law to be in violation of the Constitution, it can rule the law to be invalid.

In 1972, one woman came before the United States Supreme Court with the contention that the liberty to control her own body had been put into jeopardy by a law in the state of Texas. Her name was Norma Leah McCorvey, but at the time, in order to guard her privacy, she was known by the legal pseudonym, *"Jane Roe."* Although she has since publically disavowed the role she played in this case, *Roe v. Wade* was launched as a class action suit, which meant she technically represented any pregnant woman in the state of Texas that was being prohibited from seeking an abortion. Henry Wade, the district attorney of Dallas County, was charged with representing the respondent in this case. It was his duty to defend the Texas law disallowing abortions and thereby shield similar legislation in other states. To those who saw abortion as the murder of an unborn fetus, Henry Wade attempted to defend the right to life of millions of unborn fetuses, a position that has come to be known as *"pro-life."* By the early 1970s, twenty states had passed abortion reform or repeal laws. Hawaii, Alaska, New York and Washington State had legalized abortion. The majority of states, however, still sided with Texas.

Before going any further, a vital question regarding governmental powers needs to be addressed. Why was it that the states had restricted abortion and not the federal government?

Federalism

The simple answer to this question is that Congress never had the power to restrict abortion. This is the result of Federalism, the constitutional principle that addresses how powers are shared between the federal government and the individual states. While theoretically simple, in practice Federalism has sparked some of the most heated and contentious debates since the writing of the Constitution in 1787. In fact, it played a significant role in causing the Civil War; by far, the deadliest conflict in American history.

The powers of the federal government are written into the Constitution. Unlike Great Britain, the U.S. Constitution consists of a single, written document. While England also has a constitution, it is not one document. Instead, it consists of a series of laws, traditions and other documents such as the Magna Carta and the English Bill of Rights. With roughly a thousand years for British democracy to develop and grow, a single written contract was never deemed necessary. In contrast, since the United States emerged as a modern nation more rapidly, most Americans saw the need to put their contract into writing. The result originally was not the Constitution, but the much weaker Articles of Confederation.

The Articles were written during the turmoil of the Revolutionary War. The government created by this document barely managed to get the embryonic nation through its war for independence, and it struggled with almost everything else. Under the Articles, there was no presidency or system of federal courts. There was a Congress where each of the thirteen states had one vote, but this legislative body had few powers. Unable to collect taxes, this early Congress was forced to beg for funding from individual states. It did not take long for many to realize that the Articles of Confederation were in need of serious reform.

This governmental weakness led to the famous Constitutional Convention held in Philadelphia during the summer of 1787. The Convention, which took place in the same Independence Hall where the Declaration of Independence had been signed eleven years earlier, lasted for almost four months and was plagued by hot temperatures and even hotter debates. It was only through willingness to compromise that the Convention managed to produce a new governing document, and in retrospect, some of these compromises led to a few of the Constitution's more questionable features.

For example, the Great Compromise was intended to resolve the question of how many representatives in Congress should come from each state. While creating a bicameral legislature divided between a House of Representatives and a Senate is frequently praised as one of the document's most notable features, it has also slowed down the lawmaking process and given the states smaller in population disproportionate representation. For instance, California and Wyoming are both represented by two senators even though California has 65 times as many people. The founder's fear of giving the *"uneducated"* masses too much power in presidential elections led to the creation of the much-maligned Electoral College, a system where electors from each state choose the president (the number for each state depends on the state's population). Because most states award all of their electors to whomever wins the majority of popular votes within the state regardless of the national results, several elections have occurred where the winner did not receive a plurality of the people's votes. The infamous Three Fifths Compromise, which for the purpose of tabulating the population in the census considered a slave to count as three fifths of a person, is today recognized as unjust and patently absurd.

Nevertheless, there is no question that the Constitutional Convention produced a new government far more powerful than the one it replaced. The pendulum had swung from one end of the spectrum to the other, and there was soon mounting concern that the new government under the Constitution might infringe on the liberties of the people. This concern grew in the months of debate that followed the Constitutional Convention, since the final article of the new document required the ratification of nine states in order to become the law of the land. Immediately, people divided themselves between those who favored ratification, the Federalists; and those who were opposed, known as the Anti-Federalists. Ultimately, it took another compromise to usher in the new government under the Constitution. The founders agreed that shortly after the Constitution's ratification, ten amendments would be added to the document that would collectively be known as the Bill of Rights.

The last of these ten amendments is relatively less known, but in its language is part of the answer to the question of who should have the power to regulate abortions. It reads, *"The powers not delegated to the United States by the Constitution, nor prohibited by it to the states, are reserved to the states respectively, or to the people."* In other words, if a power is not listed as belonging to Congress in Article One, Section Eight, then it must be a state power. The words *"education"* or *"school"* are not mentioned on this list, so the power to build and maintain a school system is strictly a state power. This is what the governor of Arkansas maintained in 1957 when he refused to comply with the orders of a federal court to racially integrate Central High School in Little Rock. The word *"slavery"* is also not mentioned on this list, and southern states began to secede from the Union shortly after Abraham Lincoln was elected president in 1860— an election they saw as a direct threat to the future of this institution. As for abortion, it is also not on the list, so Texas and many other states had taken it upon themselves to regulate this practice in the name of protecting the life of an unborn fetus.

To complicate matters further, the final item on the list of powers enumerated in Article One, Section Eight of the Constitution has been dubbed the Elastic Clause because it enables the *"stretching"* of the federal government's powers. It gives Congress the authority *"to make all laws which shall be necessary and proper for carrying into execution the foregoing powers..."* This clause, combined with the Supreme Court's expansion of the Commerce Clause (the power of Congress *"to regulate commerce with foreign nations, and among the several states..."*), gives Congress the authority to regulate television stations, airlines and many other industries. Since these industries engage in commerce and operate across state lines, they are considered a form of interstate commerce. Those who favor a stronger federal government, and who tend to align with today's Democratic Party, generally like this clause and want it to be expanded. On the other hand, most modern-day Republicans favor a much stricter interpretation of these constitutional provisions.

Despite the expansion of federal power under the Elastic Clause, most constitutional scholars would state that under the principle of Federalism, and because of the Tenth Amendment in particular, the power to control public schools, decide the issue of slavery and restrict abortions must be left to the states. In order for the federal government to take any control over these powers, a different part of the

Constitution would have to apply. For example, the Fifth Amendment in the Bill of Rights provides that *"no person shall... be deprived of life, liberty, or property, without due process of law."* Here, the key question involved the definition a person. Is a slave a *"person?"* If so, to keep him or her in a state of bondage would be a violation of the Fifth Amendment, and the federal government would have a responsibility to intervene and end slavery. On the other hand, if a slave is considered to be *"property,"* then the federal government's efforts to free the slaves could be seen as violating the Fifth Amendment rights of the slave owner.

A similar line of reasoning emerged when the Supreme Court handed down its *Brown v. Board of Education* decision in 1954, the legal basis for the effort to racially integrate the public schools in Little Rock, Arkansas, three years later. While Arkansas clearly had the power to regulate its public schools, the Court voted 9-0 that a system based on the *"separate but equal"* principle was *"inherently unequal."* Why? Because the 14th Amendment, passed shortly after the Civil War in 1868, declared that no state could *"deny to any person within its jurisdiction the equal protection of the laws."* This Equal Protection Clause of the 14th Amendment has become the foundation of most modern civil rights court cases.

In the case of abortion, the Supreme Court considered other parts of the Constitution to challenge a state's unfettered power to regulate this practice. According to the Court, at least in the first trimester of a pregnancy, there is a right to privacy granted under the Due Process Clause of the 14th Amendment that extends to a woman's decision to have an abortion. Although the word *"privacy"* does not appear anywhere in the Constitution, courts have ruled that the Fourth Amendment, which protects people from *"unreasonable searches and seizures"* without valid search warrants, provides an implicit right to privacy. Courts have also noted, however, that the states' interest in protecting women's health and the potentiality of human life becomes stronger over the course of a pregnancy.

In many respects, *Roe v. Wade* reflects the strength of the Constitution. Regardless of how one feels about the issue of abortion, this case demonstrated how a document written 230 years ago remains alive and relevant today. The Constitution is surprisingly short and purposely vague in many sections. The drafters intended for parts of the Constitution to remain open to interpretation so that it could respond to a future that its authors could never imagine. This Supreme Court case recognized the powers of the state, while at the same time, balanced them against the liberty and individual rights of the people.

Individual rights

The Constitution is not only important today because it grants powers to the government and determines how those powers should be shared. Several parts of the Constitution, particularly the Bill of Rights and the 14th Amendment, are focused on individual rights. If one examines the language of these amendments, however, it might bring to mind the proverb of whether a glass of water is half empty or half full. Does the First Amendment grant five rights to the people, or does it place five limits on the powers of government? In one run-on sentence, the First Amendment provides some of our most cherished rights – freedom of religion, free speech, free press, peaceful assembly and the right to petition. Yet it begins with *"Congress shall make no law respecting..."* Regardless of whether these amendments should be viewed as rights or limits, collectively, they contribute to our understanding of why the Constitution and the liberties it bestows continue to be relevant.

Of course, none of these freedoms are absolute. It has taken thousands of court decisions, especially those handed down by the Supreme Court, to determine the scope of the freedom conveyed within the words of the Constitution. Free speech does not mean that a speaker can spread malicious lies about another that will destroy a reputation or utter threats that might put another into a state of fear. As Justice Oliver Wendell Holmes wrote in his opinion in the case of *Schenck v. United States* in 1919, *"the most stringent protection of free speech would not protect a man falsely shouting fire in a theater and causing a panic."*

This same logic applies to all of our other cherished rights. For example, the two sides in the debate over gun control dispute how far the Second Amendment extends the right to bear arms. The amendment simply states, *"a well-regulated militia, being necessary to the security of a free state, the right of the people to keep and bear arms, shall not be infringed."* This amendment does not mean that one can drive an armed tank down Main Street or that an individual with an armed robbery conviction will be able to purchase an Uzi. Similarly, although there is an implied right to privacy imbedded in the Fourth Amendment, this right is significantly curtailed the moment someone wants to board an airplane. Those accused of a crime are given many rights in the Fifth, Sixth and Eighth Amendments, but trials are not always *"speedy," "assistance of counsel"* is often unavailable to the indigent in misdemeanor cases and despite the prohibition on *"cruel and unusual punishments,"* the Supreme Court has allowed the death penalty as a criminal sentence.

To many people, such as those affiliated with organizations like the American Civil Liberties Union, our constitutionally protected individual rights retain an almost sacred quality. Nevertheless, when these rights conflict with other American values, like patriotism or national security, they have not always prevailed. Like so much that defines our democracy, there is a dynamic tension that emanates from the ongoing competition between those who strongly value our constitutional rights and those who do not. When a serious crime is committed, what is more important: bringing the offender to justice or protecting the rights of the individual who is accused of committing the offense? A similar tension exists in political campaigns, in the process of passing a bill into a law and in the struggle between the prosecution and the defense in a criminal trial. Somehow, despite the messiness, inefficiency and competing interests, leaders are chosen, legislation gets enacted and the cause of justice is usually served. The same process shapes our interpretation of the Constitution and its application to daily life.

Perceived inflexibility

Part of the genius of the Constitution is its ability to adapt to changing times. It is a *"living document,"* in that it is purposefully short and vague so that it can be open to interpretation by future generations. As previously stated, the Constitution's Elastic Clause at the end of Article One, Section Eight has enabled the federal government to govern over matters never dreamed of by George Washington, Alexander Hamilton or James Madison. When the Constitutional Convention took place in the summer of 1787, did any of the delegates imagine there would eventually be an Office of National Drug Control Policy, a National Oceanic and Atmospheric Administration or a Department of Education? Did it occur to them that the federal government would one day pay subsidies to farmers **not** to grow food, or that it would launch space probes to the outer reaches of our solar system?

The Supreme Court has had a pivotal role in helping to preserve the Constitution's malleability. Although the Supreme Court's power of judicial review is not explicitly stated in the Constitution, since the *Marbury v. Madison* decision in 1803, few have questioned the Court's authority to interpret the Constitution in order to maintain the document's relevance in contemporary times. In the recent past, there have been Supreme Court decisions over such topics as health care subsidies, same-sex marriages, pollution limits and social media. Once again, the writers of the Constitution could never have envisioned these issues. This is the primary reason why the U.S. Constitution has endured long enough to be considered the oldest living document of its kind.

Nevertheless, the writers of the Constitution did not want the document to be changed for frivolous reasons. This is why Article Five purposefully made the amending process exceedingly difficult. Some, like Sanford Levinson in his seminal critique entitled *Our Undemocratic Constitution*, have argued that the United States Constitution is the most difficult to amend or update of any constitution currently existing in the world today.

There is more than one way to enact an amendment, but they all involve multiple steps. The most common path has required both chambers of Congress to first approve an amendment by a two-thirds majority, followed by ratification of the amendment by three fourths of the states. Throughout most of American history, this process has proven to be insurmountably difficult to achieve. There are 27 amendments tacked on to the Constitution, but the first ten of these came simultaneously in the form of the Bill of Rights. The other 17, enacted sporadically over more than two hundred years, have dealt with some rather innocuous topics, such as moving up the date of the president's inauguration, giving the residents of the District of Columbia input in presidential elections and restricting the number of terms that a president can serve in office. There is no denying that some, such as the amendments that abolished slavery, empowered the federal government to collect an income tax and granted women the right to vote, were highly significant. On the other hand, the 18th Amendment led to the prohibition of alcoholic beverages, and 14 years later, the 21st Amendment nullified the 18th.

After receiving the right to vote, women suffragette leaders like Alice Paul proposed an Equal Rights Amendment that would ban all discrimination based on sex. It was first introduced into Congress in 1923 but did not receive the required two-thirds majority in both houses until 1972. (Alice Paul was still alive to see this victory.) Nonetheless, it came up three states shy of the required 38 needed for ratification. Although people might debate the merits of this amendment, one cannot deny the fact that for millions of Americans, the Equal Rights Amendment proved to be a frustrating failure. The same could be said for the proponents of other failed amendments, including those who advocated for full representation in Congress for the residents of the District of Columbia, or those who wanted to abolish the Electoral College in order to directly elect the president.

Like so many aspects of our government, the amendment process is structured to maintain a fragile balancing act. If the Constitution were easier to change, proposed amendments that would have selected the president through a lottery or banned interracial marriage might have passed. On the other hand, if it were too difficult to change, we might still be unable to directly elect our senators, or might still be living with discriminatory poll taxes. Regardless of how one feels about this delicate balance of interests, it would take an amendment to the Constitution in order to alter the amending process. This is something that will probably not occur anytime in the near future.

Conclusion

The Constitution established our current federal system and set up the ground rules for how it should operate. It created three branches of government: one to make the laws, one to enforce them and one to interpret them while in the process of dispensing justice. In addition, the Constitution created an intricate system of checks and balances to prevent any one branch of government from amassing too much power. State and local governments within the United States and many democratic nations around the world have emulated its language and principles. It is the reason why even after enduring an ugly political campaign, newly elected leaders can replace the old without a bloody coup d'état. It has been called the oldest living document of its kind in the world and after 230 years, it still reigns as the supreme law of the United States. It not only created a workable government, but set limits on the powers of that government in order to protect the individual rights of its citizenry. Most fundamentally, it has lived up to the standard established by its first three words, *"We the people…"*

Sources and further reading:

Beeman, Richard. *The Penguin Guide to the United States Constitution: A Fully Annotated Declaration of Independence, U.S. Constitution and Amendments, andSelections from the Federalist Papers.* New York: Penguin Books, 2010.

"Brown v. Board of Education." *Legal Information Institute.* Accessed June 3, 2016. https://www.law.cornell.edu/supremecourt/text/347/483.

Goidel, Kirby, Craig Freeman, and Brian Smentkowski. *Misreading the Bill of Rights: Top Ten Myths Concerning Your Rights and Liberties.* Santa Barbara: ABC-CLIO, LLC.,2015.

Greenhouse, Linda, and Reva Siegel. *Before Roe v. Wade: Voices That Shaped the Abortion Debate Before the Supreme Court's Ruling.* New York: Kaplan Publishing, 2010.

Levinson, Sanford. *Our Undemocratic Constitution: Where the Constitution Goes Wrong(And How We the People Can Correct It).* New York: Oxford University Press, 2006.

Locke, John. *Second Treatise of Government.* Indianapolis: Hackett Publishing Company, 1980.

McBride, Alex. "Schenck v. U.S." *PBS.org.* Accessed June 3, 2016. http://www.pbs.org/wnet/supremecourt/capitalism/landmark_schenck.html.

McGarvie, Grace. "Quotations About Abortion." *Quote Garden.* Accessed June 2, 2016. http://www.quotegarden.com/abortion.html.

"Roe v. Wade." *Findlaw.com.* Accessed June 2, 2016. http://casclaw.findlaw.com/us-supreme-court/410/113.html.

Saad, Lydia. "Americans Choose 'Pro-Choice' for First Time in Seven Years." *Gallup.com.* May 29, 2015. http://www.gallup.com/poll/183434/americans-choose-pro-choice-first-time-seven-years.aspx.

Chapter 3

Why does the two-party system dominate American politics?

Courtesy of Pixabay(CC0)
https:/pixabay.com/en/flag-blow-republicans-democrats-234610/

"There is nothing which I dread so much as a division of the republic into two great parties, each arranged under its leader, and concerting measures in opposition to each other. This, in my humble apprehension, is to be dreaded as the greatest political evil under the Constitution."

John Adams, Second President of the United States

In 1991, the Democrats in Louisiana nominated Edwin Edwards to run for his fourth non-consecutive term as governor. Based on his three previous terms, Edwards was known to provide strong, decisive leadership, but his administrations were repeatedly mired in charges of corruption. Edwards was remarkably candid about some of his practices. When questioned about receiving illegal campaign contributions, he once replied that *"It was illegal for them to give, but not for me to receive."* Soon after his third term began in 1985, Edwards stood trial on charges of mail fraud, obstruction of justice and bribery. While he beat these charges, later in 2001 he was found guilty of racketeering charges and sentenced to ten years in a federal prison. Needless to say, in Louisiana's 1991 gubernatorial election, Edwin Edwards was not a stellar candidate. Any outsider aware of the fact that Democratic candidates in Louisiana were no longer virtually guaranteed to win any election would think that Edwards had no chance of victory.

His opponent nominated by the Republicans, however, was David Duke. Although Duke had served one term in the Louisiana legislature, he was better known for his tenure as the former Grand Wizard of the Knights of the Ku Klux Klan. In addition, he had known ties to other white supremacist and neo-Nazi groups. All this took place in a state that was 32 per cent black. If there was ever an election where the two major parties fielded candidates so clearly unqualified for office, this was that election. Nevertheless, after the votes were counted, Edwards won the election by a 61 to 39 per cent margin. Many of the 1.7 million people that participated in the election claimed that they *"held their noses"* when they entered the voting booth, since they were forced to choose between the *"crook and the racist."*

This may be one of the most notorious examples of when America's two-party system produced limited options in an election, but it certainly is not the only one. The presidential election of 1976 offered Gerald Ford, the Republican candidate, versus Jimmy Carter, the Democrat. The highest political office that Ford had ever been elected to was as a congressman from his district in Grand Rapids, Michigan. He had stumbled his way into the White House after President Richard Nixon chose him to fill the vacancy of vice president after Spiro Agnew resigned from that position due to corruption charges. Less than a year later, Ford replaced the man who had tapped him to be vice president when President Nixon stepped down due to the infamous Watergate scandal. In a nation of almost 220 million people, there were certainly people more qualified than Gerald Ford to run for president. As a one-term governor from the state of Georgia, the same could be said for Jimmy Carter. The Democrats won a narrow victory, but Carter's one term was plagued by double-digit inflation, economic malaise and a hostage crisis in Iran. Ronald Reagan soundly defeated him four years later.

Similar comparisons might be made between the 1976 presidential election and the one held 40 years later. Hillary Clinton, who served as the First Lady for two terms before gaining valuable political experience as a Senator and a Secretary of State, certainly was qualified for the office of President, but with questions like email security hanging over her head, many people thought she may not have been the Democrats' best candidate. As for Donald Trump, he had never held any form of political office. After multiple tirades, where he managed to offend Hispanics, Muslims, women and other groups, even members of his own Republican party began to distance themselves from him. 240 years after the signing of the Declaration of Independence, how could a nation that had grown to over 324 million people be presented with such an unpopular slate of choices? How could Hillary Clinton and Donald Trump be offered as the only two viable choices for president?

Most political experts would acknowledge that there are clear problems with America's two-party political system. From president down to most local and state offices, there are generally only two choices presented to the voters, and in many cases, there are many commonalities between the two. Since the two parties frequently hold similar positions on a number of issues, the choices tend to limit voters' options. In addition, since there are many Americans who do not particularly like either of the two party candidates, some voters feel marginalized by the system. This tends to make the United States a less democratic nation. Finally, as previously stated, there are countless elections where the Democrats and Republicans clearly do *not* nominate the best people to serve in a particular office. This has significantly contributed to the rise of political apathy and a lower voter turnout in key elections.

These trends raise the question: why does America continue to cling to its two-party system? Although subject to debate, there are at least three basic responses that should be understood to answer this question.

Reason one – The winner-takes-all system

In the United States, a candidate for political office typically wins the election by securing a plurality, which means receiving more votes than any other candidate. This amounts to a winner-take-all system and there is no reward for the individual who comes in second. As a result, two political parties usually dominate to the disadvantage of smaller parties. Other parties besides the Democrats and the Republicans are free to field candidates, but this type of system generally hinders their efforts to win. After all, the Democrats and the Republicans have dominated American politics for over 150 years. They are better funded, organized and established. Perhaps most importantly, they have each managed to connect with a large block of voters by smoothing over the detailed differences between their candidates and the electorate.

For example, Claire McCaskill, a Democrat, was reelected as one of Missouri's two senators in 2012 with 54.8 per cent of the vote. As the incumbent, she had a natural advantage. On the other hand, Missouri voters have recently been drifting more towards the Republican Party, so her opponent, Todd Akin, had a good chance of winning her seat. In fact, Akin led McCaskill in pre-election polls until he made the mistake of saying that women who are victims of rape rarely get pregnant. The result of this blunder was that he earned only 39.1 per cent of the vote on the day of the election. Many people in Missouri remember this contest well. What they may not remember, however, was that Jonathan Dine, the Libertarian candidate, won 6.1 per cent of the vote. This is because almost 94 per cent of the electorate did not cast their ballots for Mr. Dine. Since he was neither a Democrat nor a Republican, most of the voters paid him little attention. They assumed that he had no chance of victory and that voting for him was comparable to throwing their votes away.

On the other side of the coin, when a candidate other than the Democrat or the Republican *does* make a significant difference in a key election, it can stir up lasting resentment amongst the general electorate. This is another factor that may discourage a larger role by third party candidates and independents. For example,

Ralph Nader, a third party choice, garnered fewer than three million votes out of more than 105 million votes cast in the 2000 presidential election and did not win a single electoral vote. In Florida, however, where almost six million votes were cast, the Republican candidate George W. Bush defeated the Democrat candidate Al Gore by just 537 votes. Since Nader won over 97,000 votes in Florida, and since his political views tended to drain more votes away from Gore than Bush, millions of angry Democrats jumped to the conclusion that Nader cost Gore the election. The lingering resentment generated by third party candidates like Nader may have thrown a wet blanket over any burning desire for there to be a more active role by those outside of the mainstream two-party system.

Related to the antipathy caused by third choice candidates that have played a spoiler's role in past elections is the *"don't throw your vote away"* argument they have generated. In the 2016 presidential election, in addition to Donald Trump and Hillary Clinton, the Libertarian Party nominated Gary Johnson as its candidate and the far-left Green Party nominated Jill Stein. Since both Trump and Clinton stirred up much enmity with millions of voters, supporters of Johnson and Stein felt this was a good year to actively seek the White House. Nonetheless, one can only imagine the millions of Republicans who told their friends tempted to vote for Johnson that you will be *"wasting your vote,"* and that a vote for Trump, *"the lesser of the two evils,"* would be better than enabling an electoral win for Clinton. A similar line of reasoning was no doubt uttered by millions of Democrats who tried to keep their fellow Democrats from voting for Stein.

The media has frequently exacerbated these obstacles blocking the path of any third party aspirant or independent. Working with the campaigns of the two major party candidates, the media has generally agreed to place limits on who can participate in the televised presidential debates. In 2016, the Commission on Presidential Debates (CPD) required that candidates poll at least 15 per cent on five national surveys leading up to the three scheduled debates and garner enough spots on state ballots in order to participate in the events. If that was not enough of an uphill struggle for Johnson, Stein or any other third party or independent candidate that might want to enter the race, there was another hidden catch. Many polling outlets only tested match-ups between Trump and Clinton in their surveys. As Gary Johnson, the former governor of New Mexico said about these requirements, *"the system is rigged."*

Most other democratic nations, such as Japan and Israel, embrace a multi-party system rather than a two-party model. In Israel, for example, twelve parties or party alliances held seats in the seventeenth Knesset. Japan has several major parties, including the Liberal Democrats, the Democratic Party of Japan, the New Komeito and the Japanese Communist Party. Since the legislative body usually chooses the chief executive in these nations, two or more parties frequently have to band together in alliances to form a government. Nations that employ the multi-party system generally use proportional representation instead of plurality to determine how seats are allocated to the political parties. In other words, parties in these nations win legislative seats in rough proportion to the percentage of popular votes won by the party.

For example, the Likud Yisrael Beiteinu Party won more votes than the other 11 parties in the 2013 election held in Israel. However, with just over 23 per cent of the votes, the party was awarded 31 seats in the 120-member Knesset. By forming a coalition with other parties, the Likud Yisrael Beiteinu Party was able to place one of their leaders, Benjamin Netanyahu, in the position of Prime Minister. Yet even the party that came in last, the Kadima Party, which earned only 2.09 per cent of the popular vote, was still awarded two seats in the Knesset. In these types of proportional representation systems, parties can achieve electoral success without winning a majority. Therefore, there is less of an incentive to form massive parties that strive for a majority.

In light of the perceived problems with the United States' two-party system, it might be tempting to abandon it in favor of the multi-party model. It should be noted, however, that there are some advantages to having only two dominant parties. First, the two-party system is often more stable than multi-party systems. Despite the current gridlock in Congress between Democrats and Republicans, imagine the frustration of trying to get legislation passed if it required cooperation between a half dozen parties. Second, since both parties must appeal to the political middle in order to win elections, they tend to be more moderate. Socialists or fascists might not see this as an advantage, but the larger percentage of people grouped toward the center of the political spectrum tend to view this trend favorably.

Finally, the two-party system may render it easier for some voters to participate. After all, most of the electorate is confronted with only two choices on Election Day. At the risk of oversimplification, Democrats in the U.S. tend to value a larger role for government, particularly the federal government, in order to provide more assistance to the indigent, the aged and the dispossessed. On the other hand, most Republicans prefer limited government, lower taxes, a protected right to property and more freedom to conduct business. The American voters who understand these fundamental differences between the two parties are therefore able to make their decision in the voting booth with greater ease. Even those who do not identify as Democrats or Republicans can be guided by these distinctions.

Reason two – The Electoral College

The U.S. Constitution was drafted during the balmy summer of 1787 in Philadelphia. The delegates from the 13 states wrestled with numerous issues, many of which were resolved by some amazingly creative compromises. One of the thorniest issues involved the appropriate amount of power to grant the average voter. In 1787, the only way most Americans could stay abreast of current events and issues was through newspapers. Yet much of the population lived in rural areas that did not have easy access to a newspaper, and of those that did, many did not possess the ability to read them. In addition, there was a deep-seated fear amongst the wealthier, more educated citizens that giving too much political power to the masses could threaten their future property interests.

The founders trusted the American people to elect their congressmen in the House of Representatives every two years, but this was largely based on the assumption that they would be selecting a neighbor with whom they were familiar. The Senate was a different matter. Knowing that states allowed all white, male property owners to elect representatives to their state legislatures, the founders gave these legislative bodies the power to choose the two senators for each state. (This was not changed until passage of the 17th Amendment in 1913, which provided for the direct election of senators.) Furthermore, the members of the Constitutional Convention did not want the president to be chosen in a popular election. They desired a system that would give people an indirect say in the choice of the president, but would not allow them to elect a demagogue or ruffian as their chief executive.

The compromise solution was the Electoral College. State legislatures would choose electors from each state, who would then be responsible for selecting the president. The number of electors from each state would reflect a combination of the state's total representation in Congress. Today, California, our biggest state in population, has 55 electors (53 representatives plus two senators). On the other hand, Wyoming has only three electors (one representative plus two senators, the minimum that a state is guaranteed). To win a presidential election, a candidate must receive a simple majority of the electors. If no one earns more than fifty per cent of the electors, however, which is certainly a distinct possibility whenever three or more people are running for the office, then the House of Representatives chooses the president from among the two candidates that earned the most votes from the Electoral College.

It should be noted that there were no political parties when the Constitution was drafted. In fact, many of the delegates to the Convention abhorred the thought of political parties. George Washington, who chaired the Constitutional Convention, later went on to say:

> *However [political parties] may now and then answer popular ends, they are likely in the course of time and things, to become potent engines, by which cunning, ambitious, and unprincipled men will be enabled tosubvert the power of the people and to usurp for themselves the reins of government, destroying afterwards the very engines which have lifted them to unjust dominion.*

Therefore, it is quite possible that the Electoral College was created to fulfill one of the primary responsibilities performed by the parties today, nominating the most viable candidates for the office. In the present, Democrats and Republicans use primaries and caucuses to pick their top choice from a list of potentially thousands of individuals who are at least 35 years old and who meet the other requirements imposed by the Constitution to run for president. Then, one of those two is chosen on Election Day. What the writers of the Constitution may have had in mind, however, is that the Electoral College would fulfill the mission of nominating the top two options, and then the House of Representatives would make the final choice.

In the early 19th century, during what historians have called *"The Age of Jackson,"* democratic reforms were made on the state level to the voting process. In particular, legislators began to drop property requirements so that considerably more people were enfranchised with the ability to vote. Another reform made by the states in presidential elections was to allow citizens to vote for any presidential candidate that could qualify to earn a spot on the state election ballot. Following the winner-takes-all principle, most of the states decided that whoever won the most popular votes in a particular state should garner all of that state's electors. Only Nebraska and Maine have systems today where electors can be assigned to more than one candidate. Therefore, even if the Democrat defeats the Republican by just a single vote within the state of California, all of California's 55 electors are expected to vote for the Democrat.

As a result, it is not difficult to imagine scenarios where the winner of the Electoral College becomes president without winning a majority of the popular votes. In fact, this has occurred four times. The most recent was in the year 2016 when Hillary Clinton, a Democrat, won the popular election by nearly three million votes but still lost the Electoral College and the overall election to Donald Trump, the Republican candidate. Complaints have been lodged against the Electoral College for decades. Not only does it allow for the undemocratic possibility that the candidate with the most votes does not win, but it also encourages most of the campaigning in the handful of larger states that are most contested.

The rules of the Electoral College also favor the two-party system because third parties have a difficult time competing under the terms of this structure. The Democrats and the Republicans have the money, manpower and organization to get their candidates on the ballots in all 50 states. Smaller parties and independents generally do not possess these resources, which makes it harder to meet state requirements for ballot access. Even a third party candidate with broad appeal may fail to win the most votes in any state, which means he or she will fail to earn a single elector. In the 1992 presidential election, independent candidate H. Ross Perot received nearly 19 per cent of the popular vote, but failed to earn a single electoral vote. Bill Clinton, the Democrat, won the election even though only 43 per cent of the electorate voted for him.

There has been frequent talk about abolishing the Electoral College, but this would require passage of an amendment to the Constitution. As discussed in the previous chapter, this is difficult to accomplish, so despite ample criticism, there has never been any significant progress in abolishing or altering the Electoral College. Regardless of how one feels about this system, its continued existence is another major reason why the United States continues to utilize the two-party system.

Reason three – Historical tradition

Americans, like virtually all human beings, are creatures of habit. In addition, many are strongly influenced by the values instilled in them by their parents. This means that if mom and dad usually vote for the Republican, their offspring are also more likely to vote Republican. Our values are implanted at an early age, and most of us generally tend to follow them throughout our lives. A Gallup Youth Survey taken in 2005 asked teens to compare their social and political views with those of their parents. While a fifth (21 per cent) said they were *"more liberal"* than their parents and seven per cent said they were *"more conservative,"* 71 per cent claimed their social and political ideology was about the same as mom and dad. Families are usually the first and most enduring influence on how people vote.

Despite the tendency for family members to possess similar values, individuals in any larger population will generally **not** share the same set of political beliefs. In other words, if you assemble a heterogeneous group of individuals together in a political state, they are bound to disagree on a number of issues. Over enough time, they will tend to coagulate around a common set of values until they have formed two or more opposing political groups. As much as George Washington, John Adams and James Madison may have disapproved of political parties or *"factions,"* they were unable to prevent them from forming. In the United States, this happened immediately after the adjournment of the Constitutional Convention. The population split into two opposing groups, and while they have changed their names and evolved over time, habit and human nature have generally maintained the tradition of two major political parties ever since.

Article VII of the U.S. Constitution specified that nine of the 13 states were required to ratify the document in order to make it the supreme law of the nation. Debates soon erupted in corner taverns, political clubs and church congregations. Articles and editorials were circulated in all of the major newspapers. Within each state, ratification conventions were scheduled. The general populace was soon split between those who were deemed Federalists and their opponents called Anti-Federalists. The word *"party"* is not even mentioned in the Constitution, but the controversy over the document's ratification became the primary impetus for America's first two political parties.

The Federalists supported the Constitution because of the stronger federal government that would emerge from its passage. Many of these men were wealthy property owners, and they wanted a centralized government with more power than the one previously existing under the Articles of Confederation. They generally believed that a government with greater power to collect taxes, regulate commerce and protect property rights was more likely to maintain a stable economy. Under this type of government, they felt there would be less risk of the masses rising up to threaten the wealth and property of America's landed aristocracy. Anti-Federalists were concerned that the new government set up by the Constitution could evolve into the same type of tyranny they had just fought a revolutionary war to escape. A government with too much power was a government more likely to abuse its power. Therefore, the Anti-Federalists only agreed to go along with the Constitution provided that shortly after its ratification, a set of amendments would be added to limit the powers of the new government and protect people's individual rights.

Within a few years, the Anti-Federalists morphed into the Democratic-Republicans, the political party of Thomas Jefferson. They continued to advocate a weaker federal government in the interest of protecting the rights of the citizen-farmers that Jefferson so cherished. In this respect, the Democratic-Republicans resembled the Republican Party of today. However, their opponents, the Federalists, also resembled modern day Republicans in that they pushed for economic policies to safeguard property ownership, like the creation of a national bank that would protect the property interests of the more affluent classes. The Federalists soon became the party dominated by Alexander Hamilton. Both Jefferson and Hamilton served in George Washington's Cabinet. While our first chief executive attempted to rise above the squabbling of partisan politics, his two leading Cabinet members did not.

When the Federalists chose to oppose the War of 1812, they soon found themselves on the losing side of history. This would not be the last time when one of the two major political parties would disappear due to a failure to keep up with the times. By 1815, the Federalists had all but vanished. This ushered in a rare decade when only one party dominated American politics, the Democratic-Republicans, in a period known as the *"Era of Good Feelings."* By the mid-1820s, however, the Democratic-Republicans had evolved closer to becoming the modern Democrats of today. At the time, it was also known as the *"Party of Jackson,"* since President Andrew Jackson dominated so much of its policies. As a foil, the Whig Party soon emerged to compete with Democratic-Republicans. The United States once again settled down into an ongoing political contest between two major parties.

The coming of the Civil War in the 1850s put added pressure on all political parties. The division over the spread of slavery between northern Whigs and southern Whigs led to the decline and fall of that party. The Democrats were also split, but since they dominated the South, they managed to hold on and survive. In place of the Whigs, the Republicans emerged as the new party in the North that was openly opposed to the spread of slavery. This *"Party of Lincoln"* was victorious in the 1860 presidential election, although with four candidates in the race, Abraham Lincoln won with just under 40 per cent of the popular vote. Nevertheless, with victories in every northern state, he dominated the Electoral College.

After the Civil War, the Democrats gradually climbed back into the position of being the second major party. From 1868 to 1912, Grover Cleveland was the only Democrat elected to the White House, but nonetheless, the Democrats managed to effectively duel with the Republicans throughout the remainder of the 19th century. During these years, however, both parties largely ignored the rising needs of millions of people. For the most part, factory workers during the heyday of the Industrial Revolution were overworked, underpaid and exploited. Meanwhile, farmers were being ripped off by the railroads they so badly depended upon, and they suffered from declining farm prices due to their success at growing larger supplies of crops. Labor unions organized, went on strike and were increasingly frustrated when the government generally sided with management in most conflicts. Their leaders begged for government relief, but there was none. Farmers also pleaded for regulation of the railroads and for the government to put more money into circulation, particularly silver in addition to gold, so that the rising inflation would provide them with higher prices for their corn, wheat and cotton. Again, with the exception of passing two pieces of legislation, the Sherman Anti-Trust Act and the Interstate Commerce Act, the leaders of both political parties looked the other way.

In this type of climate, the pattern had been to create and turn to a third party. In the 1890s, factory workers and farmers joined together to create the Populist Party. When the Populists nominated William Jennings Bryan to run for president in 1896, the Democrats opted to jump on board and nominated him as well. With this nomination, the Democrats became one of the first of the major parties to acknowledge the needs of poor workers and indebted farmers, which helps explain how they started to evolve into the modern Democratic Party and why the Populist Party would soon disappear. The fact that the Republican candidate, William McKinley, won the election may also help to explain the demise of the Populists. This is not the last time a third party would be swallowed up when one or both of the larger parties began to adopt its policies.

The onset of the 20th century saw the rise of the Progressive Movement. Although not really a single party, the Progressives typically included a collection of middle class citizens who were better educated than their Populist predecessors. The Progressives pushed for an expanded role of government to protect workers, consumers and natural resources. They also worked to break up the growing monopolies and trusts that had grown to dominate the American economy. As their popularity rose, it grew more likely that either the Democrats or Republicans would adopt their agenda. After nominating Bryan for president in 1896, the Democrats seemed to be more closely aligned with the Progressives, but an assassination in 1901 reversed the parties' ideological positioning.

The assassination of William McKinley placed his vice president, Theodore Roosevelt, into the White House. Teddy Roosevelt changed everything. His youth, charisma and penchant for reform made him naturally appealing to many Progressives. For the next seven and half years, he constantly sought legislative action to enact his relatively robust agenda, which included everything from protecting the public from tainted meat, to placing millions of acres under federal protection. In doing so, he changed and expanded the role of the U.S. President. Since he was a Republican, it only seemed natural that his party would become synonymous with Progressivism.

After stepping down from the presidency in 1908, Roosevelt was replaced by his handpicked successor, William Howard Taft. At the same time that Roosevelt was leaving the country for a safari in Africa, Taft was expected to take over the mantle of the Progressives. While Taft did make a respectable effort to break up some of the largest trusts, many people developed the perception that he was not doing enough. His wide girth and ponderous movement only fed this perception. In American politics, perception often matters more than reality. When Taft sought to run for reelection in 1912, he was viewed as too conservative, so Roosevelt decided to end their friendship and challenge him for the Republican nomination. The result was one of the most significant presidential elections in American history.

Roosevelt's challenge to Taft fractured the Republican Party. Ultimately, the Republican Convention nominated Taft, and ever since, the Republican Party (also known today as "*the Grand Old Party*" or GOP), has been the party more likely to advocate for limited federal government, lower taxes and more freedom for businesses. Roosevelt and his supporters immediately split off to form the Progressive Party, also referred to then as the Bull Moose Party (the name was derived from the characteristics of strength and vigor often used to describe Roosevelt himself). The Democrats nominated Woodrow Wilson on a platform also based on many Progressive principles. The split between Progressive Republicans and the more conservative section enabled Wilson to win. Over the next eight years, Wilson would help lead the reform of tariffs, the division of trusts and the creation the Federal Reserve System to better regulate banks. The federal government also began to collect income taxes, people gained the right to elect their own senators and women acquired the right to vote.

Under President Wilson, the Democrats had finally earned the right to portray themselves as the more Progressive party. From 1912 to the present, they have been the party more likely to create new federal aid programs, place regulations on businesses and increase taxes, especially on the wealthy. Yet despite the Democratic Party's emerging progressivism, during this period, both parties generally disregarded the concerns of African Americans and other minority communities. There is little doubt that Wilson harbored racist views, but an even bigger factor contributing to the prejudice of the Democratic Party was the white, Southern electorate that had been voting for the Democrats since before the Civil War. As a result, any Democratic politician that attempted to end segregation in the South, abolish poll taxes and literacy tests, or even support federal legislation to criminalize lynching, risked losing white southern support. This trend helps explain why presidents like Franklin Roosevelt and John F. Kennedy tiptoed around the issue of civil rights, and when Harry Truman ordered the racial integration of the military in 1948, it almost cost him his bid for reelection.

This tension was finally resolved during the 1960s, after John F. Kennedy's assassination in 1963 brought his vice president, Lyndon B. Johnson, to the White House. As a southern Democrat from Texas with years of experience in the Senate, Johnson was in a better position to advocate for the passage of a major Civil Rights Act in 1964. Soon thereafter, the majority of white southerners began to vote Republican. Relatedly, after the removal of poll taxes, literacy tests and other barriers added significantly to the number of African Americans who were able to vote, many who had sided with the Republican Party since it had been the Party of Lincoln now began to vote for Democrats. In the 2004 presidential election, 88 per cent of the African American voters opted for John Kerry, the Democrat. Even more voted for Barack Obama in 2008 and 2012.

Conclusion

In summary, several points about the two-party system can be made. First, it has dominated the American political scene from our nation's beginning. Second, the Electoral College and winner-takes-all election procedures have created systemic reasons why the two-party system has persevered up to the present. Third, Americans have grown used to their two-party system and are in no meaningful rush to make reforms. Fourth, while there are clear and obvious problems with the two-party system, the multi-party system also has its disadvantages. Finally, both of the parties that have dominated the American political scene for 230 years have proven to be remarkably fluid in how they adapt to changing times. A new party may replace one out of touch with the voters, party platforms have been adjusted, even at a glacial pace, and one or both of the two major parties have at times absorbed the agenda of third parties. Fundamentally, however, the two-party system has remained entrenched.

Winston Churchill once said, *"democracy is the worst form of Government except for all those other forms that have been tried."* Like democracy, the two-party system is far from perfect. Anyone who felt they were *"forced to choose between two evils"* in deciding between Hillary Clinton and Donald Trump in the 2016 presidential election would likely acknowledge this reality. No political system, however, is without flaws. Each has its strengths and weaknesses. The British might contend that since their prime minister is chosen by Parliament and hails from the dominant political party, they are more likely to see cooperation between their legislative and executive branches of government. On the other hand, they lose the advantages provided by the system of checks and balances that were created in the U.S. Constitution.

In the United States, there are both advantages and disadvantages that stem from its two-party political culture. Until we establish a new structure that is convincingly better, however, we will continue to live with the imperfections of the two-party system.

Sources and further reading:

Churchill, Winston. *BrainyQuote.com*. Accessed June 30, 2016. http://www.brainyquote.com/quotes/w/winstonchu164161.html.

Easley, Jonathan and Ben Kamisar. "Third-party Candidates Face Uphill Climb to Get Place on Presidential Debate Stage." *TheHill.com*. May 12, 2016. http://www.thehill.com/homenews/campaign/279624-third-party-candidates-face-uphill-climb-to-get-place-on-presidential.

Fund, John. "The Return of Edwin Edwards." *NationalReview.com*. March 18, 2014. http://www.nationalreview.com/corner/373589/return-edwin-edwards-john-fund.

"Getting the Republicans Back on Track." *NewYorkTimes.com*. January 31, 1999. http://www.nytimes.com/1999/01/31/opinion/getting-the-republicans-back-on-track.html?pagewanted=all.

Gore, D'Angelo. "Presidents Winning Without Popular Vote." *FactCheck.org*. March 24, 2008. http://www.factcheck.org/2008/03/presidents-winning-without-popular-vote/.

"Guide to Israel's Political Parties." *BBC.com*. January 21, 2013. http://www.bbc.com/news/world-middle-east-21073450.

"How Groups Voted in 2004." *Roper Center*. Accessed June 30, 2016. http://www.ropercenter.cornell.edu/polls/us-elections/how-groups-voted/how-groups-voted-2004/.

Ito, Tim. "Major Political Parties in Japan." *WashingtonPost.com*. Accessed June 29, 2016. http://www.washingtonpost.com/wp-srv/inatl/longterm/japan/japanparties.htm.

Kalb, Deborah, ed. *Guide to U.S. Elections*. Thousand Oaks: CQ Press, 2016.

Lyons, Linda. "Teens Stay True to Parents' Political Perspectives." *Gallup.com*. January 4, 2005. http://www.gallup.com/poll/14515/teens-stay-true-parents-political-perspectives.aspx.

McGerr, Michael. *A Fierce Discontent: The Rise and Fall of the Progressive Movement in America, 1870-1920*. New York: Oxford University Press, 2005.

Rivera, Ray. "State Highlights." *NewYorkTimes.com*. Accessed June 29, 2016. http://www.elections.nytimes.com/2012/results/states/missouri.

Schlesinger, Arthur Meir, Jr. *The Age of Jackson*. New York: Back Bay Books, 1988.

Washington, George. *GoodReads.com*. Accessed June 29, 2016. http://www.goodreads.com/quotes/462873-however-political-parties-may-now-and-then-answer-popular-ends.

"What Factors Shape Political Attitudes?" *UsHistory.org*. Accessed June 30, 2016. http://www.ushistory.org/gov/4b.asp.

"What is the Electoral College?" *National Archives and Records Administration*. Accessed June 29, 2016. http://www.archives.gov/federal-register/electoral-college/about.html.

Chapter 4

Why is there such diversity in the way nations govern themselves?

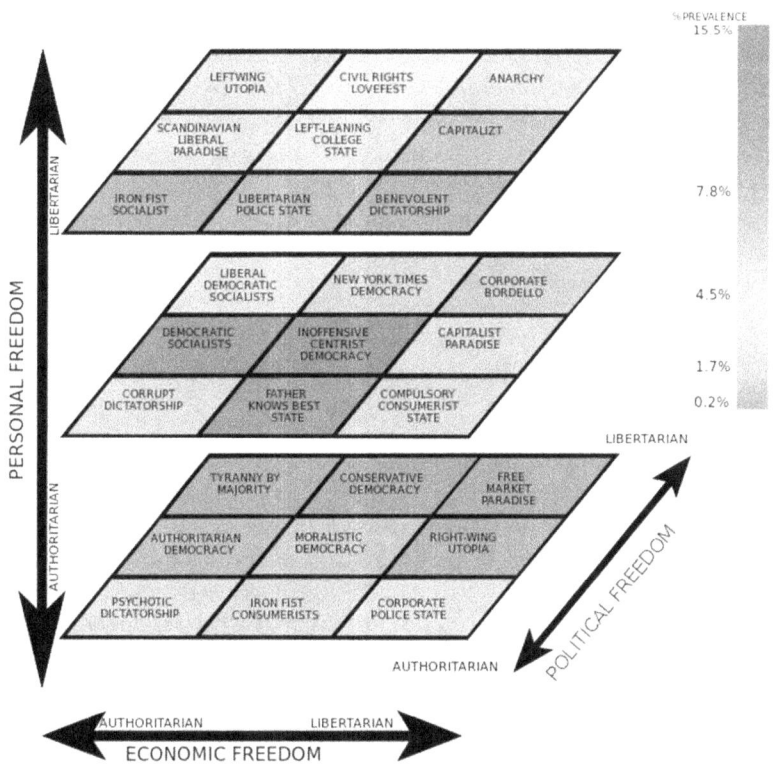

Graph of Nation States
Courtesy of Winner 42 (CC-By-SA-4.0)
https://Commons.Wikimedia.org/wiki/File:Updated_NS_Graph.svg

"Why has government been instituted at all? Because the passions of men will not conform to the dictates of reason and justice, without constraint."

Alexander Hamilton

There are 196 nations in the world today. Each has its own unique brand of government. While most can be placed under broad categories, such as monarchies, dictatorships, oligarchies, theocracies and democracies, no two are the same. Moreover, they frequently shift over time depending on the political climate and circumstances. Most would consider the United States to be a democratic republic with strong leanings toward a capitalist economic system. Yet the incredibly elaborate U.S. bureaucracy that rules over more than 320 million people today hardly resembles the simple government of two hundred years ago that did little more than collect tariffs and deliver the mail.

The origins of government parallel the origins of modern humanity. Even the earliest people were required to develop a communal society in order to survive. This meant that communal decisions had to be made on a daily basis. Those empowered to make decisions, be it one person, a few, or everyone, constituted the earliest governments. Anarchy may technically be defined as the absence of government, but no society has survived for long without establishing some kind of framework for effective decision-making. To accomplish this endeavor, four questions had to be addressed.

Question one – Who possesses the power to make important decisions?

One way to consider how societies have answered this question is to run through the options that might be placed on a spectrum. At one end of the spectrum is a system that provides only one person with all of the political power. If the individual inherits power from his or her parents or family, this form of government is called a monarchy. This holds true whether the person's title is King, Queen, Emperor, Pharaoh, Caesar, Kaiser, Czar, Sultan, Marshall, Dear Leader or Chief. Alternatively, if the individual is given or simply takes the power, his or her title can be whatever he or she chooses it to be. Those who want to pretend they are presiding over some form of democracy might call themselves presidents or prime ministers. On the other hand, Adolph Hitler was referred to as the Fuehrer, which originally was the German title for leader or guide. Benito Mussolini was called the Duce, which had a similar meaning. Regardless of the title or how the individual came to power, the simplest term for such a ruler is dictator.

At the opposite end of the spectrum is pure democracy. In theory, a pure democracy divides political power equally among all adult citizens. The city-state of Athens during the Golden Age of Greece probably came the closest to resembling a pure democracy, although women, slaves and the foreign-born were excluded from citizenship. Since it is not generally feasible for a larger population to place all of its citizens in one arena to discuss, debate and vote on every decision, most democratic societies have opted to empower their citizens to elect representatives to do this on their behalf. The representatives might meet in a Senate, Parliament,

Why is there such diversity in the way nations govern themselves?

General Assembly, Congress, Duma, Reichstag, Diet, or Council, but if they are elected to make decisions on behalf of those who chose them, this form of government is commonly referred to as a republic or a democratic republic.

Between these two extremes are different variations on allocating decision-making powers to a smaller group of people. The size of the group relative to the total population can vary from one time and place to another, but in general, this form of government is referred to as an oligarchy. If the wealthy dominate the elite group of rulers, primarily to look out for their own economic interests, this type of oligarchy is referred to as a plutocracy. If the government rules primarily on behalf of a set of religious ideas or as direct agents of a deity, it is called a theocracy.

Despite the wide variety of terms and titles, the answer to this first question seems theoretically simple. Political power in any given society will either be entrusted to one person, a numerical minority of the population or to all or most of the citizenry. In the past, most nations opted for the first option, but over the last two centuries, the principles of democracy have been spreading. According to *Borgen Magazine*, there are currently 123 democratic nations in the world.

Yet while virtually every nation on this planet except Vatican City, Saudi Arabia and Brunei claims to be a democracy, many clearly are not. When determining whether a nation is structured as a *"democracy,"* we should consider: does every adult citizen possess the right to vote? How frequently are elections held? Do the elected leaders possess meaningful powers to make decisions? Are the individual rights and freedoms of the electorate protected from the whims of the government? According to *Nobelprize.org*, more than 100 nations have non-democratic or just partly democratic governments. *Freedom House* issued a report in 2016 stating that 40 per cent of the world's population is *"free,"* 24 per cent is *"partly free"* and 36 per cent is *"not free."*

The reality is that in a world of over seven billion people and almost 200 nations, most governments defy simple labels. Terms like monarchy, dictatorship, oligarchy and democracy can be applied to different governments based on the percentage of people that possess the political power to make decisions, but when each country is examined more thoroughly, the labeling process is not so simple.

Question two – Who selects the government?

Regardless of the total number of people that possess the power to make decisions, the next question is how are these people chosen? Is their power inherited? Is it taken with the support of the masses or under the threat of military violence? Is the transfer of political power guided by a process created by a constitution or is it achieved in a haphazard fashion?

In some cases, after a rebelling group overthrows an existing structure, a new government will rise from a violent revolution. The new group might be small, such as the leaders of the military, or it could be large, as in a popular revolution. Over the last 250 years, popular revolutions have broken out in the United States, France and throughout much of Latin America, among other places. We have also witnessed economically driven uprisings in nations like Russia, China and Cuba. In each case, the leaders of the revolution eventually became the established government and remained so unless they were overthrown in another coup or rebellion.

In the case of monarchies, power is inherited. There is no guarantee that a king's son or daughter will possess the qualifications to rule, but the benefit is stability and a political order so long as the monarch extends the family tree. This is the world's oldest form of government, perhaps due to its simplicity. In many societies, the monarch's power was sanctioned by religious faith. This was the case with Egyptian pharaohs, as well as the emperors of Rome two thousand years ago and Japan in more recent times. European kings during the era of absolute monarchy ruled by *"divine right."* These monarchies provided for generally predictable successions of power, although they also often produced inconsistent quality in governance.

Dictators and oligarchs have typically gained power in one of two ways. The first is through a coup d'état in which they possess enough military support to seize control of the government. In many respects, this is similar to the revolutionary process described earlier. The second method involves appealing to the populist impulses of the people. A leader may take over through a military coup, but if he or she can win over the hearts and minds of the people, rifle bayonets are unnecessary to take and keep power. For the most part, this is a relatively recent phenomenon. Two hundred years ago, Napoleon Bonaparte exploited the chaos of the French Revolution to set himself up as popular dictator. More recently, the same path was followed by Benito Mussolini in Italy, Adolph Hitler in Germany and Juan and Eva Peron in Argentina. In many cases, *"elections"* were also held to legitimize the leadership of these dictators. More often than not, however, these elections were rigged, corrupt or were simply mandates where the only real choice was to vote for or against the leadership of the dictator.

One type of dictatorship has been defined by fascism, a system of governance that prioritizes nationalism, state interests and authoritarian leadership. The secret to the success of fascist dictators in modern times is to effectively combine three elements. The first is personal charisma. There must be something about the dictator that proves appealing to many people. Mussolini and Hitler were neither particularly tall nor handsome, but when they walked into a crowded room, everyone else took notice. Charisma is almost impossible to define, but most people will recognize it whenever they encounter a charismatic leader.

The second element is making and delivering on the right promises, particularly the promises that make people feel safe. This is the appeal of authoritarianism. After being chosen as the chancellor in 1933, Hitler promised to pull the German economy out of the Great Depression. In a nation where millions were unemployed, hungry and homeless, this promise had great appeal. More crucially, after the Fuehrer put millions to work building weapons for Germany's revamped military, assembling a new *"people's automobile"* called the Volkswagen and constructing major public works projects like the Autobahn, he had largely delivered on his promise. This made it much easier for the German people to tolerate the ugly racist policies that the Nazis were implementing at the same time.

The third element is to employ fear and propaganda to control what people know and believe. This became much easier with the new technology generated by the Industrial Revolution. Airplanes made it more convenient for Hitler to fly faster from one Nazi rally to another. Radio and film made it easier for him to communicate with the masses. Arming his military with machine guns, tanks and dive-bombers made it much more difficult for a band of organized civilians to resist his Nazi movement. Collectively, these three qualities enabled the reign of Hitler and other fascist dictators, particularly in the middle of the 20th century.

In democratic republics, representatives are selected in free elections where all or most of the adult citizens can vote and are eligible to run for office. Most of the more established democracies in the world have only gradually enfranchised all of its citizens. It was not until the first half of the 19th century that Great Britain and the United States dropped their property requirements to vote. Women did not secure the right to suffrage in these two democracies until the early 20th century. Much of the American Civil Rights Movement in the1960s was devoted to enfranchising African Americans who were prevented from voting in southern states by poll taxes and literacy tests. Even today, racial minorities and lower socio-economic classes in the United States still do not possess their fair share of political power in many key respects. Nevertheless, in theory, the people are empowered to select their governments in democratic nations.

Question three – How much power is given to the government?

Until recent times, most governments were primarily concerned with retaining power. European monarchs could theoretically do whatever they wanted, including taking complete control over the economy, the state religion and the personal lives of their subjects, but most had neither the desire nor the ability to do so. Rulers might set regulations over trade and require everyone to worship in the same Catholic or Protestant Church, but on a day-to-day basis, most subjects were left alone. There was no military draft, so monarchs employed professional soldiers and sailors to wage their wars. The average farmer, merchant or artisan was generally free to carry out their lives. The government existed to build and maintain a few roads, possibly deliver the mail and provide for military security. In most other respects, governments had little power.

In the West, much of this began to change in the years between 1648 and 1815. The Treaty of Westphalia ended the Thirty Years' War in 1648 by acknowledging the sanctity of sovereign states in Europe and creating a basis for their national self-determination. With the advent of the French Revolution in 1789 and the subsequent rise of Napoleon Bonaparte, nationalism emerged and soon began to spread. By this point, not only were the people living within the boundaries of a given nation considered to be citizens of that respective state, but they were also expected to patriotically love their country. Governments sought to grow a country's wealth, power and reputation. Conscription was instituted based on the belief that citizens should be willing to fight, kill and die for their *"fatherlands."* With the military draft, army sizes increased from thousands to millions, and as a result, the nationalistic wars of the 19th and 20th centuries became far deadlier than any fought in the past. Moreover, with the rise of industry and new technology, the powers of government were increased to better regulate economic growth and trade.

The rise of big government soon led to the question of whether limits could and should be placed on the powers of a particular regime. The British were among the first in the Western world to wrestle with this question. Great Britain has existed as a cohesive nation since 1066, the last time the British were successfully invaded. The first nation in the world to successfully enable agricultural and industrial revolutions, England was also one of the first to reign in its government's powers. This was accomplished by passage of a Bill of Rights in 1689. British kings and parliaments had vied for greater political power throughout most of the 17th century through civil war, a king's beheading and a *"Glorious Revolution."* By the dawn of the 18th century, Great Britain was not only on the path to becoming a democracy, but was also the first nation in the world to deliberately check the powers of its government.

Given its origins, it is perhaps little surprise that the United States became the second. Begun as a set of 13 English colonies, important principles about limited government were instilled by the mother country. After winning its independence in the Revolutionary War, the new nation needed a government, which was formed through the ratification of the Constitution and the incorporation of ten amendments collectively known as the Bill of Rights. These amendments were intended to limit the powers of government, as well as provide specified rights for the people. While the British constitution is more a collection of documents and traditions developed over time than a single charter, both the British and American constitutions established the principle that the powers of government must be limited in order for people to enjoy *"the blessings of liberty."*

The question over how much power should be entrusted to the government is probably the most important in attempting to explain why there is so much political diversification around the world. On one hand, a government must have enough power to provide adequate national security and meet the needs of its subjects. On the other, people who live under liberal democracies have come to expect a certain degree of personal liberty and individual rights, such as freedom of speech, the right to peaceful assembly, freedom of religion and a right to privacy. What is the ideal balance between these two interests? In creating and maintaining a government, each nation perpetually struggles with this question.

Question four – What is the government's role in providing for the production and distribution of goods and services?

How a society chooses to distribute its wealth will generally have a significant impact on how it allocates political power. Under capitalism or free enterprise, individuals possess the freedom to own property, run businesses and earn unlimited profits. Profit incentive is what underpins the capitalist system. The pursuit of wealth motivates people to create, invent and work to their maximum effort. Many believe, however, that capitalism can only operate when government does not interfere. "*Laissez faire*," the principle that the government should abstain from meddling in the workings of the free market, is one of the defining principles of free enterprise.

Accordingly, the regulatory powers of government in a purely capitalist economy should be minimal. For nearly 150 years, the U.S. government did not even collect an income tax. Most of the government's revenue came from the sale of western lands and the collection of tariffs on imports, and these existed more to protect American business interests than to generate funds. At this time, the government did not need much money because it provided few services. There were no Social Security, Medicare or food stamp programs. The military was small except during the four years of the Civil War, largely because the U.S. policy of isolationism kept it out of most international conflicts. There were also virtually no regulations on businesses to protect workers, consumers or the environment. The United States government in the 19th century was slowly evolving towards greater democracy, but the scope of its power was relatively insignificant.

On the other end of the economic spectrum, the latter half of the 19th century witnessed the rise of socialism and communism as alternatives to capitalism. As the Industrial Revolution compressed more wealth into the pocketbooks of fewer people, demands for an increased role for government began to rise, particularly in European nations. Karl Marx developed a theory that an economic revolution by the struggling masses of workers, the Proletariat, was historically inevitable. According to Marx, workers had "*nothing to lose but their chains."* His books and pamphlets called for a violent revolution to overthrow the Bourgeoisie and replace it with a classless society in which every person would share equally in the distribution of wealth.

Of course, this economic philosophy called for a colossal increase in the powers of the government. In a purely socialist or communist economic system, the government assumes control over the economy. The means of production, that is all of the farms, factories and businesses, are owned and run by the government. In addition, the government determines where people work, how much they earn, and what prices to set. The economic liberty cherished by capitalists is sacrificed to promote greater economic equality.

While the powers of the government dramatically increase as a nation moves its economy across the spectrum from free enterprise towards socialism or communism, the form of government does not necessarily have to change. Scandinavian nations like Sweden and Denmark have moved increasingly towards socialism by raising taxes on the wealthy and providing services like universal health care and free education to their citizens. Simultaneously, they have retained free elections, protected civil liberties and continued to bestow political power amongst most of their citizens. While socialism might loosely be defined as an economic theory of social organization in which the means of production, distribution and exchange are owned or regulated by the community as a whole, this is not antithetical to political freedom and democracy.

Generally, communism is simply a more extreme form of socialism. Karl Marx called for a violent revolution as the only means to equally distribute economic wealth, and historically, the communist governments that have since formed have initially proven to be dictatorships. In theory, Marx actually called for a temporary *"dictatorship of the proletariat"* that would be charged with setting up the new, communist economic system and would then *"wither away"* once people had become truly equal. Starting with the Russian Revolution in 1917, however, these communist dictatorships have hardly *"withered away."* Instead, governments in communist nations like the Soviet Union, China and Cuba have veered more toward totalitarian regimes. Since no other party has generally been allowed to compete with the Communist Party, elections in these nations have basically been a sham. Dictators like Joseph Stalin in the USSR, Mao Zedong in Communist China and Fidel Castro in Cuba have frequently appeared to be more concerned with amassing and keeping political power than they were in creating classless societies.

Economics has an enormous influence over the choice of political systems in another respect: the amount of wealth of a particular nation may be just as important as how it chooses to distribute its wealth. Affluent societies like Canada, Australia, the United States and the nations of Western Europe have the luxury of time and resources to support democratic traditions. In light of the conflicts and debates that tend to occur between competing political parties, democracy tends to be slow, messy and inefficient. In the developing nations of the world, however, growing enough food, providing safe drinking water and preventing medical epidemics often trumps the desire to hold free elections. Some nations, like India, have managed to create democratic governments in the face of massive poverty, but these are more the exception than the rule.

Democratic institutions also tend to grow slowly and need to be carefully cultivated, like a fragile plant. This requires great time and commitment. Most of the more successful democracies in the world today have been democratic for a long time. On the other hand, most of the world's developing nations were colonies controlled by a Western power until only a relatively short time ago. Their new governments are frequently plagued by political instability, as well as a lower standard of living. Many did not have input in creating their own borders. They also may have conflicting ethnic and religious groups that compete for political power. This is why the United States, Canada, Australia, New Zealand and 14 Western European nations make up 18 out of the top 20 democratic nations on the Democracy Index compiled annually by the *Economist Intelligence Unit*. At the opposite end of the ranking, the 20 least democratic nations are all located in Africa, the Middle East and the subcontinent of Asia. Furthermore, not a single one existed as a nation 100 years ago.

In the long run, what matters more, the distribution of political power or the distribution of wealth? The answer varies from nation to nation, but there is no question that each has an impact on the other. Countries that are affluent and stable have the luxury of nurturing democratic institutions like free elections and the protection of individual rights. Yet many nations of the world languish behind economically due to a host of historical reasons and circumstances. For those nations, an "enlightened" dictator who may choose a more socialistic path towards economic development may be a better option, at least in the short term.

The final determinants

In the end, why are there so many different types of governments around the world? The simplest answer is that in terms of history, religion and cultural traditions, every nation is unique. Take Kenya for example. A nation in East Africa with approximately 45 million people, Kenya only acquired its independence from Great Britain in 1963. Although Kenya wrote a democratic constitution shortly after gaining its freedom and called itself a republic, the last 60 years have witnessed bouts of dictatorial rule, attempted military coups and extensive corruption. While there is an affluent urban minority, Kenya has a Human Development Index (HDI) of 0.519, which ranks its economy 145th out of 186. Almost 18 per cent of the population lives on less than $1.25 a day, and up to a third of people's income is used to pay bribes.

In addition, Kenya has an extremely diverse population that includes most of the major ethnic, racial and linguistic groups found in Africa. There are an estimated 47 different communities residing in Kenya. Historically, Europeans drew the boundaries for Kenya, and if left alone, the modern nation of Kenya would probably not exist in its present form. The same can be said for many other nations, including Rwanda, which is also found in East Africa, and Iraq, located in the Middle East. In each of these nations, two or more subgroups with a tradition of animosity have struggled to coexist within a single nation. In 1994, a genocidal bloodbath in the nation of Rwanda took the lives of up to 1.3 million people. In more recent times, Iraq has experienced a civil war between Shiite and Sunni Muslims after the removal of Saddam Hussein as the nation's dictator. Even with written constitutions and efforts to hold free elections, the lack of democratic traditions and political stability will make the future of any elected government in these three nations tenuous at best.

For contrast, take Canada as a counter example. With 17 times more land than Kenya, Canada has ten million fewer people. Canada also has a well-developed economy and an affluent standard of living. Canada's Human Development Index has it ranked 9th in the world. Like Kenya, Canada is a former British colony. However, most of the Canadian population is primarily of European descent, with Aboriginal tribes making up only about four per cent of the population. Historically, the Canadians acquired their independence gradually, without any of the bloodshed experienced by the Kenyans. They were also given ample opportunity to establish their own local government, so the roots of democratic traditions had time to grow and develop. Today, Canada ranks among the highest in the world in international measurements of effective democratic government, such as transparency, civil liberties, quality of life, economic freedom and education. Under these circumstances, Canada's democratic government has been generally robust and stable.

On paper, Kenya and Canada are both considered to be democracies. Both were also once part of the mighty British Empire. In light of their different economic, social and cultural traditions, however, there is a world of difference between the governments in Nairobi and Ottawa. In the years to come, Canada will more than likely remain a stable democracy. Kenya's current democracy is much more fragile. A new constitution was passed in 2010 and free elections occurred in 2013. The end of 2014, however, saw passage of a Security Laws Amendment Bill that was considered necessary to guard against violence by armed groups. Opposition politicians, human rights groups and nine Western nations criticized the security bill, arguing that it infringed on democratic freedoms.

Each nation is unique. Every country has its own inimitable history and incomparable set of circumstances. Some are more tradition-bound, and a few countries like Saudi Arabia and Bahrain are still ruled by hereditary monarchies. The people in many nations are driving their countries towards free elections and democratic constitutions, but for the time being, most of the power is still retained by some kind of demagogue or tyrant. Others, like Kenya, made a conscientious choice to adopt democratic principles, but the real measure of their success will by reflected by a significant amount of time with political stability. Of course, much may depend on future events that no one can predict. Many of the newer, less developed nations of the world are only a drought, invasion, religious civil war or economic calamity away from seeing their fragile democratic apparatus overthrown in a military coup d'état.

Before concluding that the international diversity of political systems is as random as choosing lottery numbers, one might ask whether there is some overall pattern that might be discerned in modern times. Are nations, at least the majority of them, gravitating in a particular direction? If so, what is this direction, and what is its underlying cause?

Conclusion – The appeal of democracy

Democracy is 2500 years old, but it has arguably made its most significant inroads in modern times. The British may have been begun electing some kind of Parliament after passage of the Magna Carta in 1215, but until English women gained the right to vote in 1928, England was still not truly a democracy. Nevertheless, Britain's Glorious Revolution in 1688, reinforced by the American Revolution in 1776 and the Revolution in France that began 13 years later placed much of the planet on a trajectory towards liberal democracy. Written constitutions, free elections and the protection of individual human rights are all practices that are becoming increasingly universal. There are many exceptions to this overall pattern, but as previously stated, only a small handful of nations out of almost 200 do not call themselves democracies. It is likely only a matter of time before many of them start to live up that self-description.

Why is this the case? The answer lies largely in the recent advances made in technology. Thanks to the rise of radio, television, personal computers, the Internet, satellites, jet transportation, cellular phones and other forms of digital equipment, the world has become a considerably smaller place. How much longer will people agree to live under a rigid monarchy when their televisions and smart phones are brandishing the advantages of a free society right under their noses? How will military dictators continue to maintain their power when potential rebels can communicate with others through text messages and tweets? Even the most remote villages now often have multiple links with the outside world.

Three hundred years ago, the only way for the average person to know what was taking place more than a few miles from their home was to read a newspaper, and this was assuming he or she had the ability to understand it. Most people on the planet were largely kept in the dark about international events. Only a handful of people read, understood and discussed the democratic ideas being developed by pioneers of the Enlightenment like Thomas Hobbes, John Locke, Voltaire, Baron de Montesquieu and Jean Jacques Rousseau. There is no question that Enlightenment ideas had a profound influence over Americans like Benjamin Franklin, John Adams and Thomas Jefferson. Beyond the leaders of the American and French Revolutions, however, their ideas were largely unknown.

We live in a profoundly different world than the one inhabited by William Pitt the Younger, Thomas Jefferson and the Marquis de Lafayette. The principles and ideas regarding freedom and democracy may have germinated in their time, but the breezes powered by new technology have spread their seeds across the planet. We have recently witnessed this when Soviet citizens voted the Communist Party out of power, leading to the obliteration of the Berlin Wall and the spreading of democratic principles throughout Eastern Europe. We have seen this trend in the democratization of South Africa when the black majority finally won the right to vote, which led to the transfer of Nelson Mandela from prison to the president's mansion. More recently, it was seen in the Arab Spring that was unleashed by events in Tunisia in 2010, which is still having great impact throughout much of the Middle East.

There is still much diversity in how nations govern themselves today, and to a certain degree, this will always be true. Ultimately, however, the appeal of freedom and the accompanying respect for human dignity will most likely continue to spread over the Internet and people's smart phones, until much of the planet's political diversity will start to resemble genuine democracy.

Sources and further reading:

"Anxious Dictators, Wavering Democracies: Global Freedom Under Pressure." *FreedomHouse.com.* Accessed July 26, 2016. http://www.freedomhouse.org/report/freedom-world/freedom-world-2016.

Brooker, Paul. *Non-Democratic Regimes.* New York: Palgrave Macmillan, 2009.

"Democracies in the World." *Nobleprize.org.* Accessed July 26, 2016. http://www.nobleprize.org/educational/peace/democracy_map/.

"Democracy Index 2015: Democracy in an Age of Anxiety." *The Economist Intelligence Unit.* Accessed July 27, 2016. http://www.yabiladi.com/img/content/EIU-Democracy-Index-2015.pdf.

Goitom, Hanibal. "Kenya: Security Laws Bill Enacted." *Library of Congress.org.* December 30, 2014. http://www.loc.gov/law/foreign-news/article/kenya-security-laws-amendment-bill-enacted/.

Hamilton, Alexander. *Brainyquote.com.* Accessed July 26, 2016. http://www.brainyquote.com/quotes/quotes/a/alexanderh397816.html.

"How Many Democratic Nations Are There?" *BorgenMagazine.com.* September 29, 2013. http://www.www.borgenmagazine.com/many-democratic-nations/.

"Human Development Reports." *UnitedNationsDevelopmentProgramme.org.* Accessed July 27, 2016. http://www.hdr.undp.org/en/composite/HDI.

"I Have a Dream Today." *TheGuardian.com.* August 28, 2008. http://www.theguardian.com/commentisfree/2008/aug/uselections2008.constitutionandcivilliberties. Lijphart, Arend. *Patterns of Democracy.* New Haven: Yale University Press, 2012.

Marx, Karl. *The Portable Karl Marx.* Translated by Eugene Kamenka. New York: Penguin Books, 1983.

"The Rwandan Genocide." *Endgenocide.org.* Accessed July 27, 2016. http://www.endgenocide.org/learn/past-genocides/the-rwandan-genocide/.

Watts, Duncan. *British Government and Politics: A Comparative Guide.* Edinburgh: Edinburgh University Press, 2012.

Welsh, Teresa. "Democracy in Decline Around the World." *U.S.News.com.* January 28, 2015. http://www.usnews.com/news/blogs/data-mine/2015/01/28/report-democracy-in-decline.

Chapter 5

Why is wealth so unevenly distributed?

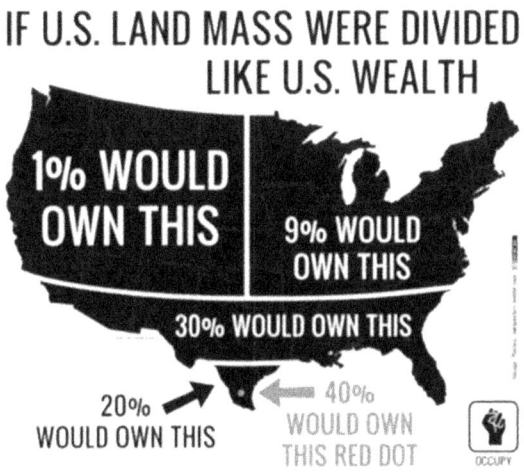

U.S. Wealth Inequality in 2013
Courtesy of Stephen Ewen(CC-By-SA-3.0)
https://commons.wikimedia.org/wiki/File: If-us-land-mass-were-distributed-like-us-wealth.png

> "An imbalance between the rich and the poor is the oldest and most fatal ailment of all republics."
>
> Plutarch

There are currently 7.4 billion people alive today. The wealth of the planet, whether it is defined as money, land or personal possessions, has never been more unevenly distributed. This has caused much debate and conflict over the centuries and has even led to the rise of competing economic systems such as capitalism, socialism and communism. How did the world reach this state?

Amongst the nations of the world, the differences in wealth are so great that it has led many to say there are actually three different worlds sharing one planet. While this division has recently fallen out of favor, it still has some relevance. The *"First World"* consists of nations who are largely led by stable, democratic governments, have fully industrialized economies and enjoy a high standard of living. One measure of a country's quality of life is to determine the sum total of all goods and services produced in a given year, the gross domestic product (GDP), and then divide this total by the nation's population. This statistic, the per capita GDP, reflects roughly how much wealth the average citizen enjoys, although it largely ignores distribution patterns. As can be seen in the chart below, the highest standards of living according to this measure are found primarily in oil rich nations like Qatar, in developed nations with diminutive populations like Luxembourg and in larger nations with fully industrialized economies like the U.S.

1	QATAR	$132,100	2015 EST.
2	LUXEMBOURG	$99,000	2015 EST.
3	MACAU	$98,200	2015 EST.
4	LIECHTENSTEIN	$89,400	2009 EST.
5	BERMUDA	$85,700	2013 EST.
6	SINGAPORE	$85,300	2015 EST.
7	ISLE OF MAN	$83,100	2007 EST.
8	BRUNEI	$79,700	2015 EST.
9	MONACO	$78,700	2013 EST.
10	KUWAIT	$70,200	2015 EST.
11	NORWAY	$68,400	2015 EST.
12	UNITED ARAB EMIRATES	$67,600	2015 EST.
13	SINT MAARTEN	$66,800	2014 EST.
14	AUSTRALIA	$65,400	2015 EST.
15	SAN MARINO	$63,900	2015 EST.
16	SWITZERLAND	$58,600	2015 EST.
17	JERSEY	$57,000	2005 EST.
18	HONG KONG	$56,700	2015 EST.
19	UNITED STATES	$55,800	2015 EST.

Country comparison: GDP-per capita
Courtesy of the Central Intelligence Agency
https://www.cia.gov/library/publications/the-world-factbokk/rankorder/2004rank.html

Why is wealth so unevenly distributed?

Life in the First World is relatively good for many people. Governments are limited by legitimate constitutions, and free elections take place on a regular basis. The economy is technologically advanced, service-oriented and highly industrialized. Machines, computers and robots do much of the manual labor, and the average citizen has more wealth and works fewer hours than ever before. More important, the standard of living is comfortable for most and affluent for many. At $55,800 per person, the average American takes for granted a lifestyle that includes two automobiles, designer labels available in most shopping malls, and refrigerators stocked with enough food. Even with 14.5 per cent of the nation living below the poverty line, most of these people still have access to clean drinking water, free public education, food on the table and a roof over their heads.

The *"Second World"* consists primarily of less developed nations that turned to communism as a means to not only generate greater wealth, but also distribute it more equitably. With the end of the Cold War, this category has grown considerably smaller. The Soviet Union voted the communists out of power in 1990 and proceeded to disintegrate into smaller states. Other nations like China, Cuba and Vietnam have slowly marched towards a free market economy. Only North Korea is still holding out, and under its unstable, dictatorial regime, it is difficult to place the Hermit Kingdom under any single category. Most of the former Second World nations are moving at various speeds toward becoming First World nations.

Then there is the *"Third World."* Since no one wants to be labeled as third in anything, a more appropriate label for this slice of the planet is *"developing nations."* Using per capita GDP as the measure once again, the list of nations at the bottom of the ranking shows countries mostly found in Africa and Oceania. Afghanistan and North Korea are the only two nations on the list found in continental Asia, and Haiti is the only one located in the Western Hemisphere.

200	MALI	$2,200	2015 EST.
201	BENIN	$2,100	2015 EST.
202	ZIMBABWE	$2,100	2015 EST.
203	SOUTH SUDAN	$2,000	2015 EST.
204	UGANDA	$2,000	2015 EST.
205	SOLOMON ISLANDS	$1,900	2015 EST.
206	AFGHANISTAN	$1,900	2015 EST.
207	RWANDA	$1,800	2015 EST.
208	ETHIOPIA	$1,800	2015 EST.
209	KIRIBATI	$1,800	2015 EST.

210	KOREA, NORTH	$1,800	2014 EST.
211	HAITI	$1,800	2015 EST.
212	BURKINA FASO	$1,700	2015 EST.
213	GAMBIA, THE	$1,600	2015 EST.
214	SIERRA LEONE	$1,600	2015 EST.
215	TOGO	$1,500	2015 EST.
216	GUINEA-BISSAU	$1,500	2015 EST.
217	MADAGASCAR	$1,500	2015 EST.
218	COMOROS	$1,500	2015 EST.
219	ERITREA	$1,300	2015 EST.
220	MOZAMBIQUE	$1,200	2015 EST.
221	GUINEA	$1,200	2015 EST.
222	NIGER	$1,100	2015 EST.
223	MALAWI	$1,100	2015 EST.
224	TOKELAU	$1,000	1993 EST.
225	LIBERIA	$900	2015 EST.
226	CONGO, DEMOCRATIC REPUBLIC OF THE	$800	2015 EST.
227	BURUNDI	$800	2015 EST.
228	CENTRAL AFRICAN REPUBLIC	$600	2015 EST.
229	SOMALIA	$400	2014 EST.

Country comparison: GDP-per capita
Courtesy of the Central Intelligence Agency
https://www.cia.gov/library/publications/the-world-factbokk/rankorder/2004rank.html

For the most part, these nations are relatively new and have little experience in self-government. Many have attempted to write democratic constitutions and hold free elections, but most remain politically unstable. They are vulnerable to military coups, corrupt politics and civil warfare. Religious and ethnic strife frequently creates social upheaval. Most important, their standard of living is abysmally low. In order to survive on just $1000 per person per year, many of the people in these nations usually rely on traditional lifestyles that include rudimentary farming, little in the way of consistent health care and education, and housing that lacks electricity, clean drinking water and safe sanitation. There are many exceptions to these rough stereotypes, but there is no denying that the distribution of wealth between nations is grossly unequal.

The same can be said for how wealth is distributed *within* most nations, including the United States. Currently, 80 per cent of the American population possesses only seven per cent of the nation's wealth. On the flip side, the top one per cent owns 40 per cent of our country's wealth. This lopsided distribution has dogged the American people throughout our nation's history, but it has recently grown worse. The share of America's wealth held by the country's richest citizens first peaked in the late 1920s, right before the Great Depression, then fell by more than half over the next three decades. Nevertheless, the equalizing trends of the mid-20th century have now been almost completely undone. At the top of the American economic summit, the richest of the nation's residents now possess as large a share of the wealth as they did in the 1920s.

Endless debates could be held as to how wealth should be fairly allocated. The question for now, however, is how did this situation arise in the first place.

Reason one – The Industrial Revolution

Generally, if a nation has completed the process of industrialization, its people will enjoy a much higher standard of living. For example, as England became increasingly industrialized in the first half of the 19th century, real wages for blue-collar employees doubled between 1819 and 1851. According to another estimate by economist N.F.R. Crafts, British income per person (in 1970 U.S. dollars) rose from about $400 in 1760 to $430 in 1800, to $500 in 1830, and then jumped up to $800 in 1860. For many centuries before the Industrial Revolution, in contrast, periods of falling income offset periods of rising income.

Another good measure of a nation's overall standard of living is its average life expectancy. After all, if there is more wealth to provide adequate food, cleaner drinking water and advanced health services, people can be expected to live longer. In 1900, the average American lived to the age of 50, and this was longer than in most other nations. Today, in just 117 years, that number has increased to almost 80. This dramatic climb coincided with much of America's industrial development. In contrast, the life span in many developing nations that have only begun the process of industrialization is significantly lower. The average person in Somalia can expect to live only to the age of 52 and in Afghanistan it is under 51.

Industrial nations clearly control a vastly disproportionate share of the world's wealth. Why is it that some nations began to industrialize over 200 years ago while many others have just begun the process? Questions of this kind were raised in Jared Diamond's famous book, *Guns, Germs and Steel*, and once again, the simplest answer boils down to one word: circumstance. As most people learn in school, the first nation in the world to industrialize was the United Kingdom, and the first major industry in the U.K. was textiles. Smaller than the state of Michigan, Great Britain emerged in the late 18th century with a combination of all the necessary circumstances to lead the world in industrial development.

First, England had already begun a revolution in agriculture that led to the growth of significantly more food. Agricultural output grew faster than the population over the century leading up to 1770, and thereafter, productivity remained among the highest in the world. Although the changes in English farming mostly involved experiments in crop rotation and an Enclosure Movement that led to the creation of larger, more efficiently run farms, other changes involving fertilization, irrigation and new mechanical equipment would later play a role as well. This increase in the food supply contributed to the rapid growth of population in England and Wales, from 5.5 million in 1700 to over 9 million by 1801.

The increase in population contributed two more circumstances to the start of an industrial revolution. Because fewer people could now grow more food, the additional population began to move to growing cities and towns where they could contribute to an expanding source of cheap labor for textile mills, mines and factories. Second, the expanding population created a larger market to purchase the increasing output of clothes and machine-made goods.

In addition, the United Kingdom, despite its relatively small size, was fortunate to possess many of the natural resources necessary to start an industrial revolution. There was ample iron ore that could be smelted into steel, the primary building material for the burgeoning industries. There was also a large supply of coal, the primary energy source for England's mills and factories. Further, the challenge of pumping water out of coalmines spurred the Scottish inventor, James Watt, to perfect the steam engine in 1781. This engine proved to be a fundamental building block in starting England's Industrial Revolution.

It might be tempting for an Anglophile to brag that one of the key circumstances behind industrialization in the United Kingdom was the creative inventiveness of the English people. A better explanation might be that the government in London kept its taxes low and involvement to a minimum so that British entrepreneurs had unprecedented freedom to build, finance and grow their fledgling industries. In addition, the awarding of patents to financially protect new inventions created a much greater incentive to innovate. In this sense, the English government was acceding to the principles of its own Adam Smith, the *"father of free enterprise"* and the author of *The Wealth of Nations* (1776).

Another necessary ingredient for an industrial revolution is investment capital. Building mills, factories and mines required more money than most individuals possessed. As an island nation, however, Great Britain had recently made great strides in the development of overseas trade, particularly with the Far East, the Indian subcontinent of Asia and its colonial settlements in North America. The Commercial Revolution that had swept across Europe going back to the 15th and 16th centuries had also led to the rise of large-scale banking and the sale of stock as a means to raise investment capital. The same investors that had purchased stock in the East India Company or colonies in Virginia would later invest their recently acquired wealth in factories and mines.

Finally, England was blessed by geographical circumstances that supported the transportation networks necessary for an industrial revolution. Raw materials needed to be transported to the factories and finished products had to be moved to the emergent marketplaces. As an island nation, ships could simply sail from one part of the U.K. to another. Navigable rivers connected interior areas, and where these did not exist, people dug canals, and later, constructed railroads. By the middle of the 19th century, Great Britain led the world in industrial output. Despite the hardships endured by coal miners, mill workers and factory laborers in terms of their long hours, harsh conditions and low pay, England was amongst the first nations in the world to achieve a significantly higher standard of living.

It was only a matter of time before other nations followed in England's sooty footsteps. France, Germany and Italy also possessed many of the right ingredients to industrialize. When Japan decided to emerge from its self-imposed isolation in the middle of the 19th century, its leaders imported industrial experts and managed to industrialize the country almost overnight. Russia lagged behind Western Europe, but after its communist revolution started in 1917, the Soviet economy advanced on an ambitious five-year plan to catch up as quickly as possible. Nations that had begun as British colonies and were largely populated by British citizens also had an advantage in their efforts to industrialize. This applied primarily to Canada, Australia, New Zealand and especially the United States.

In fact, the U.S. had all of the ingredients found in Great Britain and more. Yet in order for Americans to catch up with their former mother country, the 13 colonies first sought to gain their independence. After this was accomplished in 1783, the American people of European descent began to populate their ever-expanding borders. As long as free or inexpensive land was readily available, it was difficult for industrialists to find enough people willing to work in New England textile mills or Pennsylvania coalmines. Also, while the United Kingdom had abolished slavery throughout the British Empire by 1833, it would take another 30 years before the United States took the same step. The persistence of slavery throughout the American South tied up vast sources of capital that could otherwise have been invested in factories.

After the conclusion of the American Civil War in 1865, however, slavery was abolished and residents increasingly settled in western lands. Meanwhile, millions of immigrants continued to pour into America, providing a growing source of cheap labor. By the dawn of the 20th century, the United States had surpassed the British to become the most industrialized nation in the world. By 1900, the U.S. GDP of $312 billion dollars greatly exceeded the $185 billion found in the United Kingdom. In fewer than two centuries, a number of European nations, along with their colonial offshoots and Japan had managed to surpass the rest of the world in terms of their share of the planet's wealth. This was mostly due to the Industrial Revolution. Since then, the rest of the world has been attempting with varying degrees of success to ride the crest of industrial economic development in order to catch up.

Reason two - Imperialism

In today's world, the word *"imperialism"* has developed an ugly connotation. Literally meaning a *"policy of extending a nation's power and influence through diplomacy or military force,"* imperialism has been around for thousands of years. In essence, it has taken on two basic forms. In the first, the imperialist country establishes a colony in an area that is technologically underdeveloped. When the Phoenicians established the colony of Carthage in Northern Africa or the Greeks built the city of Syracuse on the island of Sicily, these colonies eventually grew up to become major powers in their own right. In fact, it took three Punic Wars before Rome finally defeated and destroyed the city of Carthage. In more recent times, the same pattern held true with the Portuguese colony of Brazil, the Spanish colonies of Columbia, Argentina, Venezuela, Peru, Mexico and Cuba, and the English colonies that became the nations of Australia, Canada and the United States. In each case, there were indigenous people present, but due to factors like disease and conquest, the growing populations that hailed from the mother countries eventually dominated. Ultimately, these colonies largely involved the settlement of new areas by people of European descent.

It is the second form of imperialism that has greatly contributed to the enormous disparities in wealth that currently exist between the nations of the world. Unlike the first, the second type of imperialism was characterized by the desire for new markets, the search for natural resources and the spread of Christianity. The colonies themselves remained largely populated by indigenous people and their Western rulers were always a numerical minority.

When the first colonies planted by Western European powers between the 16th and 18th centuries fought and won their independence, there was a temporary recess in the imperialist contest. By the middle of the 19th century, most of the colonies in the Western Hemisphere had gained their independence, and the European mother countries turned their attention inward to such matters as liberal political revolutions and economic industrial revolutions. While the French were creating their Second Republic, the Italians and Germans were following the principles of nationalism to unite their disparate states into unified nations. At the same time, the Russians were putting down radical groups who were assassinating czars, while the British industrialists were busy investing in new technology and factories. For a relatively brief period, the world had lost interest in overseas colonies.

By 1880, the situation had drastically changed. Aspiring entrepreneurs were seeking more secure sources of raw materials and new markets. Religious missionaries wanted to build crosses on different soil, and ardent nationalists wanted to plant their flags where the sun would never set. This New Imperialism had returned with a vengeance, and the major question was where the mother countries would attempt to form new colonies. Their answer was mostly in Africa and the subcontinent of Asia.

European nations already possessed colonies in parts of these two regions. Despite the larger populations of indigenous people that had taken thousands of years to build advanced civilizations in Africa and Asia, they were no match for modern warships and machine guns, not to mention telegraph lines and railroads. Between 1880 and 1914, the *"scramble"* for Africa took place, and when the dust settled, only Ethiopia and Liberia did not have European flags flying overhead. Meanwhile, the British controlled every acre from modern-day Afghanistan to Myanmar. The French took over what are now Vietnam, Cambodia and Laos; the Dutch were the overlords of Indonesia, and after defeating Spain in a brief war in 1898, the United States took control of the Philippines. China remained independent on paper, but virtually every Western power took control of a port city so that by 1900, the world's most populous nation resembled a whale carcass riddled with huge shark bites.

There was virtually nothing about the New Imperialism that was fair to the new colonies. India was expected to grow the cotton for the British textile mills and then buy back the manufactured clothing so that the industrialists in Manchester could reap an exorbitant profit. Congolese natives literally worked to death in Belgian diamond mines. When Philippine natives recoiled at gaining American rulers in place of the Spanish, their revolt was brutally crushed between 1899 and 1902 with the resulting loss of life estimated to be as high as 220,000. In every case, the economic interests of the colony were subservient to those of the mother country. Those with white skin looked down upon their subjects who had darker pigments. Mother nations provided centralized political leadership so that the locals developed little if any experience with self-government. Rulers redrew maps based on agreements made in Berlin without regard for different cultures that had traditional animosities towards each other. While the imperialist nations continued to modernize and raise their standards of living, the burgeoning masses in their colonies fell further behind.

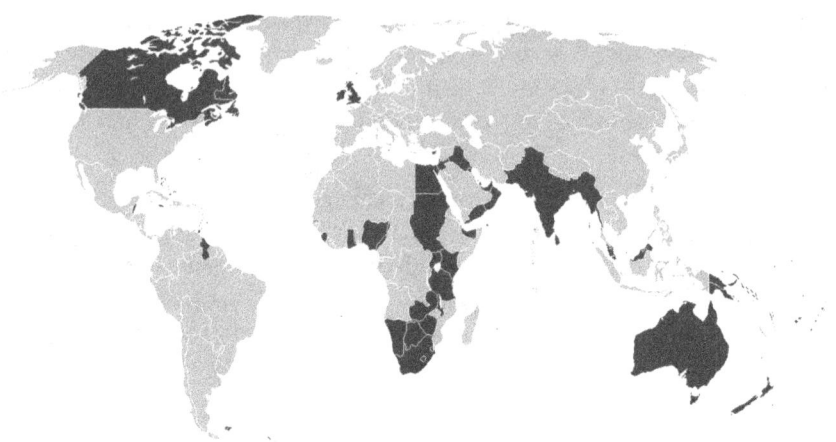

British Empire 1921
Courtesy of Vadac(PD-Self)
https://commons.wikimedia.org/wiki/File:British_Empire_1921.png

As the Second World War came to an end in 1945, pressure mounted for the colonies to gain their independence. The seeds for nationalism had already been planted years before. Now that nations like Great Britain, France and the United States had joined against fascism to win a victory for democracy, the continued domination of their colonies appeared blatantly hypocritical. Under Mohandas Gandhi's leadership, the Indian subcontinent acquired its independence in 1948. Indonesia followed suit in 1949, Libya in 1951, Vietnam in 1954, Morocco in 1956, Ghana in 1957, Nigeria in 1960, Algeria in 1962 and Kenya in 1963. Between 1945 and 1960, three-dozen new states in Asia and Africa achieved autonomy or outright independence from their colonial rulers.

For the most part, these new countries make up today's developing world. Much of the world's wealth was already under the control of Western powers long before World War Two started, so it has been a struggle for these nations just to provide the basic necessities, much less to catch up with their former mother countries. As these newly minted nations began to undergo industrial development, they also made improvements in their drinking water, sanitation and health care. At first glance, this appeared to be a tremendously positive step in the right direction. However, while vaccinations, hospitals and mosquito nets drastically lowered the death rates in these new countries, it has taken much longer for birth rates to plateau. As a result, exploding populations have absorbed much of the economic growth in developing nations. Africa's population in 1900 was approximately 133 million people. By 2050, it is projected to be up to 1.8 billion. Asia is expected to grow even more, from 904 million to over 5.3 billion. Meanwhile, Europe, which had 408 million people in 1900, is only expected to grow to 628 million by 2050.

For the average American visiting a developing nation, the disparity in wealth is more than apparent. A basic understanding of the historical roles played by industrialization and imperialism in creating this inequity will help to illuminate the reasons for this quandary. Yet when that same Americans return home to Philadelphia, Chicago or Denver, the growing gap they will see between the affluent mansions and the homeless people wandering the streets of downtown will also be starkly visible. What is the cause behind this disparity *within* the United States?

The good, the bad and the ugly side of capitalism

From the start, the United States has followed the tenets of capitalism. Adam Smith first described this economic system in his seminal book, *The Wealth of Nations*. Capitalism, also known as free enterprise, values the ownership of private property, the interests of the individual, and innovation generated by profit incentive. All means of production in a capitalist economic system should be privately owned, operated to make increasing profits and in competition against each other so that consumers can reap the benefits. Prices are set by the market's *"invisible hand,"* also known as the Law of Supply and Demand. The government should follow a laissez faire approach, which means that it should keep its role in the economy to a minimum.

Since many of the Englishmen who first settled the American colonies came in search of opportunities to gain wealth, it is perhaps unsurprising that the principles of capitalism were deeply ingrained in the American psyche from the beginning. Even when abuses of the free market became increasingly evident in the late 19th century, most Americans still clung to free enterprise traditions. By the 1890s, millions of factory workers during the Industrial Revolution were overworked, underpaid and drastically exploited. They joined politically with farmers, who were deep in debt, exploited by railroads and struggling to survive in desolate conditions. This Populist Movement of the 1890's produced several candidates for political office and two pieces of national legislation that were difficult to enforce: namely the Interstate Commerce Act and the Sherman Antitrust Act. For the most part, while European nations were creating social security programs, the United States kept the role of the federal government small and stubbornly retained its capitalist traditions.

There is no question that the role of the federal government in the United States increased in the 20th century. This began during the Progressive Era that ran up through the start of the First World War, continued during the Great Depression of the 1930s when President Franklin Roosevelt instituted New Deal programs and expanded even more in the 1960s as President Lyndon B. Johnson enacted a host of Great Society programs aimed at reducing poverty. In the end, the role of the federal government grew dramatically with the creation of such programs as the

Federal Trade Commission, the U.S. Forest Service, the Federal Reserve Bank, Social Security, the Securities and Exchange Commission, the minimum wage, 40-hour workweek, food stamps, Medicare and federal housing projects. In addition, the passage of the 16th Amendment in 1913 authorized the collection of a federal income tax that paved the way to pay for all of these new programs.

Despite this growth of the government's role in the economy, which unquestionably compromised one of the key principles of pure capitalism, the United States to this day still remains largely a free market economy. Most property is still privately owned, there are few limits placed on earned profits, and as previously stated, there are still enormous discrepancies in the amounts of wealth controlled by individual citizens. The majority of the American people still appreciate capitalism because they feel it creates an economic climate and set of incentives that will lead to more inventions, the growth of new businesses and a higher standard of living. In addition, many feel that it offers enough individual freedom and economic opportunity so that almost everyone has the chance to succeed. Besides, the main alternative to capitalism is some form of socialism, and to many Americans, socialism remains a distasteful concept.

The socialist alternative

In the late 19th century, factory conditions worsened, growing business combinations reduced competition and wealth increasingly accumulated in the hands of a tiny number of industrialists like J.P. Morgan, Andrew Carnegie, Cornelius Vanderbilt, John D. Rockefeller and Leland Stanford. As a result, a small but significant number of Americans turned to various forms of socialism as an alternative to capitalism. In a socialist economy, the government plays an active role to more equitably distribute the wealth. This can be done by imposing higher taxes on the rich and providing a wide range of programs to the poor. It can also be accomplished through government ownership of the primary means of production, including factories, farms, mines and large business enterprises. Some sought to accomplish their goals by organizing socialist political parties and working through the democratic system. Others turned to smaller utopian communities where they could share equally in the workload and wealth produced. At its most extreme, some began ascribing to Karl Marx's communist ideology.

Marx was a German economic philosopher who lived through the 19th century Industrial Revolution. He reacted to the growing inequalities he witnessed by writing books and pamphlets like *Das Capital* and the *Communist Manifesto*. According to Karl Marx, affluent capitalists would not peacefully give up their wealth and power. Therefore, the only way to truly achieve a classless society would be through a violent revolution where the oppressed proletariat would overthrow the wealthy bourgeoisie. Under the new economic system, each individual would contribute based on his or her abilities, and in turn, everyone would have their individual needs met. Marx not only wrote about his ideal economic system, but also worked to organize communist parties in many of the world's industrialized nations.

Despite Marx's prediction that communism would first take root in the most industrially advanced nations like Great Britain, Germany or the United States, it was the communist party in Russia that achieved the earliest success. The Russian Revolution of 1917 transformed czarist Russia with its traditional agrarian economy into the contemporary Soviet Union. The Russian people were brought into the modern world as the focus shifted toward heavy industries, petrochemical plants and giant collectively owned farms. There is no question that more wealth was generated and that it was more equitably distributed. Nonetheless, as depicted in George Orwell's book, *Animal Farm*, after the revolution, some people were "*more equal than others.*" In addition, a combination of economic stagnation and political oppression contributed to the demise of communism in the Soviet Union by the end of the 20th century.

While communism is clearly on the retreat, the principles of socialism are still strongly positioned to seep further into America's economic system. The populist governor of Louisiana, Huey P. Long, planted seeds during the Great Depression, when his *"Share the Wealth"* movement led to the creation of 27,000 clubs across the nation by 1935, with a total membership of more than 7.5 million. The rise of the Occupy Wall Street Movement in 2011, which called for a more equitable distribution of the wealth that has accumulated in the hands of the top one per cent, is a recent manifestation of this phenomenon. The broad appeal of Bernie Sanders and his socialist leanings in the 2016 presidential election also demonstrated that many Americans are not happy about the current distribution of wealth in the United States.

In the long run, the choice is not limited to just two options, capitalism or socialism. There are many degrees between these two extremes, and it is probably better to contextualize them on some kind of spectrum. Probably more than any other issue, the spot where people place themselves on this free enterprise-socialism continuum is the best predictor of how they will vote in elections. Most Americans who lean towards socialism as a path towards greater economic equality have tended to vote for the Democratic candidate. Whereas those who would like to preserve capitalism's emphasis on individual economic freedom, profit incentives and a smaller role for the government in the economy will generally vote for the Republican.

Conclusion

A combination of individual circumstance, industrialization and imperialism help to explain the gross international inequities that exist between the nations today.

Within nations like the United States, inequality is largely the result of choices made regarding the structure of our economic system.

Some would argue that when one person is wealthier than another, it is because he or she works harder, certain business risks were taken that paid off, or because he or she won some sort of inheritance lottery. However, this Horatio Alger notion that hard work pays off in the free market is a bit of myth. While there are plenty of personal anecdotes where this has been the case, the reality is that capitalism assigns wealth according to supply and demand. There is an extremely limited supply of pitchers who can consistently and accurately hurl a baseball at 100 miles per hour. Yet due to the business enterprise known as Major League Baseball, there is an enormous demand for such talent. This is why the talented baseball pitcher will probably earn a greater share of wealth in a single season than most individuals will garner in a lifetime. As long as economic value is determined more by supply and demand, rather than by effort, contributions or a sense of equity, wealth will always be unevenly distributed.

Sources and further reading:

C.W. "Did Living Standards Improve During the Industrial Revolution?" *TheEconomist.com.* September 13, 2013. http://www.economist.com/blogs/freeexchange/2013/09/economic-history-0.

"Decolonization After 1945." *TheMapAsHistory.com.* Accessed August 27, 2016. http://www.themap-as-history.com/maps/11-decolonization_independence.php.

Diamond, Jared. *Guns, Germs, and Steel: The Fates of Human Societies.* New York: W.W. Norton & Company, 1999.

Elkins, Kathleen. "80% of Americans Own an Unbelievably Small Portion of the Country's Wealth." *BusinessInsider.com.* June 15, 2015. http://www.businessinsider.com/inequality-in-the-us-is-much-more-extreme-than-you-think-2015-6.

"Explaining Divergent Levels of Longevity in High-Income Countries." *National Center for Biotechnology Information.* Accessed August 24, 2016. http://www.ncbi.nlm.gov/books/NBK62373/.

Headrick, Daniel R. *Power Over Peoples: Technology, Environments, and Western Imperialism, 1400 to the Present.* Princeton: Princeton University Press, 2010.

Maddison, Angus. "Countries Compared by Economy-GDP Per Capita in 1900." *Nationmaster.com.* Accessed August 25, 2016. http://www.nationmaster.com/country-info/stats/Economy/GDP-per-capita-in-1900.

Marx, Karl. *Das Kapital.* Translated by Samuel Moore. Seattle: Pacific PublishingStudio, 2010.

Nardinelli, Clark. "Industrial Revolution and the Standard of Living." *Econlib.org.* Accessed August 25, 2016. http://www.econlib.org/library/Enc/IndustrialRevolutionandtheStandardofLiving.html.

Orwell, George. *Animal Farm.* New York: Signet, 1996.

Overton, Mark. *Agricultural Revolution in England: The Transformation of the Agrarian Economy 1500-1850.* Cambridge: Cambridge University Press, 1996.

Plutarch. *Brainyquote.com.* Accessed August 17, 2016. http://www.brainyquote.com/quotes/p/plutarch109440.html.

Roser, Max. "Life Expectancy." *OurWorldInData.org.* Accessed August 24, 2016. https://ourworldindata.org/life-expectancy/.

Silbey, David J. *A War of Frontier and Empire: The Phillippine-American War, 1899-1902.* New York: Hill and Wang, 2008.

Smith, Adam. *The Wealth of Nations.* New York: Bantam Classics, 2003.

Surbhi. "Difference Between Developed Countries and Developing Countries." *KeyDifferences.com.* June 18, 2015. http://www.keydifferences.com/difference-between-developed-countries-and-developing-countries.html#ComparisonChart.

"Wealth Inequality." *Inequality.org.* Accessed August 21, 2016. http://www.inequality.org/wealth-inequality/.

"World Population to 2300." *UnitedNations.org.* Accessed August 27, 2016. http://www.un.org/esa/population/publications/longrange2/WorldPop2300final.pdf.

"Worlds Within the World." *Nationsonline.org.* Accessed August 21, 2016. http://nationsonline.org/oneworld/third_world_countries.htm.

Chapter 6

Why has the United States become such a global economic force?

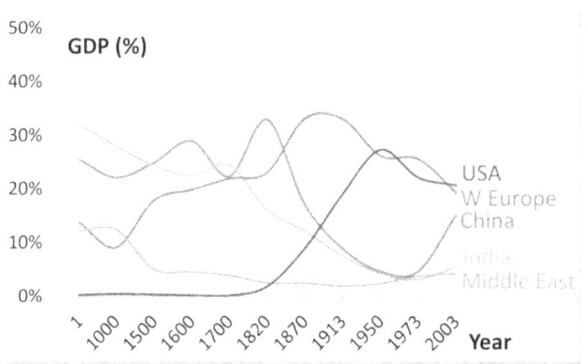

1 AD to 2003 historical trends in global distribution of GDP
Courtesy of M. Tracy Hunter (CC-BY-SA-4.0)
https://commons.wikimedia.org/wiki/File:1_AD_to_2003_AD_Historical_Trends_in_glob
al_distribution_of_GDP_China_India_Western_Europe_USA_Middle_East.png

> "Britain kept its position as the dominant world power well into the 20th century despite steady decline. By the end of World War Two, dominance had shifted decisively into the hands of the upstart across the sea, the United States, by far the most powerful and wealthy society in world history."
>
> Noam Chomsky

The gross domestic product (GDP) is the monetary value of all finished goods and services produced within a country's borders. In the year 2015, the American GDP was almost 18.5 trillion dollars. This is by far the largest the world has ever seen. China, in second place and slowly closing the gap, came in at 11.4 trillion dollars. With only 4.4 per cent of the world's population, the U.S. economy represents 25 per cent of the global GDP.

Many economists point out that China's economy is growing at an impressive rate and will soon surpass that of the United States. Yet it is not just the size of a nation's economy that matters, but also the quality. While the GDP per capita in the United States is $55,800, in China, it is only $14,100. This means that much of

China's significant economic growth is not making its way into the pockets of the Chinese people. China's growth rate, driven by massive state-owned enterprises rather than private industry, may be higher, but citizens in the United States are enjoying a much higher share of the prosperity.

There are other measures that reflect American economic hegemony. For example, of the world's largest stock markets, the top two are the New York Stock Exchange and NASDAQ, both located in the United States. Of the ten largest companies in the world, seven are American, including the top five (Apple, Google, Exxon-Mobil, Berkshire Hathaway and Microsoft). 53 of the world's largest 100 companies are also based in the United States. In fact, if the GDP's of other nations were compared to that of individual American states, one would find that the economy of North Carolina is comparable to that of Belgium, Missouri is on par with Greece, Iowa produces as much as Uzbekistan, Nevada equates with Kenya, New York with Turkey and even the small economy of North Dakota is roughly the same as that of the Democratic Republic of the Congo. At the opposite end of the spectrum, California's economy by itself equals that of the entire United Kingdom.

There are also other indirect measures that demonstrate America's dominant position on the global stage. For example, Americans have won 256 Nobel Prizes. The United Kingdom comes in a distant second at 93. Even before the 2016 Olympic games in Brazil, Americans had won 1,073 gold medals. Russia/USSR is second with 655. This legacy is by no means a reflection of American national superiority in any kind of cultural or ethnic sense. However, the Free Market economy inherited from its English mother country, as discussed in the previous chapter, does not fully explain why the United States has become such a global economic force. There are at least three other significant factors, and they all lie buried in America's past.

Reason one – Religion

Alexis de Tocqueville was a French diplomat, political scientist and historian. In 1831, he was given the mission of visiting the United States to examine its prisons and penitentiaries. While Tocqueville did visit some prisons, he traveled widely throughout the nation and took extensive notes of his observations and reflections. From these, he wrote one of the most lasting travelogues of all time, *Democracy in America*. Published in two volumes between 1835 and 1840, this tome is considered to be a fairly accurate reflection of life in the new republic. In searching for the source of America's success, Tocqueville observed:

> *I sought for the greatness and genius of America in her commodious harbors and her ample rivers, and it was not there; in her fertile fields and boundless prairies, and it was not there; in her rich mines and her vast world*

> *commerce, and it was not there. Not until I went to the churches of America and heard her pulpits aflame with righteousness did I understand the secret of her genius and power. America is great because she is good, and if America ever ceases to be good, America will cease to be great.*

Trying to establish a causal link between a nation's economic success and its religious faith is a highly dubious task. With that said, the best place to start is with America's Protestant origins. Roman Catholics have always made up a significant percentage of the U.S. population, but from the start, the vast majority of Americans have been Protestant. The first settlers in Jamestown belonged to the Church of England and were guided more by the search for wealth than by religious faith. Yet the Pilgrims in Plymouth, the Puritans in Boston and the Quakers in Pennsylvania were extremely pious and came to the New World in search of opportunities to practice their faith free of religious persecution.

As younger generations wavered from the dogmatic faith of their elders in the first half of the 18th century, this stimulated the Great Awakening, which spread like wildfire throughout the English colonies. It was characterized by rousing sermons, delivered by men like Jonathan Edwards and George Whitefield in open fields to audiences of up to 20,000 people, without the aid of microphones or amplifiers. The Great Awakening pulled Americans away from ritual, ceremony, sacraments and hierarchy, and made Christianity intensely personal to the average person. It deepened and reinforced America's Protestant roots.

The same phenomenon occurred again during the Second Great Awakening that originated in the Burnt-Over District of upstate New York and swept the nation roughly one hundred years after the first. This religious revival saw the birth of a uniquely American Christian denomination, the Church of Latter Day Saints, better known as the Mormons. Protestant evangelism and fundamentalism have periodically bubbled to the surface of American society throughout the 20th century as well, particularly in the 1920s and the 1980s. There is an unbroken religious thread that runs through American history linking the early 17th century to the present. Its impact extends far beyond the walls of America's churches.

One way to better understand the incredible power of religious faith is through a simple observation. In Europe, the wealthier nations tend to be in the North. Germany and the United Kingdom have greater GDP's than either Italy or Spain. In fact, the top 15 European nations in terms of per capita GDP are all located in Northern Europe. This is not just because the colder weather of the north encourages a stronger work ethic or greater productivity. With the exception of Ireland, Austria and France, these Northern European nations have another variable in common; they all possess Protestant religious majorities.

At the risk of making an overly zealous generalization, there is some merit to the historical notion of the Protestant Work Ethic. Throughout Europe's Middle Ages, when the Roman Catholic Church had a monopoly on the spiritual life of virtually all Europeans, most forms of gaining profits were largely frowned upon. Earning wealth at the expense of your neighbors, even through hard work and determination, was considered to be sinful.

This all changed with the advent of John Calvin's Doctrine of Predestination. Preaching that an all-powerful God has known since the beginning of time which people would achieve salvation, it was left up to individuals on their own to determine if they were amongst the chosen few. How could this best be accomplished? One method that grew increasingly popular was to pursue a *"calling."* This meant that if a Calvinist worked hard at the task God had chosen, it could be taken as a sign of salvation. The calling applied not just to those who entered the ministry, but also to anyone who vigorously worked at their task in an honest and moral fashion. Suddenly, a craftsman, a merchant, even a banker could be seen as one of the most holy stalwarts in a Protestant Christian community. It was no longer a sin to earn big profits or to become rich; in fact, combined with a pious lifestyle, it could be taken as an indicator of sanctity.

Shortly after the start of the 20th century, the German sociologist and economist, Max Weber, published a book that described this connection between religion and economics. Titled *The Protestant Ethic and the Spirit of Capitalism*, Weber wrote that capitalism in Northern Europe advanced when the Protestant, and particularly the Calvinist, work ethic influenced large numbers of people to engage with the secular world. This link between salvation and business success encouraged individuals to develop their own enterprises, engage in trade and accumulate wealth for investment. According to Weber, this Protestant Work Ethic was a vital force behind the emergence of capitalism.

Pilgrims, Puritans and Quakers were all strongly influenced by Calvinist theology and the rise of this Protestant Work Ethic. So were French Huguenots and Scottish Presbyterians. Devout communities spread throughout the English colonies, particularly in New England. Boston became what Massachusetts Governor John Winthrop called, "*a city upon a hill*," that is, a theocracy intended to serve as an example for the rest of the world in rightful living. This early religious background provided a firm foundation for the nation that was thoroughly examined by Alexis de Tocqueville two hundred years later. Even today, among some international observers, Americans have a reputation for prioritizing work over play, often sacrificing personal time in favor of their careers.

This religious background also contributed to the rise of another uniquely American attribute in the early years of the republic: aggressive land expansion. One of the factors behind the dazzling economic success of the United States has been its plentiful land containing a wide array of natural resources. From 1776 to the middle of the 19th century, the United States overspread the North American continent from "*sea to shining sea.*" This phenomenal growth involved a series of purchases, wars, treaties and land grabs so that the boundaries of the lower 48 states were completely filled out by the time of the Gadsden Purchase from Mexico in 1853. This included the Treaty of Paris that ended the Revolutionary War, which granted the U.S. all of the acreage up to the Mississippi River, the Louisiana Purchase of 1803 which stretched America's boundaries to the Rocky Mountains, the Adams-Onis Treaty with Spain that led to the purchase of Florida in 1819, the signing of the Oregon Treaty with England in 1846 bringing in the entire Northwest and the Mexican-American War at roughly the same time that brought in the entire Southwest. Meanwhile, the indigenous people that had inhabited this land for centuries were pushed out of the way and eventually forced to settle on small allotments called reservations, usually inferior ground that most white settlers did not want to claim.

How could this expansion be intellectually defended? In 1845, the newspaper editor, John O'Sullivan, wrote "*our manifest destiny is to overspread the continent allotted by Providence for the free development of our yearly multiplying millions.*"

In addition, he went on to say:

> *The far-reaching, the boundless future will be the era of American greatness. In its magnificent domain of space and time, the nation of many nations is destined to manifest to mankind the excellence of divine principles; to establish on earth the noblest temple ever dedicated to the worship of the Most High -- the Sacred and the True. Its floor shall be a hemisphere -- its roof the firmament of the star-studded heavens, and its congregation a Union of many Republics, comprising hundreds of happy millions, calling, owning no man master, but governed by God's natural and moral law of equality, the law of brotherhood of peace and good will amongst men.*

During the mid-19th century, millions of Americans eagerly accepted this spiritual justification of America's rapid land growth. They believed that they were special— that their democratic constitution, resourceful use of the land's natural wealth, and especially their religious and moral values, distinguished them from indigenous cultures and European mother nations. In their minds, certainly they would make better use of the land than the indigenous tribes who had lived in the West for thousands of years. Many settlers believed that under the American flag, this new territory would flourish and the people living there, including the various tribes and the Mexicans who were suddenly residents of a new nation, would have better lives. The same religious compulsion that brought the Puritans aboard the *Arbella* in 1630 to settle in Boston inspired millions of their descendants to travel the Oregon Trail two centuries later. In between and ever since, the power of America's religious faith added an explosive fuel to the nation's economic growth.

Reason two – The frontier experience

The United States' rapid land expansion contributed to its economic dominion in another way. In 1893, Frederick Jackson Turner, a historian from the University of Wisconsin, introduced his famous Turner Thesis in a paper entitled "*The Significance of the Frontier in American History*," delivered to the American Historical Association in Chicago. In this paper, Turner argued that much of America's past was defined by its frontier experience. Since the 1890 census revealed that, for the first time, there was no longer a definitive frontier line that could be drawn across the map, it was now appropriate to review the impact that the frontier had had on shaping the United States' character. According to Turner, the traits that originated from the frontier were

> *Coarseness and strength combined with acuteness and inquisitiveness; that practical, inventive turn of mind, quick to find expedients; that masterful grasp of material things, lacking in the artistic but powerful to effect great ends; that restless, nervous energy; that dominant individualism, working for good and evil, and withal that buoyancy and exuberance which comes from freedom...*

While this is just the view of one historian, which has been amply criticized from many perspectives for more than a century, it seems reasonable that throughout the first half of America's history, the frontier acted as a magnet that attracted certain character traits within the populace. Those with a greater propensity towards freedom, risk-taking and economic opportunity continued to push westward. Facing the risks that accompanied venturing into the unknown, these individuals tended to leave the more cautious behind them. Over time, they passed down these pioneering traits to future generations. As Turner said, "*the advance of the frontier meant a steady movement away from the influence of Europe, a steady growth of independence on American lines.*"

Some of these traits included greater egalitarianism, a disinterest in "*high culture*" and a proclivity toward violence and guns. In the economic arena, it has also meant greater materialism and a willingness to be more aggressive in the pursuit of wealth. Admittedly, these are generalized stereotypes, but as is often the case, there is at least a kernel of truth to be found in the source of these characteristics.

These traits are reflected throughout America's history. They are seen in the Yankee ships that ventured out of New England ports during the 19th century, seeking new markets in China, forcing the opening of Japan and hunting down whales throughout the Pacific. They motivated the acquisition of Alaska in 1867, Hawaii in 1898, and the decision to go to war against Spain at the turn of the century in order to join the race for overseas colonies. They formed the underlying basis behind the frantic Oklahoma Land Rush in 1889, particularly those Sooners who snuck out early to grab the land parcels that had just been taken from the surrounding Indian reservations. They can also be found in the international aggression of American corporate interests, like the American Fruit Company in Latin America or J.P. Morgan's investments in Chinese railway construction that led to the rise of Dollar Diplomacy during the administration of William Howard Taft. Many of the same character traits that Frederick Jackson Turner identified with the frontier experience are linked with America's unique economic growth up to the present.

In terms of character, are there certain traits that distinguish one national culture from another? Turner not only suggested that there were, he made an effort to explain the historical causes behind them. If one accepts the premise that the American people lean towards such characteristics as ambition, materialism and aggression, this will form one piece of the puzzle that explains American economic domination. Another major piece, however, is the land itself. In this regard, it can be argued that in terms of location, natural resources and physical attributes, the United States is truly blessed.

The upside of geography

When George Washington stepped down as the nation's first president in 1796, he stated in his Farewell Address that the new nation should "*have as little political connection as possible*" to the other nations of the world. In regard to Europe, he advised that the United States should avoid entangling our "*peace and prosperity in the toils of European ambition, rivalships, interest, humor, or caprice*" and that it should be our "*policy to steer clear of permanent alliances with any portion of the foreign world.*" Out of this belief emerged the foreign policy tradition called isolationism, an approach that the United States generally followed for the next century and a half.

This did not mean that the United States operated like a hermit nation. There was still prodigious trade with other countries, and land was often taken from others. Wars were fought with England in 1812, Mexico in 1846 and Spain in 1898. In 1823, the United States issued the Monroe Doctrine that warned European states that any further efforts to control of the emerging nations in North or South America would be viewed as "*the manifestation of an unfriendly disposition toward the United States.*" In 1917, primarily to protect U.S. shipping rights from German submarine attacks, the United States entered World War One. Throughout these years, however, the U.S. avoided entangling alliances and clung to its policy of isolationism. With the Atlantic Ocean protecting one side and the Pacific on the other, and with smaller, weaker nations to the north and south, the United States could exploit its removed location. Left alone, it was able to grow and economically prosper. Isolationism did not really end until the Japanese attack on Pearl Harbor in 1941, as it showed that the oceans could no longer be relied on for protection.

What were the economic consequences of America's geographic isolation? With the exception of the bloody carnage of the Civil War years between 1861 and 1865, America's wars between the end of the Revolution and the attack on Pearl Harbor were relatively brief. Moreover, several of them brought in immense amounts of new land with rich natural resources. The dominant theme of the first half of America's story was expansion, and left alone to expand, the American economy witnessed extraordinary growth. After the Civil War, the issue of slavery had finally been resolved, removing a major impediment to economic expansion. Mining, cattle, farming and railroad construction attracted millions of settlers to the West, and the frontier soon disappeared.

Meanwhile, immigrants continued to pour into the United States. Between 1871 and 1901, 11.7 million entered the U.S., more than the total number that had arrived during the preceding three centuries combined. As western lands became increasingly less affordable, more of the newly arrived immigrants remained in eastern and mid-western cities to look for jobs in America's burgeoning factories. The increased supply of available labor lowered its cost, so while millions labored long hours for little pay, the American middle class began to grow and a small number became millionaires. Immigrants came to the United States believing that its streets *"were paved with gold."* While this was largely a myth for most, the image of America as an opulent citadel far removed from the crowded quarters of Europe helped to swiftly build its population. For a nation experiencing the climax of its Industrial Revolution, the timing could not have been better. There were now more people not only available to work in factories but also to consume their goods.

In addition to location, the other resource the United States was incredibly fortunate to possess involves what lies beneath the land. In terms of minerals and natural resources, there are few spots on the planet as auspicious as America. The land and its climate offered the chance to grow plenty of food, and its waters teemed with fish and other forms of sea life. The forests were so packed with trees that it was said that at the time of Jamestown and Plymouth, a squirrel could travel from Maine to Florida without ever touching the ground. Today, the United States still possesses over 31 per cent of the planet's coal reserves, by far the most of any nation. The U.S. is also in the top five nations globally for natural gas, copper and gold, and almost 20 per cent of the earth's iron ore is located in the United States. Recently, the U.S. reemerged as the world's top producer of petroleum. While energy resources like coal, oil and natural gas are certainly not renewable, their prodigious quantities helped fuel America's Industrial Revolution and are another historical factor that explains the United States' global economic supremacy.

Conclusion – The future

How much longer can the United States hope to remain one of the world's most productive economies? After all, other nations have been gaining ground for the last 70 years. America's share of the world's GDP in 1945, the year World War Two ended, is estimated to have been about 50 per cent. This was more than halved by 1980. It was only a matter of time before the other nations that had been decimated by the war rebuilt their economies and increased their own production. Ironically, the United States and its allies had defeated two of the nations that experienced the most phenomenal growth in the 1950s: West Germany and Japan. While each has become close political allies with the United States, they soon became two of America's leading economic competitors. More recently, China, with the planet's largest population, has stepped into the role of the nation most likely to overtake the U.S in economic production. Eventually, it is only a matter of time before developing nations in Africa and the Asian subcontinent also make significant strides. Fewer than five people out of 100 around the world are American. U.S. economic dominion cannot last forever.

Additionally, the United States has been on a downward trajectory in a number of other areas over the last several decades. Emerging as the leader of the Free World during the Cold War, the U.S. government felt compelled to spend inordinate amounts on costly wars in such places as Korea and Vietnam. It is estimated that for every dollar President Lyndon B. Johnson spent to fight poverty within the United States, ten dollars were spent to fight the communists in the jungles of Vietnam. The more recent war against terrorism has also led to expensive military ventures into nations like Iraq and Afghanistan. Today, the United States not only spends more on its military than any other nation, but its spending equals more than numbers two, three, four, five, six, seven and eight combined. There are American troops currently stationed in over 150 nations, including more than 35,000 in Germany and over 50,000 in Japan. This military supremacy has contributed to the Pax Americana that has brought relative peace and freedom to many quarters of the world, while simultaneously opening up new markets for U.S. businesses, but it has also diverted significant amounts of capital from the American economy.

Meanwhile, the United States has experienced costly problems at home. Racism and poverty still plague many parts of the nation. The top one per cent of America's income earners has more than doubled their share of the nation's income since the middle of the 20th century, while more than 45 million Americans still live below the poverty line. In addition, deep-seated racial tension has recently fueled riots in Baltimore, Milwaukee and Ferguson, Missouri. Crime has been gradually declining, but the United States still has over two million of its people locked up behind bars, considerably more than any other nation in the world. A 2016 study at Washington University in St. Louis maintains that the cost of incarceration in the United States is more than one trillion dollars a year, and more than half of this burden falls on the families and the communities of the incarcerated.

As for the U.S. economy, the growing prosperity over the last century has meant considerably higher wages, but it has also raised the cost of American labor. As a result, many American corporations have moved jobs overseas in order to save money. Coupled with a trade deficit that has been steadily growing for the past few decades, and a national government debt that will soon top twenty trillion dollars, it is not hard to see why some prognosticators hold a fairly pessimistic view of America's economic future.

In all likelihood, the United States will hardly take a nosedive into economic calamity. Due to its land, resources, people, endemic wealth, and political values, the United States will likely remain an economic titan for many generations. Nonetheless, other nations were bound to catch up. Relative to the rest of the world, America's economic stature will gradually wane. This is a reality that will ultimately have to be accepted by the American people.

Sources and further reading:

Bremmer, Ian. "These are the 5 Reasons Why the U.S. Remains the World's Only Superpower." *Time.com.* May 28, 2015. http://www.time.com/3899972/us-superpower-status-military/.

Bronaugh, Whit. "North American Forests in the Age of Man." *AmericanForests.org.* Accessed September 8, 2016. https://www.americanforests.org/magazine/article/north-american-forests-in-the-age-of-man/.

Carroll, Lauren. "Obama: US Spends More On Military Than Next 8 Nations Combined." *Politifact.com.* January 13, 2016. http://www.politifact.com/truth-http://www.politifact.com./truth-o-meter/statements/2016/jan/13/barak-obama/obama-us-spends-more-military-next-8-nations-combi/.

Chomsky, Noam. *Brainyquote.com.* Accessed September 1, 2016. http://www.brainyquote.com/quotes/n/noamchomsk635721.html.

"Countries With the Largest Number of Prisoners Per 100,000 of the National Population, as of April 2016." *Statista.com.* Accessed September 8, 2016. http://www.statista.com/statistics/262962/countries-with-the-most-prisoners-per-100-000-inhabitants/.

"Country Comparison: GDP-Per Capita." *CIA.gov.* Accessed September 1, 2016. https://www.cia.gov/library/publications/the-world-factbook/rankorder/2004rank.html.

"Distribution of Natural Resources." *EschoolToday.com.* Accessed September 8, 2016. http://www.eschooltoday.com/natural-resources/distribution-of-natural-resources.html.

"Gadsen Purchase, 1853-1854." *Office of the Historian, Bureau of Public Affairs.* Accessed September 5, 2016. https://www.history.state.gov/milestones/1830-1860/gadsen-purchase.

"GDP Ranking 2016." *Statisticstimes.com.* April 14, 2016. http://www.statisticstimes.com/economy/countries-by-projected-gdp.php.

Gongloff, Mark. "45 Million Americans Still Stuck Below Poverty Line: Census." *HuffingtonPost.com.* September 16, 2014. http://www.huffingtonpost.com/2014/09/16/poverty-household-income_n_5828974.html.

Hammermesh, Daniel. "Why Americans Work Around the Clock." *HuffingtonPost.com.* September 16, 2014. http://www.huffingtonpost.com/2014/09/16/americans-workplace-burnout_n_5828866.html.

Kidd, Thomas. *The Great Awakening: The Roots of Evangelical Christianity in Colonial America.* New Haven: Yale University Press, 2009.

Kiersz, Andy. "16 Charts that Illustrate America's Global Dominance." *BusinessInsider.com.* July 4, 2015. http://www.businessinsider.com/charts-that-illustrates-americas-global-dominance-2015-7/#americas-economy-is-so-large-that-the-economies-of-individual-states-are-big-enough-on-their-own-to-be-comparable-to-major-countries-1.

Layson, Hana, and Daniel Greene. "Immigration and Citizenship in the United States, 1865-1924." *The Newberry.* Accessed September 8, 2016. http://dcc.newberry.org/collections/immigration-and-citizenship.

Manzi, Jim. "A Post-American World?" *TheAmericanScene.com.* May 7, 2008. http://www.theamericanscene.com/2008/05/07/a-post-american-world.

"Massachusetts Bay-'The City Upon a Hill'." *USHistory.org.* Accessed September 9, 2016. http://www.ushistory.org/us/3c.asp.

O'Sullivan, John. "The Great Nation of Futurity." *The United States Democratic Review* 0006, no. 23(Nov 1839): 426-430.

Priester, Marc, and Aaron Mendelson. "Income Inequality." *Inequality.org.* Accessed September 8, 2016. http://www.inequality.org/income-inequality/.

Sauter, Michael B., Charles B. Stockdale, and Paul Ausick. "The World's Most Resource-Rich Countries." *WallSt.com.* April 18, 2012. http://www.247wallst.com/special-report/2012/04/18/the-world's-most-resource-rich-countries/.

Selderhuis, Herman J. *John Calvin: A Pilgrim's Life.* Downers Grove: Intervarsity Press, 2009.

Sexton, Jay. *The Monroe Doctrine: Empire and Nation in Nineteenth-Century America.* New York: Hill and Wang, 2011.

Taketa, Kristen. "WU Study: Incarceration Costs Top $1 Trillion." *St. Louis Post-Dispatch,* September 10, 2016.

Tocqueville, Alexis de. *Democracy in America.* Translated by Gerald Bevan. New York: Penguin Books, 2003.

Turner, Frederick Jackson. *The Significance of the Frontier in American History.* Eastford: Martino Fine Books, 2014.

"The U.S. Acquires Spanish Florida." *History.com.* Accessed September 5, 2016. http://www.history.com/this-day-in-history/the-u-s-acquires-spanish-florida.

"United States Balance of Trade." *TradingEconomics.com.* Accessed September 8, 2016. http://www.tradingeconomics.com/united-states/balance-of-trade.

Veeser, Cyrus. *A World Safe for Capitalism: Dollar Diplomacy and America's Rise to Global Power.* New York: Columbia University Press, 2002.

Washington, George. "Washington's Farewell Address 1796." *Yale.edu.* Accessed September 7, 2016.
http://www.avalon.law.yale.edu/18th_century/washing.asp.

Weber, Max. *The Protestant Ethic and the Spirit of Capitalism.* New York: Penguin Classics, 2002.

Chapter 7

Why is capitalism increasingly prevalent around the world?

The fall of the Berlin Wall 1989
Courtesy of Lear 21 at English Wikipedia(CC-BY-SA-3.0)
https://commons.wikimedia.org/wiki/File:Thefallofthe berlinewall1989.JPG

"In the end we beat them with Levi 501 jeans. Seventy-two years of communist indoctrination and propaganda was drowned out by a three-ounce Sony Walkman."

P.J. O'Rourke (U.S. humorist and journalist)

The year 1989 saw momentous changes sweeping across Eastern Europe. People had grown weary of communist rule. In Berlin, a great city partitioned by an ugly wall, people on both sides wanted the wall torn down. On November 9th, in a move that surprised everyone, the communists in East Germany opened up the borders. More than two million Berliners scampered from one side of the city to the other that weekend. In a two-day revelry, people climbed on top of the wall, danced and chipped off souvenirs. Over the next year, the wall was reduced to rubble. By October of 1990, East and West Germany were reunited as one nation. The Union of Soviet Socialist Republics had also been transformed back into

Russia, the communists were voted out of power and the Cold War was finally over. Freedom and capitalism had triumphed over tyranny and communism, or so it seemed.

A long and complicated story had come to an end. Lurking beneath this story, however, was a simple question: How should wealth be ideally distributed? Every society has worked to produce the goods and services that each member wants or needs. Should people compete on an individual level to create, produce and pass on their share of the wealth, or should the government intervene to distribute wealth in a more equitable manner? In the Western world today, probably no other question is more politically divisive. Within the United States, there are a multitude of seemingly unrelated issues that divide modern-day liberal Democrats from conservative Republicans, but first and foremost is the issue of wealth distribution.

Republicans generally favor a minimal economic role for the federal government in order to maximize an individual's freedom to earn profits. This means taxes should be low, rules regulating private industry should be kept to a minimum and there should be little federal assistance, even with such basic necessities as housing, education or health care. The ownership of property is seen as a sacred right and the market place should be allowed to fully operate without government interference. The free market's *"invisible hand"* should be left alone to determine what people produce and how it is distributed. Under this perspective, if some are considerably richer than others, this is only fair, because each individual *"earns"* his or her share of a society's wealth. In other words, today's Republican prefers the capitalist principles first expounded upon by Adam Smith more than 240 years ago.

Conversely, Democrats lean further to the left end of the spectrum, toward the socialist principles that support dividing wealth more equitably among individuals. They argue that no one chooses to be poor, and that more often than not, poverty is the result of circumstances beyond an individual's control. This view holds that many of those who possess a disproportionate share of the wealth only hold it because of the lottery of being born to advantageous circumstances. They see real wealth stemming from labor. Therefore, the person who works on the factory floor is entitled to a fairer share of the company's earnings. In order for the wealth to be apportioned more reasonably, Democrats usually favor higher progressive taxes on the rich in order to finance programs to help the poor, and they favor a larger economic role for the federal government.

Today, neither capitalism nor socialism really exists anywhere in the world in its pure form. Within the United States, Republicans and Democrats continue the ongoing tug-of-war pulling the nation more towards one extreme or the other. While this political wrestling match goes on in other democracies as well, the recent ending of the Cold War has marked the overall ascendency of capitalism. The Soviet Union has ceased to exist, and in its place, Russia and the other former

Soviet republics have dramatically moved toward free enterprise. Capitalist prin-principles have even crept into the national economies of such communist bastions as China, Vietnam and Cuba. How did this change come about? Why did the communist revolutions that began almost a century ago veer so far away from their original objectives?

The Marxist dream

The Commercial Revolution that shoved Europe out of its Dark Ages focused on the ownership of private property and the acquisition of unlimited profits. Unleashing the human desire to earn wealth led to the creation of new financial instruments designed to raise investment capital. These included business partnerships, joint stock trading companies and banks. Soon after, European nations sent out explorers to find new trade routes, and their flags were then planted in distant colonies all across the planet. Mercantilism, with its emphasis on government support in order to produce a favorable balance of trade, quickly took hold of each nation's financial policies. Fortunes were earned by a few and the dream of riches motivated almost everyone else. By the end of the 18th century, these developments solidified into Adam Smith's principles of capitalism.

In the 19th century, some of the same measures that had produced huge fortunes through trade, commerce and agriculture were applied to the construction of mills and factories. The new wealth that gradually began to displace old money was created by the Industrial Revolution. At the same time, this wealth was increasingly concentrated in fewer hands. Many working class people, as they made the transition from farming and skilled craftsmanship to factory labor, often found themselves at the mercy of industrialists. Hours were long, pay was low and conditions were abysmal. Even when miners or factory workers managed to form unions to increase their negotiating power, the lack of any government support put them at an enormous disadvantage. 19th century strikes frequently turned violent, but few made significant improvement in providing the workers, the proletariat, with a greater share of the wealth they were producing.

It was under these dire circumstances that socialism emerged as an alternative to capitalism. Some attempted to spur change through political organization and democratic processes. Others sought to withdraw into isolated utopian communities. On an international level, however, many began to heed the words of Karl Marx; that true socialism would only occur when the proletariat rose up in open rebellion against the bourgeoisie, which meant overthrowing the wealthy classes and their allied political rulers. "*Workers of the world unite; you have nothing to lose but your chains.*" Marx saw the communist revolution as the final stage in the ongoing class struggle between those who possessed wealth and power and those who did not. These ideas were encapsulated in his writings and helped to guide the creation of the Communist International, a global organization that advocated worldwide communism. Karl Marx died stateless and poverty-stricken in 1883. There were fewer than a dozen mourners at his funeral. Yet his dream lived on well into the 20th century.

Revolution!

Marx had always predicted that the first communist revolutions would occur in the most industrially advanced nations. Imagine his shock to know that the first successful revolt occurred in the less developed nation of Russia. Weighed down by a relatively primitive economy, choking in the quicksand of the First World War and led by a reactionary monarch called the czar, the Russian people were more than ready for change. While the czar was away trying to raise the morale of his troops along the front, food riots broke out in St. Petersburg. A brief experiment with a democratic constitution soon faltered when the new government maintained its determination to keep Russia fighting in the war. By autumn, a Marxist named Vladimir Lenin and his Bolshevik followers seized control of the revolution. Several more bloody years followed, and when the dust settled, the czar and his entire family had been shot and Russia had been transformed into the Soviet Union, the world's first experiment in modern communism.

Lenin died in 1924 and Joseph Stalin soon took his place. Much has been written about the deeds and even the sanity of Joseph Stalin. There is no question that his determination to modernize and industrialize the Soviet Union led to the deaths of millions of people. Stalin remained in power until he died in 1953, and during his quarter century of rule, the USSR was transformed into a colossus of heavy industry and a military superpower. In addition to the millions who died from Stalin's purges and efforts to collectivize agriculture, at least another twenty million Russians were killed in the Second World War. The Soviets emerged from the war victorious in 1945, but no country in the history of the world had ever suffered such horrific casualties.

Many blamed Joseph Stalin for destroying the Marxist dream. George Orwell, a socialist in his own right, portrayed the betrayal of this dream in his allegorical and dystopian novella, *Animal Farm*. When the animals overthrew Farmer Jones to affect the communist dream of Old Major (Marx), one of the pigs, Napoleon (Stalin) initiated a coup of his own. He then steered the revolution in a new direction, one that enhanced his own status and power. By the end of the parable, Napoleon and his crony pigs had simply come to replace the same human farmers that had previously exploited the animals. In fact, the pigs had even formed a friendly alliance with the farmers living in the surrounding area. "*The creatures outside looked from pig to man, and from man to pig, and from pig to man again; but already it was impossible to say which was which.*"

Why is capitalism increasingly prevalent around the world? 83

While historians are still debating the extent to which Joseph Stalin destroyed the Marxist dream, there is no denying that under his watch, communism spread. Even before the end of World War Two in 1945, the Soviet Red Army had already begun to *"liberate"* the nations of Eastern Europe and soon started to erect communist governments in national capitals, stretching from Warsaw in Poland to Tirana in Albania. Germany was split in half, with the United States, Great Britain and France occupying West Germany, while the Soviets set up a communist government in the East. Even though Berlin was located in the eastern sector, it too was divided so that the western half of the city fell under the control of the western half of the German nation. Sixteen years later, the Soviets and the East Germans erected the reviled wall in order to stem the tide of refugees crossing over to the West.

The spread of communism did not result only from Stalinist aggression. By 1949, a cadre of Chinese communists led by Mao Zedong had brought Marxism to the world's most populous nation. Within a decade, there were communist revolutions in North Korea, Vietnam and Cuba. Several more countries, primarily in Africa, also declared themselves to be socialist or communist states by 1983, the period marking the greatest territorial expansion of communist states. In the new countries emerging as part of the developing world, the growing gap between a handful of wealthy magnates and the millions who were struggling was substantially larger than in the western nations. A communist revolution that would significantly redistribute the wealth, at least in theory, was seen as justified. This division between the spreading communist nations and the industrially developed countries led by the United States formed the crux of the Cold War. In places like Korea, Vietnam and Cuba, this tension exploded, and with the rise of a nuclear arms race, it took on a terrifying dimension.

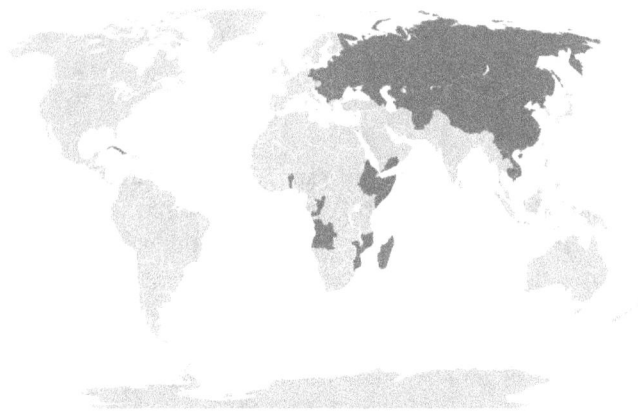

Communist countries 1979-1983
Courtesy of Smurfy(PD-self)
https://commons.wikimedia.org/wiki/File:Communist_countries_1979-1983.png

How should wealth be ideally distributed? This question not only serves as the biggest wedge dividing Democrats and Republicans, but at the height of the Cold War, it also pushed the world to the brink of nuclear Armageddon. However, just as the start of the 20th century witnessed the birth of the first communist states, the final decades saw them start to fade. How can this be explained? Like many other questions, this one does not have a single answer that will generate any form of consensus. In fact, liberals and conservatives often hold conflicting views on how to best answer this query.

The conservative answer

Conservatives tend to focus on human nature. They argue that most people need a tangible incentive in order for them to expend more energy creating, inventing or just applying greater effort to their work. Without the opportunity to earn larger profits, the economy will stagnate. In the 72 years that the communists controlled the Soviet Union, the Russian GDP never climbed higher than 40 per cent of the American GDP. In addition, while there were significant advances in terms of agriculture and heavy industry, it largely came at the expense of consumer buying power. The Soviet economy was rarely a wellspring of invention or creativity in any area that might have improved the quality of life for their people.

In addition, conservatives see an inherent unfairness imbedded in any socialist model. They argue that those who invent, invest, or work harder should be able to reap the benefits, and to tax those away for the good of the masses is a form of government-sponsored larceny. Conservatives generally see property as a hallowed right. Therefore, to place considerable taxes on earned wealth clearly violates one of the three natural rights first identified by John Locke during the Enlightenment. The bottom line is that if you earn it in any legal fashion, it should be yours to keep, to spend or to pass down to your progeny. It should not be taxed away to support complete strangers. Besides, going back to their view of human nature, most conservatives feel that government assistance will only encourage lethargy and slothfulness.

Finally, the conservative view on the capitalist versus socialist question is based largely on the value of liberty. This means that they want to be free from government intrusion in the economic arena. In other areas, such as personal morality, many conservatives support a larger government role. But most feel that entrepreneurs who use their property to develop businesses should not be overly burdened by restrictive measures designed to protect workers, consumers or the environment. After all, we all benefit from the success of the entrepreneur in the form of higher-paying jobs, new products on the market and a rising standard of living.

These were the views that led conservatives to elect Ronald Reagan by a large margin into the White House in 1980. Reagan, the Republican candidate, defeated the incumbent, Jimmy Carter with 489 electoral votes to Carter's 49. Four years later, Reagan was reelected with the support of every state except Minnesota and the District of Columbia. During his eight years, President Reagan oversaw a *"revolution"* within the United States that involved massive tax cuts, major reductions in social spending and widespread economic deregulation. As for the Soviet Union, Reagan referred to it in a 1983 speech as *"an evil empire."* He called for a major escalation in military spending to match Soviet capabilities and a rollback strategy that would *"write the final pages of the history of the Soviet Union."*

To conservatives like Ronald Reagan, communism was never destined to last. While the free market is based on natural impulses and human nature, any form of socialism goes against the grain of progress. Many of Reagan's supporters felt that he deserved credit for bringing an end to the Cold War and for pushing the ascendency of free market capitalism. They argued that the pressure for reform in the Soviet Union had built for decades, particularly because of the sacrifices made by Soviet consumers. While the Soviets were pouring their economic potential into military hardware and heavy industry, consumers in the West were driving the latest automobiles, dancing to rock and roll and wearing the hippest fashions. Now President Reagan was applying even more pressure by increasing the U.S. military budget and propagating a new missile defense technology called the Strategic Defense Initiative, better known as Star Wars. Mikhail Gorbachev may have slightly opened the door to the possibility of reform in the USSR, but the pressure applied by President Reagan led the Soviet people to demand a change.

The late 1980s witnessed a chain reaction of events. Free elections within the Soviet Union led to the ouster of the Communist Party. The USSR soon splintered into Russia and 14 other republics, including the Baltic states of Latvia, Estonia and Lithuania, as well as others such as Ukraine, Belarus, Georgia and Kazakhstan. Russia still had more land and people than the other 14 new nations combined, but communism largely disappeared from all of them. Meanwhile, there were arms control negotiations that considerably lowered the number of nuclear missiles aimed between the two super powers. Free elections were held throughout the nations of Eastern Europe, and people voted the communists out of office. Freedom and capitalism prevailed as the Cold War finally came to an end. The Berlin Wall, the most obvious and hated symbol of the Cold War, was torn down while millions partied in the streets and listened to the music of Beethoven's *Ode to Joy*. To the Republicans in the United States and conservatives throughout the Western world, this was the result of socialism's inherent flaws and the more natural benefits that flow from the free market.

The liberal response

As might be expected, most liberals see the recent rise of capitalism in an entirely different light. They look back at the last 125 years of American history and see a distinctly expanding role for the federal government in the nation's economy. This is a positive pattern that they would like to see carried on into the future.

In the late 19th century, millions of farmers were imploring the government to raise agricultural prices by increasing the nation's money supply. They also called for the government to regulate railroads that were charging exorbitant prices. By the 1890s, the farmers had linked up politically with the growing number of industrial workers who were being exploited by big money interests. The result was the Populist Movement, which advocated the free coinage of silver, the abolition of national banks, a graduated income tax, government ownership of all forms of transportation and communication, the direct election of senators, civil service reform, an eight-hour working day and pensions. While the Populist Party failed to displace either the Democrats or the Republicans, and their list of legislative accomplishments was limited, their call for an increased role for the government in order to alleviate many of the problems of the poor and the dispossessed laid a foundation for the future.

The start of the 20th century witnessed a continuation of the Populist agenda by Progressive reformers on the local, state and federal levels. Since the Progressives built on the foundation established by the Populist Movement, they proved to be much more successful. All three presidents between 1901 and 1920, Theodore Roosevelt, William Howard Taft and Woodrow Wilson, left behind a Progressive record of legislative accomplishments that included anti-trust legislation, the Pure Food and Drug Act, the Meat Inspection Act, the abolition of child labor, the National Park Service, the Federal Reserve System, the income tax and the right to vote for women. By 1920, the Democratic Party had more or less adopted the Progressive agenda, and to a large extent, they have been guided by it ever since.

In the 1920s, the government took a giant step backwards in terms of expanding its role in the economy. There was considerable economic growth during this decade, but it was exceptionally uneven. The 1920s ended with a stock market crash that ushered in the longest and most severe economic depression in the nation's history. By 1932, with the nation's unemployment rate hovering around 25 per cent, the United States turned to a Democrat, Franklin D. Roosevelt, to bring the government back into the epicenter of the nation's economy. The result was more than two-dozen new government programs collectively called the New Deal. Among the more lasting reforms were stock market regulation, agricultural subsidies, federal insurance of bank accounts, Social Security pensions, the minimum wage, the 40-hour workweek and the construction of massive public works projects to provide millions of new jobs. To many conservatives at the time, FDR's New Deal was a gigantic step towards socialism.

The 1960s witnessed another round of new government programs. By this point, the richest people could see up to 93 per cent of their income taxed by the federal government. During President Lyndon B. Johnson's *"War on Poverty,"* the lower classes received government assistance in the form of federal housing projects, Medicare, Medicaid, food stamps and subsidized preschool education. Johnson's Great Society also passed legislation in such areas as immigration reform, civil rights and environmental protection. Even today, many liberals look back fondly on the 1960s as a period of progress. This decade included not only a significant movement towards socialism, but also a greater communitarian spirit, marches for nonviolence, the rise of a new liberating moral code and rock festivals like the one held at Woodstock in 1969.

There have been some noteworthy setbacks, particularly during the Reagan years of the 1980s, but most liberals are proud of the accomplishments from the previous century. There are now hundreds of new government programs to help the poor, the aged and the dispossessed. While the gap between the richest and poorest Americans is huge and has recently grown even larger, there is also a safety net under that prevents most Americans from starving to death. The U.S. government is now motivated by a compassionate value that largely did not exist prior to the late 1800s.

As for the Soviet Union, most liberals see the demise of communism in that nation as an aberration. The socialist experiment in Russia failed more because of the power-hungry tyranny of its leadership than because of any incompatibility with human nature. Liberals point out that it is fairer to compare the differences *within* nations like Russia, China, Cuba or Vietnam before and after their Marxist revolutions rather than comparing them with nations that had already industrialized in the 19th century. A nation like Cuba was never really democratic or economically advanced, so rather than highlighting Cuba's economic stagnation, liberals would likely argue that many Cubans today have decent housing, educational opportunities and access to health care. As for Russia, liberals would assign more of the credit for ending the Cold War to Mikhail Gorbachev, rather than President Reagan. Some might even contend that life in the Soviet Union during the 1980s was preferable to the corruption, civil rights violations and economic inequities that dominate current life in Vladimir Putin's Russia. Moreover, socialist reforms throughout the Western world have improved the standard of living for hundreds of millions, and many of these new programs that involve better access to housing, food, education and health care can hardly be considered failures.

Additionally, just as conservatives emphasize the inherent unfairness of socialism, liberals have their own moral concerns regarding capitalism. To many liberals, the idea that wealth reflects an individual's choices or hard work is largely an illusion. No one has the freedom to choose their parents, pick from a menu of hereditary attributes or select the environment in which they are raised. Whether an individual ends up running a company, keeping its books, assembling the product on the factory line, or sweeping up the floor at night is largely the result of forces beyond each person's control. Therefore, dividing up the economic pie so that one person receives an enormous piece while another is given only crumbs hardly seems fair. If a worker spends a full day sweating on the factory floor, that person is entitled to a fair share of compensation relative to the CEO who spends the same day in an office making phone calls, running meetings and negotiating contracts. To do otherwise is morally unconscionable.

Most liberal Democrats in the United States do not call themselves socialists. Yet on any spectrum that places pure capitalism at one end and pure socialism on the other, many liberals would likely place themselves closer to socialism. To liberals, capitalism has not won an overwhelming victory against socialism. They may not support a violent overthrow of the state by a small cadre of communists, but that does not mean they have given up their goal of greater economic parity. These liberals would argue that governments in every western nation today, including the United States, play an expanded role in the national economy in order to provide vital programs and greater equality.

Conclusion

Nations like China, Cuba and Vietnam are still not conducting free elections, but over the last few decades, they have adopted a number of free market principles to improve their economies and raise their standards of living. The former Soviet states and nations of Eastern Europe vary in the amount of political freedom they grant their citizens, the level of economic liberty they provide their entrepreneurs and the standard of living enjoyed by their people. None of these states, however, can be accurately labeled as communist anymore, and it is perhaps doubtful they ever will be again. The Cold War has ended, and with only the United States still standing as a superpower, it would seem that free enterprise has prevailed over communism.

How did this happen? Without constitutional safeguards or democratic traditions, any nation is susceptible to the whims of a tyrant. Adolph Hitler and his Nazi cronies came to power in 1933 promising Germany a Third Reich (empire) that would last a thousand years. Yet without any tangible limits to the abuses of his power, it barely lasted a dozen. The same can be said about the Soviet Union under Joseph Stalin, China under Mao Zedong, Vietnam under Ho Chi Minh and Cuba under Fidel Castro. Mahatma Gandhi once said that "*there have been tyrants, and murderers, and for a time they can seem invincible, but in the end they always fall...*" By definition, communism is an extreme form of socialism that can only begin when an established government is overthrown. Problems arise, however, when it comes time to provide a replacement. Historically, a tyrant has often filled the vacuum. Perhaps more than anything else, the inevitable fall of these tyrants helps to explain the downfall of communism.

While the remnants of communism may only exist in a handful of nations like North Korea, today, one can no longer find pure capitalism anywhere on the planet. Even nations like Germany, Australia, the United Kingdom, Canada, Japan and the United States, all of which have a high degree of economic freedom, still maintain a safety net that provides food, education and health care to most citizens. The days of laissez faire free enterprise, as seen in Dickensian Great Britain two hundred years ago or in the United States' Gilded Age during the second half of the 19th century, are long over. It is highly doubtful they will ever return.

Sources and further reading:

Alchin, Linda. "Progressive Movement." *American-Historama.org*. Accessed September 14, 2016. http:www.american-historama.org/1881-1913-maturation-era/progressive-movement.htm.

Andrew, John A. III. *Lyndon Johnson and the Great Society*. Chicago: Ivan R. Dee, 1999.

Badger, Anthony J. *The New Deal: The Depression Years, 1933-1940*. New York: Hill and Wang, 1989.

Barghini, Tiziana, and Valentina Pasquali. "Economic Freedom by Country 2015." *GlobalFinance.com*. November 18, 2015. https:www.gfmag.com/global-data/economic-data/economic-freedom-by-country.

Bartlett, Bruce. *The New American Economy: TheFailure of Reaganomics and a New Way Forward*. New York: St. Martin's Press, 2009.

Carr, E. *The Russian Revolution from Lenin to Stalin 1917-1929*. Basingstoke: Palgrave Macmillan, 2004.

Friedman, Milton. *Capitalism and Freedom: Fortieth Anniversary Edition*. Chicago: University of Chicago Press, 2002.

Gandhi, Mahatma. *BeliefNet.com*. Accessed September 15, 2016. http:www.beliefnet. com/quotes/inspiration/m/mahatma-gandhi/when-i-despair-i-remember-that-all-through-history.aspx.

Karlin, Anatoly. "The Soviet Economy-Charting Failure." *AnatolyKarlin.com*. June 22, 2012. http://www.akarlin.com/2012/06/the-soviet-economy-charting-failure/.

Marx, Karl. *Karl Marx: Selected Writings*. New York: Oxford University Press, 2000.

"1980 Presidential Election." *270towin.com*. Accessed September 13, 2016. http://www.270towin.com/1980_Election/.

O'Rourke, P.J. *Quoteland.com*. Accessed September 12, 2016. http://www.quoteland.com/author/P-J-ORourke-Quotes/287/.

Orwell, George. *Animal Farm*. New York: Signet, 1996.

Tousignant, Marylou. "The Berlin Wall Fell 25 Years Ago." *WashingtonPost.com*. November 7, 2014. https://www.washingtonpost.com/lifestyle/kidpost/the-berlin-wall-fell-25-years-ago/2014/11/06/4d2a900c-5fab-11e4-9f3a-7e28799e0549.

Whittemore, Jessica. "The Commercial Revolution: Economic Impact of Exploration and Colonization on Europe." *Study.com*. Accessed September 12, 2016. http://www.study.com/academy/lesson/the-commercial-revolution-economic-impact-of-exploration-and-colonization-on-europe.html.

"Why are Conservatives Firmly Against Socialism While Liberals are Not?" *Quora.com*. Accessed September 13, 2016. https:www.quora.com/Why-are-Conservatives-firmly-against-Socialism-while-liberals-are-not.

Chapter 8

Why has the world population exploded and why is it so unevenly distributed?

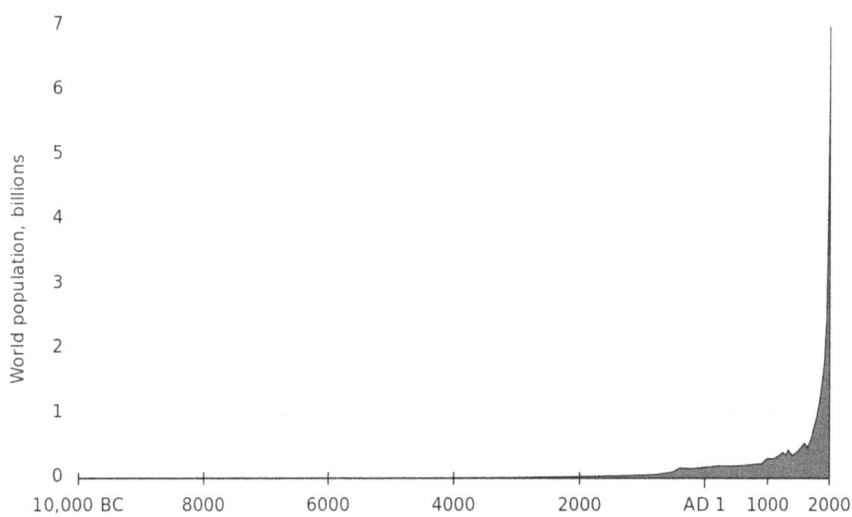

World human population 10,000BC-2000AD
Courtesy of El T at English Wikimedia(PD-user)
https://commons.wikimedia.org/wiki/File:Population_curve.svg

"Population, when unchecked, increases in a geometrical ratio."

Thomas Malthus

"Man begets, but land does not beget."

Cecil Rhodes

Two thousand years ago, the human population of the entire planet, about 300 million, was less than the current number of people living in the United States today. One thousand years later, it had only increased by about ten million, and well into the second millennium, it grew less than 0.1 per cent each year. By the

1300s, it actually dropped due to the Black Plague, which took the lives of 50 million people, 60 per cent of Europe's population. Beginning in the late 18th century, however, the Industrial Revolution raised the standard of living, spurred growth and radically changed everything. By 1800, the world's population had climbed to the unprecedented level of one billion people. Almost 65 per cent lived in Asia, 21 per cent were European and less than one per cent inhabited North America.

It took only 127 years for the world's population to double. It then took only another 33 years to reach three billion. From 1920 to 1950, the population growth rate averaged approximately one per cent a year, and this was despite the 60 million or more people that died from the Second World War. In the late 1960s, the growth rate hit an all-time peak of 2.04 per cent a year. The growth rate then began to gradually decline, but with so many people already on the planet waiting to give birth, the world's population continued to explode. It hit four billion in 1974, and five billion only 13 years later. By 1999, the population topped six billion, and it climbed to over seven billion in 2011. As for distribution, Europe and Africa each has about 12 per cent of the world's population, although the rate of growth is considerably higher in Africa. Nine per cent live in Latin America and only five per cent reside in North America. Just as in 1800, Asia is home to the majority of the planet's population, roughly 61 per cent.

These massive demographic transformations have completely reshaped the lives of the 7,340,370,000 people that currently call Earth their home. These changes have occurred slowly enough that, from one day to the next, most people do not seem to notice. Relative to the amount of time that humans have occupied the planet, however, these changes came in the blink of an eye. It is estimated that 6.5 per cent of all people ever born are alive right now. Between 1900 and 2000 the increase in the world's population was three times greater than the entire previous history of humanity – an increase from 1.5 billion to 6.1 billion in just 100 years.

Based on these observations, the history of the world can be divided into three distinct but vastly uneven periods. The first, the pre-modern, lasted millions of years and witnessed only glacial population growth. The second period, beginning with the start of the modern Industrial Revolution, lasted until the 1960s and was characterized by a steadily expanding rate of population growth. Now that this growth rate has stabilized and even started to decline, the earth has entered the third period. Nevertheless, population growth is like a colossal ship that builds tremendous momentum before losing power. The ship requires a great distance before it will come to a natural stop. Demographic experts believe that it will take until the end of the 21st century before the world's population will stop growing.

In ecological terms, what does this mean to our overall quality of life? In 1798, the English cleric and scholar, Thomas Malthus, published his book, *An Essay on the Principle of Population*. Malthus argued that although the Agricultural

Revolution in England grew unprecedented quantities of food and improved the wellbeing of the populace, the gains were only temporary. He reasoned that more food would spur more people and that population growth would eventually outpace resource production, which in turn would exacerbate famine and disease.

Despite these Malthusian predictions, worldwide agricultural production today has actually outpaced human population growth. There is more than enough food today to feed every human being on the planet, and this will probably remain true throughout the rest of the century. The famines that devastate certain developing nations today do not stem from a lack of food but from its vastly uneven distribution.

That said, the exploding world population will likely strain many of the world's resources. It will contribute to rising air pollution, shortages of clean drinking water and all of the problems associated with global warming. The growing population will also likely increase political tension, with people in the most crowded quarters scrambling for limited land and resources. This may spur more conflicts, wars and refugee immigration. Psychologically, population growth might even cause more mental illness. As the science fiction writer, Robert A. Heinlein, pointed out, "*animals can be driven crazy by placing too many in too small a pen. Homo sapiens is the only animal that voluntarily does this to himself.*" In light of these consequences that stem from the world's population growth, it is crucial to understand the causes behind these titanic demographic changes.

The good news and the bad news

There is no question that the world has benefitted from the Industrial Revolution. There were short-term costs for millions in the form of longer hours, lower pay and excruciatingly bad working conditions. Due to the rise of labor unions and such government reforms as worker's compensation, minimum wage, the eight-hour workday and Social Security pensions, the quality of life for the average industrial worker gradually improved. Thousands of new inventions and cheaper factory-made goods also improved the overall standard of living. People around the planet had more commodities than ever before, and because machines were doing the work that used to be performed by hand, many people could work less. The middle classes grew, and by the outset of the 20th century, the average American family was thrilled to enjoy products that are taken for granted today. These include electric lights, indoor plumbing, movies, recorded music and even the first automobiles.

In addition to the plentiful consumer products pouring out of mills and factories, industrialization brought other positive changes. Crop rotation, new irrigation techniques, steel-tipped plows, fertilizers and mechanized farm equipment meant that one farmer could now feed more people, and food became more plentiful and affordable. The burgeoning field of public health led to improved sanitation, better waste removal and cleaner drinking water. The lethal epidemics of typhus and cholera, which had once plagued any city where human or animal waste infected water sources, all but disappeared in the more technologically advanced nations. Advances in vaccinations, surgical procedures and the adaptation of germ theory also produced a dramatic reduction in premature deaths. In 1900, for every 1000 live births, six to nine women in the United States died of pregnancy-related complications. By 1997, the maternal mortality rate had declined almost 99 per cent to less than 0.1 deaths per 1000 births. In addition, the infant mortality rate, that is the number of babies out of every 1000 that will not live to see their first birthday, declined 90 per cent from 100 per thousand in 1900 to 7.2 in 1997.

The end result was that people, particularly in the more industrially advanced nations like the United States, were living healthier and longer lives than ever before. In 1850, the average American could expect to live to the age of 38. By 1900, it had climbed to 50, and today, it is over 79. As previously indicated, this notable change had many complex causes, but most of them boiled down to environmental interventions, improvements in nutrition, advances in clinical medicine, enhancements in access to health care, upgrades in the surveillance and monitoring of disease, increases in education levels and a significantly rising standard of living. One hundred years ago, few could foresee the downside to all of these positive developments.

Demographically speaking, the only way that any population throughout the history of the world could ever remain stable is if its birthrate was on par with its death rate. In developed nations, this requires a birth rate of 2.1 children per woman in order to maintain current population. In Colonial America, life expectancy was only 36, although this was still higher than in much of the world. To compensate, the average American family in the late 1700s had between six and seven children. Several may never have survived to adulthood, but as long as two were able start families of their own, the population remained stable. Combined with the large number of immigrants pouring into Colonial America, not to mention thousands of slaves brought over in chains, this high birth rate contributed to a steadily growing population.

The problem was that people tended to be creatures of habit. If large families became the norm over many centuries, each new generation was likely to continue this pattern. These cultural mores were deeply rooted, and changing them took a concerted effort as well a modicum of time. For generations, people had a propensity to marry shortly after reaching childbearing ages and to continue procreation until no longer able. Birth control, if it was practiced at all, typically involved primitive rhythm methods and withdrawal. There were a few devices available, such as condoms, but most people were not in the habit of using them. More convenient methods, like the birth control pill, did not come along until the 1960s.

This meant that just as industrializing nations started to enjoy their longer life spans, new consumer products and enhanced standards of living, they also witnessed an explosion in their populations. In the second half of the 19th century, Japan went so far as to import experts from Western nations to help them modernize their economy as well as their military. Japan built new industries such as shipyards, iron smelters and spinning mills. Railroads and telegraph lines crisscrossed the nation. They modernized their military so successfully that, to the shock of the Western world, they defeated Russia in a war in 1905. During this same period, however, their population doubled.

The same pattern was repeated to a certain extent in most of the Western nations as well. Between the second half of the 19th century and the first half of the 20th century, nations like Great Britain, France, Belgium, Holland, Germany, Austria and Italy witnessed similar growth in their populations. Those countries that had begun as European colonies and were now attracting large numbers of immigrants, like Canada, Australia and especially the United States, witnessed even greater population growth. Gradually, over time, their population expansion began to plateau. To a large degree, growing affluence tended to breed the desire for even more affluence. As the middle classes began to steadily increase in western societies, people began to realize that one of the fastest ways to dissipate their newfound wealth was to maintain the tradition of large families. With more people surviving to become grandparents, many people did not feel the need to continue having so many children. In addition, higher levels of education accompanied the growing wealth. More people chose to delay marriage in order to complete their educations, and once done, many used birth control at higher rates. The waning influence of religion and the rise of increasingly secular values also contributed to a growing willingness to use birth control. It took a couple of generations, but gradually, the birth rate declined to match the lowered death rates.

By the middle of the 20th century, the population growth in industrialized Western nations began to taper off. These nations had experienced phenomenal increases throughout the previous century, and by 1950, the United States, Japan, Germany, Italy and the United Kingdom were all among the top nations in the world in terms of their population. By 2000, the United States still held its ranking, but this was largely due to immigration. Japan had fallen from 5th to 9th, and the other three had dropped out of the top ten. During this same period, women in most of these Western nations were experiencing a rise in economic freedom that led many to delay the start of families in lieu of career aspirations. In several industrialized nations, some people even began to raise concerns about declining population numbers.

Meanwhile, much of the developing world today has been experiencing the same demographic phenomenon that characterized the Western world more than a century ago. From 1950 to 2013, China's population grew from 544 million to almost 1.4 billion, and this would have been considerably higher had the government not instituted a one-child-per-couple policy that placed a large tax on families that chose to have two or more children. The population of India grew from 376 million in 1950 to 1.25 billion in 2013. Bangladesh and Nigeria both had populations of approximately 38 million apiece in 1950. By 2013, Bangladesh was up to 157 million and Nigeria had climbed to a staggering 174 million. While these nations have witnessed recent explosions in their populations for many of the same reasons that spurred growth in Western countries 150 years ago, most have not experienced comparable growth in their economic development. The end result is that housing shortages, lack of educational opportunities, inadequate access to health care and famine have plagued several of these developing nations.

The Top Twenty:

Rank:	Nation:	Population:	Percentage of the World's Population:
1.	China	1,378,870,000	18.8%
2.	India	1,298,200,000	17.7%
3.	United States	324,531,000	4.42%
4.	Indonesia	260,581,000	3.55%
5.	Brazil	206,687,000	2.81%
6.	Pakistan	194,315,000	2.64%
7.	Nigeria	186,988,000	2.54%
8.	Bangladesh	161,120,000	2.19%
9.	Russia	146,654,000	2.00%
10.	Mexico	128,632,000	1.75%
11.	Japan	126,920,000	1.73%
12.	Philippines	103,045,000	1.40%
13.	Vietnam	92,700,000	1.26%
14.	Ethiopia	92,206,000	1.25%
15.	Egypt	91,622,000	1.25%
16.	Dem. Rep. of the Congo	82,310,000	1.12%
17.	Germany	82,176,000	1.12%
18.	Iran	79,552,000	1.08%
19.	Turkey	78,742,000	1.07%
20.	France	66,763,000	.88%

The question of distribution

As can be seen from the list above, there are major discrepancies in the distribution of the world's population. The contrast is most stark when comparing two nations geographically side by side. For example, Nigeria has almost eight times as many people as Australia, but only one eighth the amount of land. Compared to Canada, Bangladesh has almost four and a half times as many people, but over 67 nations the size of Bangladesh would fit into Canada. There is not necessarily a direct correlation between the population density of a nation and its standard of living. There are several smaller nations, such as Singapore and Bahrain that are densely populated but rank quite high in their per capita GDP. On the other hand, high population density is a significant hindrance to the economic growth of most developing nations. Why is the world's population so unevenly distributed?

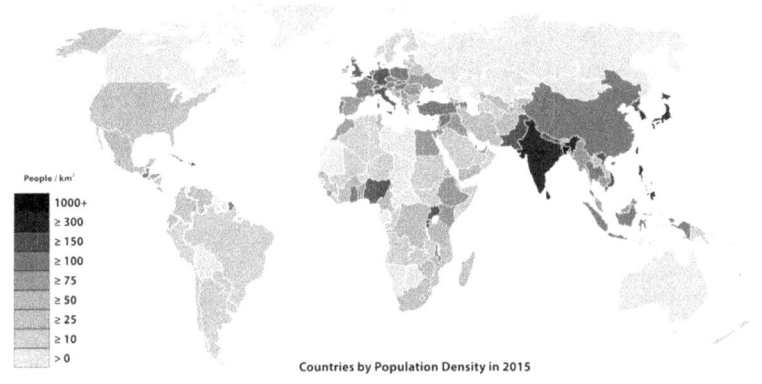

Courtesy of Ali Zifan (CC0)
https://commons.wikimedia.org/wiki/File:Countries_by_Population_Density_in_2015.svg

The influence of geography

The distribution of people across the planet has never been even. Based on the remains of ancestral humans uncovered in the Great Rift Valley, it can be postulated that the earliest people evolved in East Africa and have since dispersed across the globe. For millions of years, they hunted and gathered in the forests and savannahs of Africa, Asia and Europe. Natural land bridges exposed during the earth's more recent ice ages enabled them to meander their way into North America, South America and Australia somewhere between ten and forty thousand years ago. Throughout this Paleolithic Era, people traveled in small clans in search of wild game. Their numbers did not coagulate into small land areas because the food supply could never have sustained a larger population. Then, about 12,000 years ago, a revolution occurred that changed everything.

Beginning in the Middle East, humans began to cultivate crops and domesticate certain animals. The Neolithic Revolution meant that people could rely on a larger, steadier supply of food, and their numbers could begin to grow. This in turn led to the establishment of permanent settlements, increased specialization of labor and the beginnings of modern civilization. The primary preconditions for this agricultural revolution were relatively large areas of fertile soil and a reliable source of fresh water. This is why most world history textbooks begin their examination of the origins of modern civilization in the four major river valleys: the Nile River in Egypt, the Tigris and Euphrates Rivers in Mesopotamia (the modern nation of Iraq), the Indus and Ganges Rivers in the Asian subcontinent and the Yellow and Yangtze Rivers located in China.

Why these particular rivers? Not only did each provide ample water for consumption and crop irrigation, but they also flooded often enough to leave behind a healthy residue of fertile soil. Today, the population of Egypt is approximately 82 million people while there are just under 38 million in Iraq. Neither falls into the top ten nations of the world today in terms of population, but it should be noted that both are essentially located in deserts. Without the fresh water and fertile soil provided by the Nile, Tigris and Euphrates Rivers, the population of Egypt and Iraq might be more comparable to a West African nation today like Mauritania, which has roughly four million people.

On the other hand, what if these early river valley civilizations also enjoyed the advantages of consistent rainfall and moderate temperatures? This is essentially the case for the empires that developed in India and China. These two areas have led the world in population from the start, and nothing has really changed. Largely because of China's recent measures regarding one child per couple, the United Nations is predicting that India's population will surpass that of China by 2022. Regardless, India and China are clearly the world's two most populous nations. The United States comes in a distant third, but for every American alive today, there are 3.9 Indians and 4.25 Chinese.

Another geographic factor behind the uneven distribution of population is the presence of natural barriers that protect and isolate. India is shielded from the south by the Indian Ocean and from the north by the world's highest mountain ranges. There are passes through the mountains that outside invaders have been able to exploit, such as Alexander the Great in 326 BCE, but for the most part, India has been largely left alone to nurture its steady population growth for thousands of years. Natural barriers such as the East and South China Seas, mountains and deserts also surround China, but where the Chinese were most vulnerable, they managed to shield themselves off from the outside world by constructing a Great Wall that extended for 5500 miles.

Conversely, Israel has never possessed natural barriers to keep out invaders. Sitting on the crossroads of Europe, Asia and Africa, Israel has been subjected to invasions by the Egyptians, Babylonians, Assyrians, Persians, Greeks, Romans, Turks and most recently, the British. After the Romans crushed their revolt in the first century, the majority of Jewish residents were forced to scatter into a diaspora that drifted across the planet for the next 1900 years. Even after the United Na-Nations created the modern state of Israel in 1948, the nation still suffered from invasions from almost every direction. Therefore, it should come as no surprise that Israel possesses a relatively small population of about eight million people, and only 75 per cent are Jewish. Granted, Israel is not a large nation in terms of land and does not sit in the midst of a sizable river valley. All of these geographic factors have combined to keep its population down for the last several centuries. In 1900, what is now Israel had only 600,000 people.

On a smaller scale, these same geographic factors help to explain the location of at least some heavily populated cities. For people to congregate in a highly dense urban area, there is often a topographical explanation: the presence of a natural port, like in New York City, the confluence of navigable rivers, as in Pittsburgh or a central location connecting an enormous lake with surrounding farmland, like in Chicago. The growth of human transportation networks, such as river ports, rail lines and heavily traveled highways have also played a vital role in the location of major urban areas. This was certainly a factor in the location of such cities as Atlanta, St. Louis and Denver. More recently, the rise of industrialization has forced large numbers of people to concentrate around particular business enterprises. Would Seattle have become America's 15th largest urban center without the aerospace industry? Would Houston be 5th without petroleum?

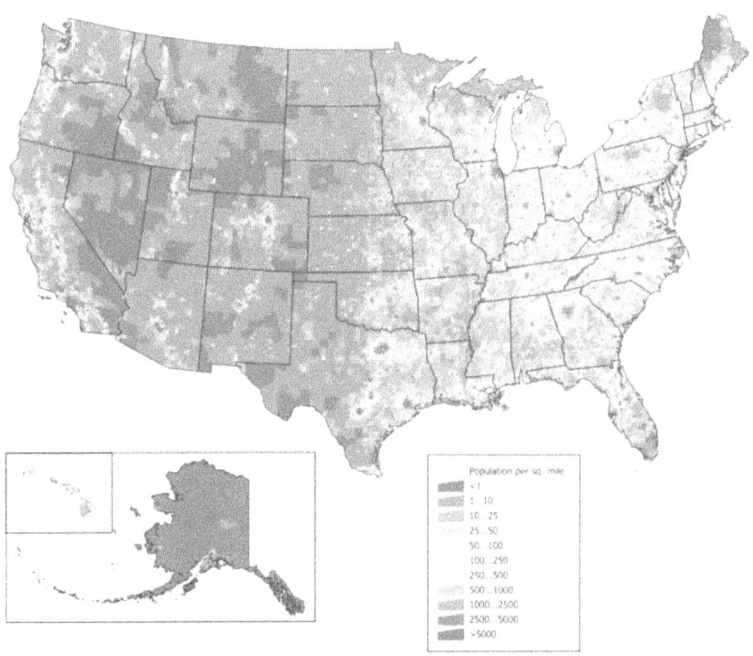

U.S. population map based on 2010 data
Courtesy of Jim Irwin (CC-BY-SA-3.0)
https://commons.wikimedia.org/wiki/File:US_population_map.png

The human factor

Finally, there are the political causes. A revolution, a civil war or the inability of a government to deal with a natural disaster has frequently forced people to vacate an area. According to the United Nations High Commissioner for Refugees, the total number of refugees by the end of 2015 had reached 65.3 million people, one out of every 113 people on Earth. Long term conflicts in nations like Afghanistan, South Sudan and Syria have greatly added to this number, which now exceeds the total number of refugees generated by the Second World War. Since 2011, the Syrian civil war alone has contributed almost five million people to this total.

Those nations that have traditionally opened their doors to migrants have undergone the opposite experience. Most of America's 324 million citizens can trace at least a major part of their ancestry to either people who arrived as immigrants or were dragged to the United States wearing the chains of slavery. A similar story helps to explain much of the population distribution found throughout the rest of North America, South America, Australia and New Zealand. Some of these nations, like Canada and Australia, have deliberately placed much tighter limits on immigration in order to maintain considerably smaller populations. As a result, despite their enormous acreage, each of these two nations has a population smaller than that of California.

Human migration throughout history has typically resulted from a combination of pushing and pulling forces. People might be pushed out of an area by wars, oppression, extreme poverty or natural disasters. On the other hand, a nation offering greater freedom or economic opportunities can act like a magnet attracting millions of immigrants. Of course, the policies of a nation that determine the openness of its borders also have a major impact on the shifting of human populations. Each nation has a unique story to explain its demographics, but in most cases, there is a combination of geographic, economic and political causes.

Conclusion

The tiny nation of Monaco has almost 44,000 people per square mile. Of course, this diminutive country has less than half the acreage of Central Park. Bangladesh, with a landmass just smaller than the state of Illinois, has approximately 2500 people per square mile. In contrast, despite the crowded megalopolis of Chicago, Illinois has only 232 people per square mile. Alaska averages about 1.3 people per square mile, making it the least crowded of America's 50 states. There are 8.8 people per square mile in Canada and 8.5 in Australia. In other words, in terms of the distribution of the world's population, there is astounding diversity between one place and another.

There is no question that the planet's population has been significantly expanding for the last 200 years, and that a larger percentage of the earth's residents have been increasingly packed into smaller areas of land. Much of this is best explained by the juxtaposition between geography and the forces of history. There is also little doubt that the continuation of rapid population growth into the future will seriously threaten the ecology of the planet. Besides the more immediate concerns about food and water, the world population explosion is likely to contribute to global warming and other environmental calamities, as well as a rise in political tension, terrorism and warfare. The increased concentration of people into smaller areas will have similar deleterious effects, at least in many nations.

This does not mean, however, that the future lies beyond the grasp of the planet's inhabitants. While there may have been some randomness guiding the past, that does not have to be the case in the future. The world's population today has more knowledge, better communication and greater opportunities for international cooperation than ever before. Therefore, the future lies squarely in the hands of the world's 7.4 billion people.

Sources and further reading:

"Achievements in Public Health, 1900-1999: Healthier Mothers and Babies." *CDC.gov.* October 1, 1999. https://www.cdc.gov/mmwr/preview/mmwrhtml/mm4838a2htm.

Benedictow, Ole J. "The Black Death: The Greatest Catastrophe Ever." *History Today* 55, no.3(March 2005). Accessed September 19, 2016. https://www.historytoday.com/ole-j-benedictow/black-death-greatest-catastrophe-ever.

Birdsall, Nancy, Allen C. Kelley, and Steven Sinding, ed. *Population Matters: Demographic Change, Economic Growth, and Poverty in the Developing World.* New York: Oxford University Press, 2001.

"Countries With the Most Population for the Years 1950, 2000, 2013, 2050 and 2100." *GeoHive.com.* Accessed September 21, 2016. https://www.geohive.com/earth/ population3.aspx.

"Demographics of Israel: Population of Israel/Palestine." *JewishVirtualLibrary.org.* Accessed September 23, 2016. https://www.jewishvirtuallibrary.org/jsource/History/demographics.html.

Friedman, Lauren F. "One of Society's Greatest Achievements in a Simple Chart of the Past 175 Years." *BusinessInsider.com.* June 19, 2015. http://www.businessinsider.com/how-has-life-expectancy-changed-throughout-history-2015-6.

Greene, Jack P. and J.R. Pole ed. *Colonial British America: Essays in the New History of the Early Modern Era.* Baltimore: The Johns Hopkins University Press, 1984.

Hanes, Michael. "Fertility and Mortality in the United States." *EH.net.* March 19, 2008. http://eh.net/encyclopedia/fertility-and-mortality-in-the-united-states/.

Heinlein, Robert A. *GoodReads.com.* Accessed September 18, 2016. https://www.goodreads.com/quotes/167995-animals-can-be-driven-crazy-by-placing-too-many-in.

"Human Numbers Through Time." *PBS.org.* Accessed September 19, 2016. https://www.pbs.org/wgbh/nova/worldbalance/numb-nf.html.

"Human Population: Population Growth." *PopulationReferenceBureau.org.* AccessedSeptember 21, 2016. https://www.prb.org/Publications/Lesson-Plans/HumanPopulation/PopulationGrowth.aspx.

King, Russell. *Atlas of Human Migration.* Buffalo: Firefly Books, 2007.

"The Largest U.S. Cities: Cities Ranked 1-100." *CityMayors.com.* Accessed September23, 2016. https://www.citymayors.com//gratis/uscities_100.html.

Malthus, Thomas. *An Essay on the Principle of Population.* New York: Oxford University Press, 2008.

Mazoyer, Marcel and Laurence Roudart. *A History of World Agriculture: From theNeolithic Age to the Current Crisis.* New York: Monthly Review Press, 2006.

McKirdy, Euan. "UNHCR Report: More Displaced Now Than After WWII." *CNN.com.* June 20, 2016. https://www.cnn.com/2016/06/20/world/unhcr-displaced-peoples-report/.

Ortiz-Ospina, Esteban and Max Roser. "World Population Growth." *OurWorldInData.org*. Accessed September 19, 2016. https://www.ourworldindata.org/world-population-growth/.

Pavitt, Nigel. *Africa's Great Rift Valley.* New York: Harry N. Abrams, 2001.

Rhodes, Cecil. *GoodReads.com.* Accessed September 19, 2016. https://www. http://www.goodreads goodreads.com/quotes/236881-man-begets-but-land-does-not-beget.

"U.S. States Area and Ranking." *EnchantedLearning.com.* Accessed September 23, 2016. https://www.enchantedlearning.com/usa/states/area.shtml.

"World Population Prospects: The 2008 Revision." *UnitedNations.org*. Accessed September 21, 2016. https://www.un.org/esa/population/publications/wpp2008/wpp2008_text_tables.pdf.

"World Population Prospects: The 2015 Revision." *UnitedNations.org*. Accessed September 21, 2016. https://esa.un.org/unpd/wpp/Publications/Files/Key_Findings_WPP_2015.pdf.

Chapter 9

Why does race and gender still play such a large role in modern society?

	White	Black
Median Household Wealth	$91,405	$6,446
Home Ownership	72.9%	43.5%
Median Household Income	$59,754	$35,416
Unemployment Rate	5.3%	11.4%
Poverty Rate	9.7%	27.2%

Courtesy of U.S. Census Bureau, 2014
https://money.cnn.com/2014/08/21/news/economy/black-white-inequality

"It is incontrovertible that race relations have improved significantly during my lifetime and yours, and that opportunities have opened up, and that attitudes have changed. That is a fact. What is also true is that the legacy of slavery, Jim Crow, discrimination in almost every institution of our lives – you know, that casts a long shadow. And that's still part of our DNA that's passed on. We're not cured of it."

President Barak Obama

June 22, 2015

If you are a white American, you can expect on average to live to the age of 78.9. If you are an African American, you should subtract 4.3 years from that lifespan. If you are a black person living in at least 70 different police jurisdictions scattered across the nation, according to a 2014 article in *USA Today*, your chances of being arrested are ten times higher than if you are white. If you are an African American student in school, you are three times more likely to be suspended than if you are white. These disturbing statistics go on and on.

There are also a number of significant differences when comparing men to women. For example, while American women have made significant progress when compared to the developing nations around the world, the United States was ranked last out of 20 industrialized countries in measures that included family leave, part-time employment and alternative work arrangements. In education, while there are now more women than men attending U.S. colleges and universities, the degrees earned by women are statistically more correlated with lower income careers. Around the house, research shows that women on average still perform a disproportionate share of the chores, particularly with child rearing. More women are now working fulltime than ever before, but unlike many men, a woman's work often does not end when she arrives home after a long day. In addition, women earn only 79 per cent of what men are paid.

The United States has a long and ugly history when it comes to the prejudice and discrimination it has doled out to its different minority groups. For African Americans and women, there has been dramatic improvement over the last 60 years, but racism and sexism have hardly disappeared. Their presence today is deeply rooted in the nation's past, but there are additional reasons why race and gender still linger on as factors that detract from the quality of life for millions of Americans.

The influence of the past

America's original sin lies in the institution of slavery. The idea that one individual might *"own"* another dates back to ancient times. Slavery played a vital role in the societies of Egypt, Mesopotamia, Greece and especially Rome. At one point, between 30 and 40 per cent of the Italian population during the days of the Roman Empire was held in bondage, and conditions for many grew so dire that in 73 BCE, a gladiator slave named Spartacus led an uprising that eventually involved between 90,000 and 120,000 slaves. Several Roman legions were destroyed before Spartacus was defeated.

In different forms, slavery continued to thrive into the Middle Ages. Slaves were present in societies as far-flung as Africa, the Middle East and among many of the American indigenous cultures. The Byzantine-Ottoman wars resulted in the taking of a large number of Christian slaves, and slavery became common within the British Isles during the Middle Ages. During the 9th century, the Muslims of Spain captured so many slaves from Eastern Europe that the word *"slave"* originated from the word *"Slav."* Slavery is mentioned in both the Bible and the Koran. For thousands of years, slaves have been bought, sold and worked to death. However, up until the discovery of the New World by the Spanish at the end of the 15th century, the horror of slavery was generally only bestowed upon those captured in a war or as a means to pay off a debt.

The enormous demand for a cheap source of labor in European colonies changed everything. Europeans were motivated by the desire to gain quick wealth through trade, mining gold and silver or by cultivating cash crops like sugar or tobacco. Yet they did not want to perform all of the work that was required. One option was to capture and enslave the locals, but many of the indigenous people either ran away or succumbed to the diseases brought over from Europe. This left another option.

Between 1525 and 1866, 12.5 million Africans were enslaved and carried to the New World via the slave trade's Middle Passage. Since most of these people were not captured in a major war nor sold into slavery to pay off a debt, something had to be invented to intellectually justify this new form of slavery. Latching on to the notion that animals such as horses or oxen could be purchased as property for their labor due to their inferior status in relation to humans, modern racism was invented. White Europeans convinced themselves of the Africans' apparent lack of humanity. What much of the world sees today as a beautiful style of abstract art was misunderstood and unappreciated by Europeans 500 years ago. Today, the traditional village homes in West Africa are admired for their functionality, but 500 years ago, the Europeans saw primitive, dirt-floor shacks. The rich tradition of storytelling did not dispel the European perception of African illiteracy. As for religion, the Europeans convinced themselves they were saving souls by converting African slaves from their spiritual traditions to Christianity. To many of the Europeans, the Africans were an inferior race, and this was used to justify the modern slavery that persisted in North and South America until the late 19th century. Slavery did not officially end in Brazil until 1888.

The passage of the 13th Amendment to the Constitution in 1865 officially abolished slavery in the United States. Yet it hardly eradicated the racism that had been its justification since the first slaves were auctioned in Jamestown, Virginia in 1619. The dozen or so years that followed the end of the American Civil War in 1865 were known as Reconstruction, and while there was some success in reconstructing a partitioned nation, little was done to help the four million former slaves. The right to vote was granted to former male slaves, and some even managed to gain political office, but for many, life was not that different from what it had been before the Civil War. African Americans were terrified by the ferocity and violence of the Ku Klux Klan, disenfranchised by poll taxes and literacy tests, and socially removed by Jim Crow segregation.

In almost every respect, African Americans lived separate lives. They attended separate schools, prayed in separate churches and drank from separate water fountains. This was all legally sanctioned in 1896 when the U.S. Supreme Court handed down its *Plessy v. Ferguson* decision that interpreted the Equal Protection Clause of the 14th Amendment to mean that as long as facilities like railcars or classrooms were *"equal,"* it did not violate the Constitution to mandate that the races be kept apart. Of course, in reality, the races were miles apart. For about 100 years, African Americans continued to endure inadequate housing, underfunded schools and pathetic health care. On paper, they may have been equal, but in reality, they were forced to live under the worst form of apartheid. Most of their efforts to rectify the situation were met with race riots, lynchings and other forms of terrorism.

The end of the Second World War in 1945 brought a hint of better days to come. In 1948, President Harry Truman issued an executive order to integrate the military, and even though this cost him millions of white Southern votes, he still managed to barely get himself reelected. Six years later, the Supreme Court handed down the *Brown v. Board of Education* decision where it unanimously reversed the *"separate but equal"* judgment it had made 58 years earlier and ordered the integration of the nation's public schools with *"all deliberate speed."* This in turn laid the foundation for the pinnacle event that occurred two years later in Montgomery, Alabama.

When Rosa Parks, an African American seamstress, refused to give up her seat on a bus in direct defiance to Jim Crow tradition, she was promptly arrested. The African American community quickly rallied around her, and led by a 27-year-old minister named Martin Luther King, conducted a boycott of that city's busses that lasted for over a year and finally culminated in a victory. Since millions soon joined in the efforts to march, demonstrate and protest, the Montgomery Bus Boycott can be considered the official start of the modern Civil Rights Movement. Over the next decade, there were hundreds of protests that ranged from lunch counter sit-ins to freedom rides on interstate busses to marches on Washington, D.C. There were thousands of arrests and quite a few African Americans were injured or even killed in church bombings and vicious assassination attempts. While many followed Martin Luther King's admonitions to refrain from the use of violence, others like Malcolm X, the Nation of Islam and the Black Panthers used more militant and confrontational tactics.

By the end of the 1960s, the Civil Rights Movement began to splinter. Legislation like the Civil Rights Act of 1964 and the Voting Rights Act of 1965 had removed most of the legal barriers, but the economic gap between whites and people of color was still stark, particularly in terms of jobs, pay and poverty rates. While the movement shifted towards a more economic direction in the late 1960s, it suffered an irreparable loss on April 4, 1968 when Martin Luther King was brutally gunned down. His assassination occurred in Memphis, where he had come to support a strike by sanitation workers who were looking to improve their economic lot.

Since the 1960s, there has been significant progress. The barriers to voting are considerably smaller, more African Americans are graduating from college and moving up into the nation's middle class and in 2008 the United States elected its first African American president. Yet despite these gains, racism still plagues most institutions in American society. While most Americans, black and white, acknowledge that racism remains a problem, there is a stark difference in perceptions. When a Gallup poll in 2013 asked if new civil rights laws were needed to reduce discrimination against blacks, 53 per cent of blacks said yes compared with 17 per cent of whites. When asked if the justice system is biased or not, 68 per cent of blacks but only 25 per cent of whites said yes.

In fact, often when Americans start to believe that racism and prejudice may be on the decline, our original sin resurfaces. In 1992, a race riot broke out in Los Angeles in response to the failed effort to convict the police officers that had been videotaped viciously beating an African American, Rodney King. By the end of that riot, there was over a billion dollars in property damage, 11,000 people had been arrested, 2000 were injured and 53 people were dead. On October 3, 1995, a jury in Los Angeles returned a not guilty verdict in the trial of O.J. Simpson. In a poll taken shortly after the verdict, 73 per cent of whites said that Simpson should have been found guilty of the murder of his former wife, Nicole Brown Simpson and Ronald Goldman. However, the fact that only 27 per cent of blacks agreed indicated that there was still an enormous abyss separating racial perceptions of the U.S. justice system. More than 30 years after passage of the Civil Rights Act of 1964, most African Americans still felt that there were two systems of justice in America, one for whites and one for everyone else. The advent of strict mandatory sentencing rules in the 1990s, which greatly contributed to the large number of people of color in our nation's prisons, was another factor that fueled this perception (this topic will be explored at length in the next chapter).

Almost 20 years later, another dramatic event occurred in the north St. Louis suburb of Ferguson, Missouri that once again revealed America's festering abscess of racism. On August 9, 2014, Michael Brown, an 18-year-old unarmed African American male, was gunned down by a white Ferguson police officer, Darren Wilson. The event sparked protests and riots that lasted for several days, and these were renewed a few months later when a grand jury failed to indict Officer Wilson. Combined with other killings by police in such places as Cleveland, New York City, Baltimore, St. Paul, Baton Rouge and Charlotte, a new civil rights movement coalesced again entitled Black Lives Matter. While its overall goals are sometimes ambiguous, the Black Lives Matter Movement has vigorously campaigned against violence and systemic racism toward people of color. It has employed clever forms of protest against the killings of black people by law enforcement personnel, and it has confronted racial profiling, police brutality and racial inequality in the U.S. criminal justice system.

Modern racism was invented more than 400 years ago to justify the slavery that literally helped to build the United States. While slavery ended more than 150 years ago, the racism that provided its intellectual foundation has hardly disappeared. A large part of the reason lies imbedded in our history. If an individual suffers a psychologically traumatic event, such as physical abuse as a child or extreme violence on the battlefield, years of therapy may still not provide a lasting cure. After all, each person is largely the sum total of their past experiences. The same holds true for a particular society or culture. Four centuries of ugly racism have divided American society and stifled the advancement of generations of people of color. It has become deeply imbedded into the nation's consciousness and even its cultural DNA. Why does race still play such a vital role in American society? A quick glance into a historical mirror will provide much of the answer. The same account can be applied to the experience of American women, but it should be noted that their story differs in a number of significant ways.

The vexing experience of American women

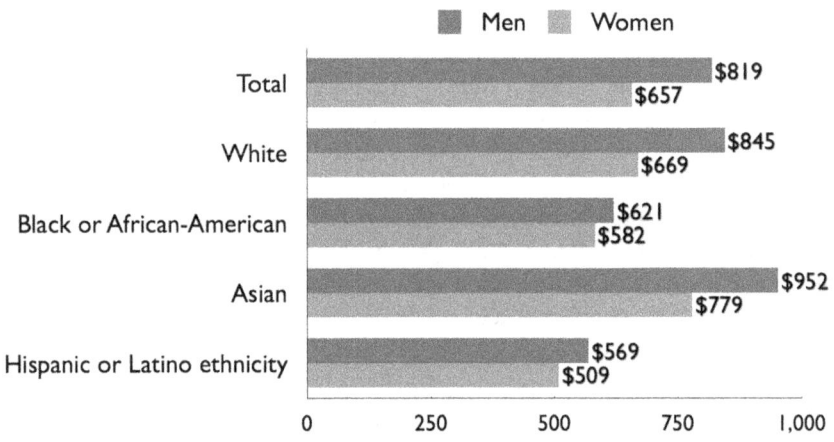

Median weekly earnings of full-time wage and salary workers, by sex, race, and ethnicity, 2009
Courtesy of U.S. Bureau of Labor Statistics. *Highlights of Women's Earnings in 2009.* Report 1025, June 2010
https://en.wikipedia.org/wiki/Gender_pay_gap_in_the_United_States#/media/File:US_gender_pay_gap,_by_sex,_race_ethnicity-2009.png

Comparing the historical experiences of women to that of African Americans is like holding a banana next to a pineapple and attempting to note their similarities and differences. There is no denying that both are grown as a type of fruit, but that is about the full extent of their common ground.

During the early years of American history, women were not entitled to vote and had to surrender control of their property to their husbands upon marriage. They were also extremely limited in their educational and occupational opportunities. It was traditionally believed that a woman's place was in the home, raising children and tending to domestic affairs. This was their *"sphere of influence,"* while men dominated the political and economic realm. Unless she also happened to be of African descent, an American woman could not be bought or sold as legal chattel. In terms of the limits placed on their individual liberty, however, the quality of life for many women was not much better than that of a slave toiling on a Southern plantation. Furthermore, life for women of color was particularly brutal.

One of the major differences in the experience of early American women with that of black Americans resided in their own self-awareness. African Americans clearly knew they were the victims of racism. In contrast, many women acknowledged their differences from men and were sometimes more willing to accept their status. Even today, there are still women who believe that feminism leads to higher divorce rates and threatens traditional family values. Throughout American history, the leaders of any woman's movement that sought greater equality not only had to contend with the men who refused to give up their status or power, but also with the women who were satisfied with the status quo.

Nevertheless, an important step was taken in July of 1848 when the first women's convention was held in Seneca Falls, New York. Led by several Quakers, as well as women like Elizabeth Cady Stanton and Lucretia Mott, 300 women and men spent two days laying out an agenda for a movement that is still ongoing. Writing a *Declaration of Sentiments*, the participants in Seneca Falls stated "*that all men and women are created equal...*" The focus of their movement was to attain suffrage, that is, the right to vote. Once this was secured, women would grasp the power they would need to acquire all other forms of political and economic equality.

Ironically, one of the chief impediments in the path towards women's suffrage was the Abolition Movement. The abolition of slavery sometimes competed with the goal of women gaining the right to vote, and when the slaves were finally freed with the passage of the 13th Amendment in 1865, the aim of many reformers shifted to securing civil rights for former slaves rather than for women. The 15th Amendment ratified in 1870 legally provided suffrage to former slaves, but still not women. Many of the women who had worked as abolitionists felt cheated. As the nation transferred its gaze towards other interests in the second half of the 19th century, like westward expansion and industrial development, the Suffragettes lost much of their momentum. Additionally, some of the gains made when new western states like Wyoming, Colorado and Utah granted women the right to vote in the 1890s undermined public support for a constitutional amendment that would grant women the right to vote nationwide.

By the dawn of the 20th century, women were generally divided into two camps. The older generation of Suffragettes, led by women such as Carrie Chapman Catt and Anna Howard Shaw, were willing to work for the right to vote one state at a time. Their organization, the National American Woman Suffrage Association (NAWSA), employed more moderate political tactics in the process of securing the right to vote. Meanwhile, a younger generation of women had come of age influenced by the more militant Suffragettes in the United Kingdom. Alice Paul and

Lucy Burns formed the National Women's Party, and they soon shifted their focus to the passage of a constitutional amendment that would immediately grant women the right to vote nationwide. The NWA led massive parades, picketed the White House and staged hunger strikes while locked up in jail. Although common today, no group had ever marched in front of the White House before, and to do so after the United States had entered the First World War in 1917 was even more audacious.

In this instance, the more militant tactics worked. President Woodrow Wilson finally recognized the hypocrisy of fighting a war in Europe to defend democracy, while denying suffrage for half of America's citizens back home. With his support, Congress passed the 19th Amendment in 1919, and it was ratified by the states the following year. 72 years after the Seneca Falls Convention, women finally had the right to vote. Once again, however, their momentum waned in the decades that followed. Although a few women such as Alice Paul turned their attention to the passage of an Equal Rights Amendment, other women felt that with the acquisition of the right to vote, victory had been achieved.

By the 1950s, the state of the women's movement on the whole had declined. There had been progress during the Second World War, as millions of women took jobs in defense industries. Subsequently, however, while Martin Luther King was leading the bus boycott in Montgomery, two thirds of American women still did not have jobs. Many women were expected to marry young and stay home to raise a family. Those that did work earned only 64 cents for every dollar earned by a man. Since the cult of domesticity that had dominated so much of the 19th century still prevailed in the 1950s, there was little in terms of leadership, direction, or energy to improve the status quo of women.

This began to dramatically change in the following decade with the 1963 publication of *The Feminine Mystique* by Betty Friedan. Read by millions of American housewives, it described what Friedan called *"the problem that has no name."* *The Feminine Mystique* drew attention to the widespread unhappiness of women, even those who possessed material comfort and the *"bliss"* of being married and raising children. Betty Friedan's landmark book helped to raise the consciousness of millions of women who began to more boldly question their second-rate status. Combined with the advent of the birth control pill in 1960, *The Feminine Mystique* helped to launch a modern women's liberation movement that continued to gain steam throughout the 1960s and 1970s.

In 1972, the movement hit its apex when both houses of Congress passed the Equal Rights Amendment (ERA). First proposed back in 1923, the ERA read, *"Equality of rights under the law shall not be denied or abridged by the United States or by any state on account of sex."* Sent to the states for ratification, it seemed headed for quick approval despite the opposition it would face from conservative men. However, after Phyllis Schlafly mobilized conservative women in opposition, arguing that the ERA would be disadvantageous to housewives and to the sanctity of the American family, the amendment ran out of time. Congress had set March 22, 1979 as the deadline for states to ratify the ERA. By that date, 35 states had ratified the amendment, but since 38 were necessary, the amendment went down in defeat.

Despite this setback, most would agree that women have made genuine progress up through today. Women have overcome most educational barriers, and after the passage of Title IX in 1972, this success has extended to the athletic fields. Women now make up about half of the workforce and earn a higher percentage of college degrees than men. Women constitute more than half of the students attending America's law schools and almost half of those attending medical schools. The pay gap is still significant, but even this number has improved a bit. More fundamentally, society's expectations have evolved so that women today do not feel as much pressure to define themselves exclusively as housewives and mothers. Today, women comprise 47 per cent of the nation's workforce. In almost every area of life, women no longer feel as many of the constraints that had held back their mothers and grandmothers for so long.

Nevertheless, sexual discrimination has not disappeared. It may be subtler, but in the economy, men still dominate the upper echelons of management and are still more likely to receive promotions into higher paying jobs. Only 5.2 per cent of the CEO's of Fortune 500 companies are women. In the political arena, women hold only 26 per cent of the high government positions in the United States, and less than 20 per cent of the seats in Congress. On college campuses and in the military, women are still frequently subjected to sexual harassment and even rape. And then there is the pay gap. It may have improved over the last several decades, but compared to many other Western nations, the United States still lags behind. These systemic inequalities are even worse for women of color.

With only a few exceptions, women around the world have faced gender inequality for thousands of years. They have been exploited, denied equal opportunity and in many cases, physically and sexually abused with impunity. Just as with racism, sexism and misogyny will not disappear because of the progress made over a few decades. Stereotypes and prejudices from the past are deeply ingrained. The more their historical background is understood, however, the easier it becomes to recognize their enduring presence in today's world.

Immigration restrictions

There are other factors deeply rooted in the past that help address the question of why race and gender still play such a large role in modern society. Nativism is technically defined as "*the policy of protecting the interests of native-born or established inhabitants against those of immigrants.*" A pattern of nativism developed in the first half of the 19th century that has lasted through the present. A number of Americans whose parents or grandparents had migrated to the United States developed arguments in favor of a policy that would close the door on future immigrants. Some were concerned about competition for jobs or worried that too many immigrants would reduce wages. Others simply believed that their native birth put them in a superior position relative to the newcomers. By the 1840s, many railed against the huge waves of Irish immigrants that were fleeing the deadly famine in the Emerald Isle. By the 1850s, millions joined or supported the American Party, who many called the Know-Nothing Party that advocated for major reductions in the numbers of immigrants allowed into the United States, particularly the Roman Catholics coming from Ireland. Divisions over slavery led to the demise of the Know-Nothings, but not the nativism from which it spawned.

In 1882, similar sentiments led to passage of the Chinese Exclusion Act, which slammed the door in the faces of virtually all immigrants who sought admission into the United States from China. A less formal arrangement was struck in the form of a *"gentleman's agreement"* with the emperor of Japan in 1907 that significantly reduced the number of Japanese immigrants. The rationale underlying both developments was clearly based on racism directed towards Asian immigrants, as no similar restrictions were placed on the tidal wave of immigrants coming from Europe. In 1924, however, Congress enacted legislation setting quotas on immigrants coming from all nations. Since these quotas were applied to the total number of immigrants that had entered the United States from each individual nation prior to the 1890 census, they placed much tighter restrictions on those coming from Eastern Europe, since their numbers had only started to swell over the past three decades. Without using the racist language that had been directed at the Chinese, this Immigration Act was still motivated by racism and nativism. Unfortunately, President Franklin D. Roosevelt strictly enforced these immigration quotas in the 1930s. The result was that the door was slammed shut in the faces of thousands of European Jewish refugees who sought to escape the Nazi Holocaust that eventually took the lives of over six million Jews.

Immigration reform in the 1960s removed some of the more blatantly inequitable policies, but major restrictions still remain to this day. Immigration law has become so complex that there are many attorneys today that do nothing but handle immigration cases. While the laws themselves have been largely cleansed of racist language and policies, there is still a direct link between the continuing calls for immigration reform today and the nativist traditions of the past. Every time a politician calls for building a wall on the Mexican border, or the need to kick out every man, woman and child who does not possess the legal status to remain in the United States, it reflects an undercurrent of intolerance. Whenever the fear of rising crime or terrorism is cited as a reason not to accept refugees from war-torn Muslim nations like Syria, it raises the ugly specter of nativism.

There are few people today that call for America to completely open its doors to all immigrants that might want to enter. However, many of those that push for the most extreme limits on immigration are still motivated by feelings of superiority, and there is still a lingering prejudice underlying many of their calls for immigration reform. There may be valid economic or national security reasons cited to justify their positions, but quite a few are also motivated by the vestiges of racism that still survive today. For some, this racism may be repressed or even subconscious. For others, they still openly wear it on their sleeves.

Hate groups

According to the Southern Poverty Law Center, there are currently 892 hate groups operating in the United States. 190 of these are openly affiliated with the Ku Klux Klan, a secret racist organization first founded during the period of Reconstruction that followed immediately after the Civil War. More recently, after the World Trade Center and the Pentagon were attacked on September 11, 2001, there has been a rise in the number of hate groups that direct their vitriol specifically at Muslims. Other hate groups include Neo-Nazis, White Nationalists, Racist Skinheads, Christian Identity groups, Neo-Confederates and even Black Separatists.

There is obviously a huge gulf separating the interests of Neo-Nazis from those of Black Separatists, but what all of these groups share in common is a keen awareness of the rather superficial differences that separate one group from another. Martin Luther King may have dreamed of a day when everyone would be judged more by the "*content of their character*" than by "*the color of their skin,*" but these groups clearly do not share his vision. They try to guard their own interests at the expense of others, and each in their own way thrives on America's longstanding tradition of racism. As the last bastions of prejudice in the modern world, they attempt to keep racism alive by recruiting new members and spreading hateful propaganda.

The First Amendment protects the free speech rights of these hate groups. In fact, in a 1977 case entitled *National Socialist Party v. Skokie*, the U.S. Supreme Court ruled that as long as their demonstrations were peaceful, the Neo-Nazi Party based in Chicago had a constitutional right to march in the village of Skokie, a predominantly Jewish suburban community located on that city's north side. This protection included their right to wear Nazi uniforms and swastika armbands. Supreme Court Justice Louis Brandeis once stated "*that fear breeds repression; that repression breeds hate; that hate menaces stable government; that the path of safety lies in the opportunity to discuss freely supposed grievances and proposed remedies; and that the fitting remedy for evil counsels is good ones.*" While the continuing existence of hate groups is a significant factor in explaining why race still plays such a large role in our modern society, the courts have recognized that putting up with their protected expressions of speech is a necessary price to preserve our constitutional liberties.

The need to maintain racial consciousness

At first glance, it would seem that the surest path towards the elimination of racism and sexism in modern times would be to minimize the superficial differences that divide white people from people of color and men from women. After all, why should skin color and differences in sex be the source of so much conflict? Due to the numerous advantages gained by white men over the last several centuries, however, there are many people today who support policies that, by definition, must acknowledge differences in race and gender. In order to correct inequities deeply rooted in the past, some institutions recently created affirmative action programs to expand opportunities to people of color in such areas as school admissions, scholarships, and employment.

Controversy has swirled around these programs since they first appeared in the 1960s. Opponents have frequently labeled affirmative action as a form of reverse discrimination, and a number of cases challenging their legality have made their way to the U.S. Supreme Court. While the court has ruled that reserving a specific quota of seats for minorities in a medical school is an infringement on the constitutional rights of prospective white students, it also supported the principle that race could be one of several factors considered in deciding whom to admit into a highly competitive educational program. Supporters of affirmative action programs argue that these efforts are necessary in order to address the discrimination people of color have suffered in the past, as well as to ensure greater diversity.

Affirmative action, integrative school bussing and other comparable programs are designed to offer an advantage to groups that have been the victims of prejudice in the past. Most of these programs were intended to be temporary, but due to the continuing presence of discrimination in modern society, many may persist for some time.

Evolving views of gender and sex

There is one other recent development that has amplified the role of gender in our modern society. While the Supreme Court ruled in its 1967 case entitled *Loving v. Virginia* that any prohibition of interracial marriage violated the U.S. Constitution, nothing was said about the marriage between two men or two women. It would take another 36 years before Massachusetts became the first state to legalize gay marriage. Anticipating this possibility, Congress had already passed the Defense of Marriage Act (DOMA) in 1996. This legislation had defined marriage for federal purposes as strictly the union of one man and one woman and allowed states to refuse to recognize same-sex marriages granted under the laws of other states. As additional states steadily joined the ranks of those that would allow gay marriage, others dug in their heels and even added prohibitions on same-sex marriage to their state constitutions. Gay marriage suddenly became one of the most controversial issues in the nation.

The Supreme Court seemed to resolve the issue in 2015 by handing down a decision that legalized gay marriage. Yet despite this landmark case, there were soon businesses and even local government officials that refused to cater to the needs of gay couples seeking to get married. This was even supported by proposed legislation in states such as Mississippi and Indiana in an effort to protect the *"religious freedom"* of those who saw gay marriage as an affront to their moral values. Front-page headlines were generated not only from the passage of these laws, but also by the boycotts and protests that ensued.

In addition, U.S. society has slowly become aware that gender is not as simple as distinguishing between male and female, straight or gay. A growing number of people began to recognize a continuum in between, which includes people who are bisexual, transgender and gender neutral. Schools have wrestled with such issues as the provision of bathrooms for students who were born into one gender but identify with the opposite gender. On March 23, 2016, North Carolina passed the Public Facilities Privacy and Security Act mandating that students throughout the state use school bathrooms according to the gender to which they were born. This stirred up a firestorm of boycotts and protests, and because of this law, the National Basketball Association decided to move its 2017 All-Star Game from Charlotte to New Orleans.

At the present, issues continue to emanate from the movement towards greater equality for those who identify as lesbian, gay, bisexual and transgender (LGBT). The laws and values of our society are also continuing to evolve with the recent changes in gender identification. As these developments progress, the role of gender in our society will continue to change as well.

Conclusion

Societies, like individuals, are shaped by their pasts. American culture today is the offspring of centuries where prejudice, discrimination and intolerance have been more the rule than the exception. It took many generations to create the racism and sexism that still persist in modern society, and it will take many more generations to reduce their influence.

There is some good news, however. According to a study published in 2015 in the journal *Social Forces*, Americans have grown increasingly tolerant of people with views and lifestyles that differ from their own. The study found that the average American's tolerance has been improving steadily since the early 1970s. The biggest generational shift occurred between Baby Boomers (born between 1946 and 1964) and their *"Greatest Generation"* parents (1925-1945). Yet subsequent generations— Generation X (1964-1981) and Millennials (born after 1982) — have continued this pattern of accepting opinions and lifestyles different from their own. This trend is reflected by a number of recent developments, such as the legalization of gay marriage, the granting of full access for women to combat positions in all branches of the military and the rise in interracial dating. By 2010, 1.8 per cent of all new marriages were between black people and white people, nearly 20 times higher than in 1950. In fact, the growing acceptance cited in the *Social Forces* study came with just one exception: Americans are not more tolerant of people with racist beliefs.

Sources and further reading:

Bush, Mia. "US Women Make Strides Towards Equality, But Work Remains." *VOANews.com.* March 8, 2016. https://www.voanews.com/a/international-womens-day-us-women-gender-equality-work-remains/3223162.html.

Cahill, Bernadette. *Alice Paul, the National Women's Party and the Vote: The First Civil Rights Struggle of the 20th Century.* Jefferson: McFarland, 2015.

Chang, Jeff. *We Gon' Be Alright: Notes on Race and Resegregation.* New York: Picador, 2016.

Chappell, Bill. "We Are Not Cured: Obama Discusses Racism in America with Marc Maron." *NPR.org.* June 22, 2015. https://www.npr.org/sections/the-two-way/2015/06/22/416476377/we-are-not-cured-obama-discusses-racism-in-america-with-marc-maron.

Cobb, Jelani. "The Matter of Black Lives." *NewYorker.com.* March 14, 2016. https://www.newyorker.com/magazine/2016/03/14/where-is-black-lives-matter-headed.

Czech, Kenneth P. "Ancient History: Spartacus and the Slave Rebellion." *HistoryNet.com.* July 31, 2006. https://www.historynet.com/spartacus.htm.

Eil, Philip. "We're at Peak 'White Racial Apocalypse': The Enduring Toxic Myths Fueling Obama Backlash, All Lives Matter, and Donald Trump." *Salon.com.* September18, 2016. https://www.salon.com/2016/09/18/were-at-peak-white-racial-apocalypse-the-enduring-toxic-myths-fueling-obama-backlash-all-lives-matter-and-donald-trump/.

Ferguson, Susan J., ed. *Race, Gender, Sexuality, and Social Class: Dimensions of Inequality and Identity.* Thousand Oaks: Sage Publications, 2016.

Freedman, Estelle. *No Turning Back: The History of Feminism and the Future of Women.* New York: Random House, 2002.

Friedan, Betty. *The Feminine Mystique.* New York: W.W. Norton & Company, Inc., 2001.

Gates, Henry Louis Jr. "How Many Slaves Landed in the US?" *TheRoot.com.* January 6, 2014. https://www.theroot.com/articles/history/2014/01/how_many_slaves_came_to_america_fact_vs_fiction/.

"Gender Discrimination-History." *JRank.org.* Accessed September 29, 2016. https://www.law.jrank.org/pages/22615/Gender-Discrimination-History.html.

"Hate Groups: State Totals." *Southern Poverty Law Center.* Accessed September 30, 2016. https://www.spicenter.org/hate-map.

Health, Brad. "Racial Gap in U.S. Arrest Rates: 'Staggering Disparity'." *USAToday.com.* November 18, 2014. https://www.usatoday.com/story/news/nation/2014/11/18/ferguson-black-arrest-rates/19043207/.

"History-Brown v. Board of Education Re-Enactment." *UnitedStatesCourts.gov.* Accessed September 27, 2016. https://www.uscourts.gov/educational-resources/educational-activities/history-brown-v-board-education-re-enactment.

"Jim Crow Stories." *PBS.org.* Accessed September 27, 2016. https://www.pbs.org/wnet/jimcrow/stories_events_plessy.html.

Kopf, Dan. "Why is Interracial Marriage on the Rise?" *Priceonomics.com.* September 1, 2016. https://www.priceonomics.com/why-is-interracial-marriage-on-the-rise.

"The L.A. Riots: 24 Years Later." *LATimes.com.* April 28, 2016. https://www.latimes. latimes.com/los-angeles-riots/.

"Life Expectancy at Birth(in years)by Race/Ethnicity." *KaiserFamilyFoundation.org.* Accessed September 26, 2016. https://www.kff.org/other/state-indicator/life-expectancy-by-re/?currentTimeframe=0&sortModel=%7B"cold":"Location,"sort":asc"%7D.

"Loving v. Virginia." *Legal Information Institute.* Accessed October 12, 2016. https:// www.law.cornell.edu/supremecourt/text/388/1.

Luhby, Tami. "5 Disturbing Stats on Black-White Inequality." *CNN.com.* August 21, 2014. https://money.cnn.com/2014/08/21/news/economy/black-white-inequality/.

Miller, Kevin. "The Simple Truth About the Gender Pay Gap(Fall 2016)." *AAUW.org.* Accessed September 27, 2016. https://www.aauw.org/research/the-simple-truth-about-the-gender-pay-gap/.

Mullen, Shaun D. "Trial Exposed a Gulf in Racial Perceptions Some Still See 2 Justice Systems." *Philly.com.* June 12, 1996. https://articles.philly.com/1996-06-12/news/25628796_1_racial-gulf-racial-perceptions-blacks.

Perry, Susan. "Americans Have Become More Tolerant with Each Generation, Study Finds." *MinnPost.com.* March 23, 2015. https://www.minnpost.com/second-opinion/2015/03/Americans-have-become-more-tolerant-each-generation-study-finds.

Rider, Flynn. "10 Worst Race Riots in American History." *TopTenz.net.* January 5, 2015. https://www.toptenz.net/10-worst-race-riots-american-history.php.

Sanders, Katie. "NBA Legend Abdul-Jabbar: 'More Whites Believe in Ghosts Than Believe in Racism'." *Politifact.com.* May 4, 2014. https://www.politifact.com/punditfact/statements/2014/may/04/kareem-abdul-jabbar/nba-legend-abdul-jabbar-more-whites-believe-ghosts/.

Shoichet, Catherine E. "Is Racism on the Rise? More in U.S. Say it's a 'Big Problem,' CNN/KFF Poll Finds." *CNN.com.* November 25, 2015. https://www.cnn.com/2015/11/24/us/racism-problem-cnn-kff-poll/.

Stone, Geoffrey R. "Remembering the Nazis in Skokie." *HuffingtonPost.com.* May 25, 2011. https://www.huffingtonpost.com/geoffrey-r-stone/remembering-the-nazis-in_b_188739.html.

"The Story of Africa: Slavery." *BBC.com.* Accessed September 27, 2016. https://www.bbc.co.uk/worldservice/Africa/features/storyofafrica/9chapter1.s html.

Williams, Juan. *Eyes on the Prize: America's Civil Rights Years, 1954-1965.* New York: Penguin Books, 2013.

"Women's Bureau: Latest Annual Data." *United States Department of Labor.* Accessed September 27, 2016. https://www.dol.gov/wb/stats/latest_annual_data.htm.

"Women's History in America." *Women'sInternationalCenters.org.* Accessed September 29, 2016. https://www.wic.org/misc/history/htm.

Chapter 10

Why has the prison population in the United States grown so large?

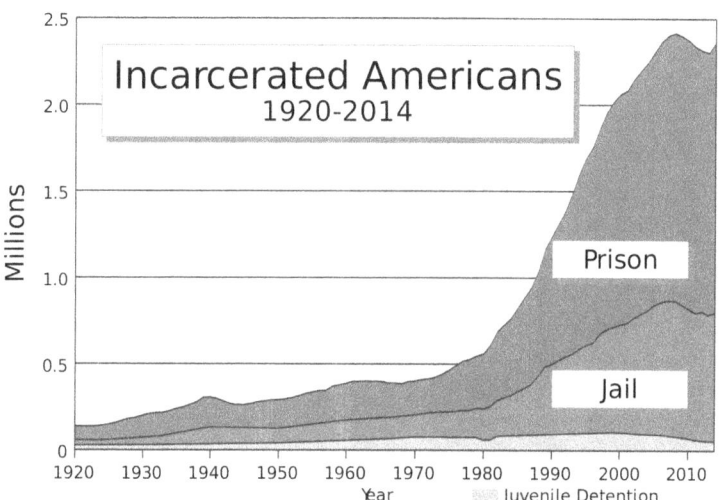

Timeline of total number of inmates in U.S. prisons, jails, and juvenile facilities
Courtesy of U.S. Bureau of Justice Statistics
https://commons.wikimedia.org/wiki/File:US_incarceration_timeline_clean.svg

"It is said that no one truly knows a nation until one has been inside its jails. A nation should not be judged by how it treats its highest citizens, but its lowest ones."

Nelson Mandela

The United States currently locks up more people, per capita, than any other nation in the world, past or present. The American criminal justice system currently holds more than 2.3 million people in 1,719 state prisons, 102 federal penitentiaries, 942 juvenile correctional facilities, 3,283 local jails and 79 Indian Country jails. In addition, there are others confined to military prisons, immigration detention facilities, civil commitment centers and prisons located in U.S. territories. In a nation of just over 324 million people, this means that for every 1,000 Americans, more than seven are incarcerated behind locked doors.

Beyond the walls of our prisons, there are even more people on probation, parole or under some other form of judicial supervision. In 2014, there was an estimated 6,851,000 people under the supervision of U.S. adult correctional systems, and this was actually a decline of about 52,000 from the previous year. About one in 36 adults in the United States was under some form of correctional supervision by the end of 2014.

These numbers reflect a staggering increase of about 500 per cent over the last 40 years. They also represent the culmination of almost 200 years of American penal reform. How did we ever reach this point, and what does it say about the current state of American culture and society?

Background history

During colonial times and for the first few decades after gaining independence, criminal punishments in the United States usually consisted of fines and various forms of public humiliation, including the pillory, stocks and ducking stools. Whippings were common, as were other types of corporal punishment, and the death penalty, usually taking place on the gallows, was handed out for serious felonies. Jails were small and frequently packed with inmates awaiting trial or the dispensing of their punishments, but very few housed felons for any length of time. Incarcerating people convicted of crimes in a prison for a specified number of years was not yet seen as a viable option.

This all began to change in the early 1800s. The first half of the 19th century saw a wave of social reform spread across the United States. Influenced by the Enlightenment principles of the previous century, the religious sentiments of the Second Great Awakening and the rise of Unitarianism and Transcendentalism, many people began to believe that society held the capacity to seek progress and improve the human condition. Leading the way in these reform movements were the abolitionists who blamed the institution of slavery for many of America's social ailments. Women followed in their wake by seeking greater equality in such areas as health care, education and especially the right to vote. From the 1820s to the start of the Civil War in 1861, there were also efforts to expand public education, house the mentally ill in humane treatment facilities, abolish alcoholic beverages and reform the treatment of people convicted of crimes.

This last area largely involved the proliferation of a more deterministic approach to how people viewed crime. There was a growing recognition that such background factors as the lack of an education, bleak poverty and family dysfunction all played a larger role in creating criminals than the individual free will of the law-breakers. Therefore, if convicted felons could be isolated and removed from the culture that had led them to lives of crime, they could be rehabilitated and then returned to society as law-abiding citizens. This thinking led to the rise of the modern-day penitentiary, a place where law-breakers could do their penance, reform and then receive forgiveness. The one remaining question, however, which has yet to be resolved to this day, is what should take place inside the walls of a penitentiary to best assure their chances for rehabilitation.

One of the earliest of these modern prisons was the Eastern State Penitentiary, which opened up on the outskirts of Philadelphia in 1822. Despite its decaying form today, Eastern State Penitentiary was conceived inside the home of Benjamin Franklin as a reform ahead of its time. Laid out in neat rows that emanated in every direction from a central building, the cells that held inmates guaranteed solitary confinement. The prisoners were given a work detail that consisted of handicrafts, but this was accomplished without any talking or socialization. The guiding premise was that without any contact with other people or the outside world, inmates would not only be removed from the societal influences that turned them into criminals, but they would also have ample time to reflect on how to become model citizens.

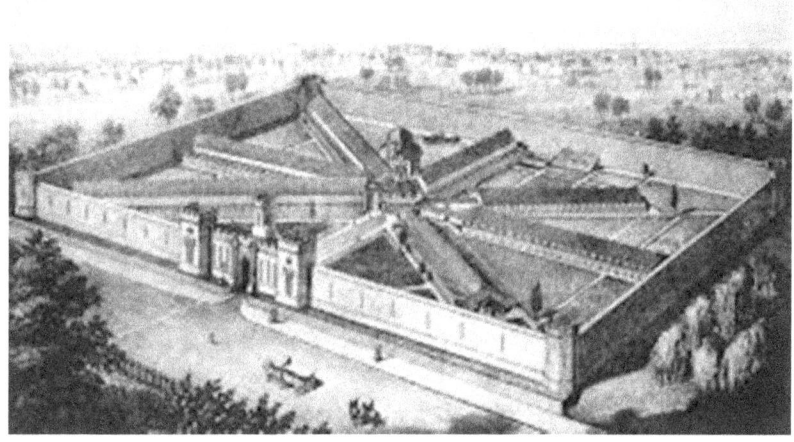

Aerial view of Eastern State Penitentiary
Courtesy of Mike Graham (CC-BY-2.0)
https://commons.wikimedia.org/wiki/File:Eastern_State_Penitentiary_aerial_crop.jpg

Three years later, the Auburn and Sing Sing Penitentiaries were opened in upstate New York. Like Philadelphia, guards enforced a strict rule of silence to keep prisoners from corrupting one another. However, inmates under this system were allowed out of their cells by day to participate in some form of work. There was strict control over every daily routine. Discipline was quite severe and whippings were common. Today, the early 19th century prisons in Pennsylvania and New York would provoke a spate of lawsuits over the violation of the inmates' rights, but in the first half of the 1800s, they were both seen as competing types of humane reform.

As the 19th century came to a close, penitentiaries grew more industrial to reflect the revolution sweeping across the country. Many grew more sterile and antiseptic in appearance. On the inside, however, they continued to veer between punitive conditions, which were based on the corrections philosophies of retribution and deterrence, and a focus on education and job training that was the mainstay of the rehabilitative approach. In addition, probation had been created as an alternative to sending an individual to prison for committing a minor offense, and parole was created as a path to supervised early release. An entirely separate corrections system was then created in the late 19th century for juveniles, which was based on the assumption that in people's early formative years there was a greater likelihood for rehabilitation. Finally, by 1890, the electric chair had been developed as a *"more humane"* method for carrying out capital punishments.

The 20th century

The population of the United States grew from 76 million in 1900 to 282 million in 2000. With this tremendous growth in the number of people came a corresponding rise in the number of crimes they would commit. This led to a dramatic increase in the number of prisons. Yet in the interest of reducing the rate of recidivism, which is the number of crimes committed by those released from incarceration, there was also a concerted effort to build prisons that would provide classrooms, job-training, counseling and other forms of rehabilitation. The term *"corrections"* was increasingly used during this time to describe a system built around the effort to *"correct"* the factors that had led someone to a life of crime. In fact, the purpose of opening the federal prison on Alcatraz Island in 1934 was to provide a secure, clean, efficient facility that could house those inmates who were the most resistant to rehabilitation. By removing them onto *"the Rock,"* more than a mile from San Francisco's wharves, they would be less likely to interfere with the efforts in other federal penitentiaries to transform criminals into law-abiding citizens.

By the middle of the 20th century, many of the reform efforts aimed at rehabilitation gave way to a get-tough-on-crime approach. Sentences tended to lengthen, and policymakers placed greater emphasis on retribution and deterrence over efforts to rehabilitate. With high guard towers, razor wire topping their increasingly lofty walls and the use of tiny isolation rooms to maintain order, most of America's prisons placed less emphasis on the goal of rehabilitating inmates. This approach was not always effective, and in many cases, the resulting rise in recidivism increased overall prison populations.

It was during this period that Louisiana's Angola State Penitentiary grew to become the largest prison in the United States. Situated on 18,000 acres at a bend in the Mississippi River, Angola has grown to house more than 6,300 inmates. Some reform came to Angola in the 1950s after 31 inmates cut their Achilles' tendons in order to protest the hard work and brutality. This did not last for long, however, largely because Angola's contracted inmate labor had proven to be such a lucrative revenue source. The Louisiana State Penitentiary has often embodied the worst brutality in America's modern prisons.

Similar changes occurred during the 1900s in regard to the use of the death penalty. Several states made an effort to make executions more painless and *"humane"* by replacing their electric chairs with gas chambers, and in more recent times, by using different forms of lethal injection. Others abolished its use altogether (as of this writing, 18 states plus the District of Columbia do not use the death penalty). In the 1970s, the Supreme Court stopped its use nation-wide, but this was largely because people of color and indigent people were much more likely to receive the death penalty, and not because of a judicial determination that its use violated the *"cruel and unusual punishment"* clause of the Constitution's Eighth Amendment. Consequently, when states rewrote their capital punishment laws in the late 1970s to address the due process issues, the Supreme Court gave the green light to the resumption of its use.

Today, even though there are still almost 3,000 Americans on death row, this is a tiny fraction of the total number of people incarcerated in our jails and prisons. The incarcerated population in the U.S., which has been steadily growing throughout our history, has skyrocketed since the 1970s. In attempting to determine why, there are three basic explanations.

Reason one – More crime

Overall, violent crime in the United States has held steady since colonial times. During the early 20th century, however, crime rates in the U.S. were considerably higher than those in Western Europe. For example, in 1916, Chicago, with a population slightly over two million, recorded 198 homicides. While this was not exceptional when compared to other American cities such as New York, it was significantly higher than European cities. In that same year, London recorded only 45 homicides even though it had three times the population of Chicago. Crime rates in America continued to climb during the Roaring Twenties and then leveled off a bit in the 1930s and 1940s. After World War Two, however, they began to steadily increase again, peaking from the 1970s to the early 1990s. Violent crime nearly quadrupled between 1960 and its peak in 1991. Property crime more than doubled over the same time period. Nonetheless, in the 1990s a new trend developed that shocked and mystified the experts. Crime rates began to decline.

Nothing will generate more debate amongst a group of criminologists than to raise the question about why crime increased so dramatically before 1991 and then began its inexplicable descent. This dramatic increase in crime, particularly in the 1960s, has been frequently linked to two causes. First, since the birth rate in the United States spectacularly increased in the twenty years following World War

Two, the baby-boomers were hitting their teens and early twenties during this period. Since people are most likely to commit crimes during this stage in their lives, more crimes resulted simply because there were more young people in the population to commit them. Second, this new generation of baby-boomers tended to hold a different set of values from the *"Greatest Generation"* that had preceded them. The vast majority had never known the hardship of suffering through the Great Depression or fighting in a world war. Instead, they experienced the affluence brought on by the longest period of economic growth and prosperity in the nation's history. However, not everyone shared equally in this burgeoning prosperity. Therefore, some of those left behind turned to crime as a quick means to catch up.

In addition, there is little doubt that America's values were dramatically shifting in the 1960s. Higher rates of crime were accompanied by higher rates of divorce, teenage pregnancy and drug abuse. The Youth Counter Cultural Movement spurred a number of changes where younger people purposefully chose to reject the traditions and values of their parents. This could be seen in their hair and clothing styles, in their rock and roll music and particularly in their marches and protests against the war in Vietnam. While hippies converged on communes in the Haight-Ashbury District in San Francisco, the Chicago police confronted thousands of youthful demonstrators when they came to protest the 1968 Democratic National Convention. The joyful exuberance and growing freedom that revolved around music, sexual liberation and drugs hit its cultural apex at the Woodstock Festival in upstate New York in August of 1969.

The surging emphasis placed on values such as love, peace and freedom came with a dark underside. Malevolent emotions were unleashed four months later at another rock festival held at the Altamont Speedway in Northern California that featured the Rolling Stones. Unlike Woodstock, this event was marred by considerable violence, including the killing of one person by the Hells Angels that had been hired to provide security. There were multiple injuries, numerous cars were stolen and then abandoned and there was extensive property damage.

In the same summer of 1969, while the nation was transfixed to televisions watching the first Americans walk on the moon, members of the *"Manson Family,"* a cult built around the quasi-commune established by Charles Manson, committed a series of nine brutal murders at four locations over a period of five weeks. At about the same time, a militant left-wing organization known as the Weather Underground formed as a faction of Students for a Democratic Society (SDS). Better known as the Weathermen, their goal was to create a clandestine revolutionary party intent on the overthrow of the U.S. government. With radical positions focused on black power and opposition to the Vietnam War, this group conducted a campaign of bombings that lasted through the mid-1970s.

While it may not be possible to pinpoint the exact causes behind the steep rise in crime between the 1950's and the early 1990s, there is no question that society's evolving moral structure played a vital role. The growing freedom to experiment with narcotic drugs led to a massive rise in the illegal drug trade. The growing affluence of the rich was continuously broadcasted on inexpensive televisions to millions of people who still lived below the poverty line, cultivating a materialistic desire to shortcut the American dream. Looking to expand the freedom from societal mores as well as the government, the National Rifle Association (NRA), along with other supporters of the Second Amendment, pushed to make guns progressively more available. In 1953, there were 40 firearms for every 100 Americans. By 1970, that number had climbed to 55, and ten years later, it had reached 76. As of 2014, it had grown to 116, meaning that there are now more guns in the United States than there are people. All of these developments reflected America's evolving values, and all of them could be linked to increased crime rates.

Since crime had steadily grown for almost a half century, many criminologists were surprised when rates began to decline in the 1990s. Conservatives wanted to credit this development to the significant increases in law enforcement, as well as stricter sentencing guidelines and the massive construction of additional prisons. Others pointed to a reduction in the use of crack cocaine that had skyrocketed in the previous decade. One hypothesis even suggested that a reduction in exposure to lead poisoning contributed to lower crime rates.

Probably the most creative explanation involved demographic changes. The Baby Boom had come to an end in the mid-1960s, and by the early 1990s, there were simply fewer young people around to commit crimes. An interesting wrinkle was added to this account in 2005 when two authors published a book called *Freakonomics: A Rogue Economist Explores the Hidden Side of Everything*. Written by University of Chicago economist Steven Levitt and *New York Times* journalist Stephen J. Dubner, it suggested that the decrease in crime was linked to the legalization of abortion, which was established by the *Roe v. Wade* Supreme Court case of 1973. According to this hypothesis, the drastic increase in abortions after 1973 meant that millions of unplanned babies were never born, and as a result, never had the chance to become criminals. If not for *Roe v. Wade*, millions of children would have been born in the mid-1970s to parents that did not want them or were not prepared to raise them. How many of these children would have turned to lives of crime by the 1990s? This thesis remains controversial to this day.

Regardless of the causes behind the increases and decreases in crime rates, the link between rising crime rates and incarceration rates seems straightforward up until the 1990s. As crime rates began to fall, however, prison populations did not. Therefore, we must consider other explanations.

Reason two – Longer sentences

Crime has declined in the United States over the last 25 years, but prison populations have continued to swell. America is home to just under five per cent of the world's population, but houses 25 per cent of its prisoners. This staggering fact is largely attributable to its War on Drugs, stricter enforcement of life sentences, prosecutions of juveniles in adult courts and the expansion of the penal code.

The federal government and the states have long provided sentencing guidelines to judges for most crimes. Yet in the past, judges were free to consider a host of mitigating factors that might lead to shorter sentences for many criminals. However, mandatory minimum sentences began to emerge in the 1970s as the United States commenced its War on Drugs. This meant that judges were forced to impose a designated sentence or one that was even harsher. In the 1980s, Congress passed even longer mandatory minimum sentences, primarily in connection with drug possession crimes. Many state governments soon followed this trend. Since then, these laws have also been applied to sex and gang-related crimes. Few would disagree that these mandatory minimum sentences have significantly contributed to the rise in prison populations.

Related to this development was the advent of *"three strikes"* laws in about half of the states. Generally, under these laws, if an individual has already been convicted of two previous crimes, the conviction of a third will result in a prison sentence of 25 years to life. This law not only added to the prison populations, but has also led to some extremely questionable outcomes. In California, for example, Leandro Andrade was convicted of stealing $153 in videotapes from Kmart stores in San Bernardino. In the past, Andrade had a few run-ins with the law. He was a drug addict, and he had committed some residential burglaries years before. Therefore, when he stole the videos, it was his third strike, which meant a minimum of 25 years in prison. Because he had grabbed the videotapes in two different Kmart stores, he was prosecuted for two third strikes. As a result, Andrade was sentenced to life in prison with no parole for 50 years.

The *"three strikes"* rule became federal law in 1994 when President Bill Clinton signed the Violent Crime Control and Law Enforcement Act. Covering a wide range of topics, this law proved to be the largest crime bill in U.S. history. It provided almost $10 billion in funding for prisons and expanded federal criminal law in a number of directions. It also defined new federal crimes in such areas as immigration, hate crimes, sex crimes and gang-related crime. The bill required states to establish registries for sexual offenders and greatly expanded the use of the death penalty by the federal government. Coming on the heels of the recent surge in crimes, the law made sense to many elected leaders at the time, but it significantly increased federal incarceration rates and led to prison overcrowding. It also inspired many states to adopt similar policies. President Bill Clinton later expressed regret over the provisions of the law that led to this increased prison population, including the three strikes provision.

The decline in the use of parole is another contributing factor to the explosion in prison populations. Historically, parole was a stepping-stone that moved an inmate out of prison and back into society under the supervision of a parole officer. Even a life sentence did not always equate to spending a life in prison. Many federal prisoners who received life sentences were given their first parole review after just 15 years. This lenient attitude toward life sentences changed, however, when the Supreme Court initiated a temporary ban on capital punishment in 1972. In response to that ruling, many states began using life-without-possibility-of-parole sentences. Since the 1970s, the federal government and the states of Illinois, Iowa, Louisiana, Pennsylvania and South Dakota have eliminated parole altogether. As of 2012, nearly 160,000 Americans were serving life sentences in prison without the hope of parole.

Along with this recent get-tough approach to crime came a movement to withdraw from the juvenile justice system that has been in use for more than 100 years. Due to their youth, juveniles were more likely to encounter a justice system that focused on rehabilitation, counseling and training. Because of the rise in violent crime amongst young people in the late 1980s, the public increasingly supported policies that treated older juveniles as adults. Juvenile offenders tried as adults were more likely to receive prison sentences in adult correctional facilities. In the past ten years, the number of people under 18 serving time in adult prisons has more than doubled.

Another related development has been the plethora of new crimes added to the statute books. When the U.S. Constitution was written, it listed just three federal crimes: treason, piracy and counterfeiting. Since then, the number of acts considered federal crimes has increased to 4,500. Legislators have also written many new laws that do not require proof of a person's intent. As a result, between 2000 and 2010, more than 780,000 people were convicted of federal crimes and received prison sentences.

Finally, there has been the War on Drugs. While few Americans were originally opposed to the justice system's tougher approach to dealing with the nation's illegal drug problem, the last three decades have seen the War on Drugs evolve into a war on non-violent drug-related crime. In 2011, nonviolent drug offenders made up 25 per cent of the nation's prison population. In that same year, one in every 28 children had a parent in prison and two-thirds of these parents were incarcerated for non-violent crimes. Only in the last few years has there been a growing movement to either legalize or decriminalize certain drugs like marijuana and to provide those addicted to drugs with rehabilitative options rather than prison sentences.

2.3 million people are locked up in American jails and prisons, a number larger than ever before. To a large extent, this figure has resulted from the confluence of rising crime rates and society's determination to reduce these rates. However, there is another factor that we must take into account, one that has left its ugly imprint on almost every facet of American society. Unlike the previous two reasons that explain the relatively recent rise in the nation's prison population, this feature has been present in American history from the very beginning.

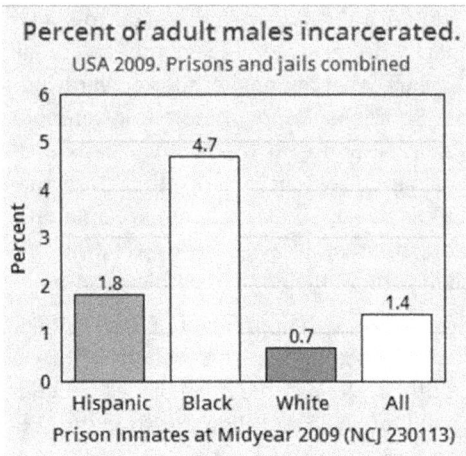

USA 2009 per cent of adult males incarcerated by race and ethnicity
Courtesy of U.S. Bureau of Justice Statistics
https://commons.wikimedia.org/wiki/File:USA_2009._Per
cent_of_adult_males_incarcerated_by_race_and_ethnicity.png

Reason three – Racism

In the United States, African Americans make up 13 per cent of the total population. Yet 40 per cent of the nation's prisoners are black. While there are 450 white inmates for every 100,000 people, there are 2,306 African Americans per 100,000. What has driven these appalling statistics?

Many people tend to offer one of three explanations for this anomaly. The first, which has absolutely no validity, is that African Americans are somehow genetically predisposed to commit more crimes. This one reeks of racism and is not even close to accurate. The vast majority of African Americans never commit crimes, and if other extenuating circumstances, such as the two discussed below, were taken into account, black people would not be overrepresented in our nation's prisons. The only reason to even mention this theory is that it was once believed by a large segment of the population, similar to how racist views were popularly accepted in order to justify slavery, Jim Crow segregation and other vestiges of America's prejudiced past.

The second explanation is also linked to American racism. As stated in the last chapter, there are still significant differences between white people and people of color in terms of net worth, income, educational opportunities, poverty rates, unemployment, access to health care, and average life span. These disparities are due to a legacy of discrimination. If a group of people is subjected to hundreds of years of prejudice and oppression, they can hardly be expected to catch up in just one or two generations. Therefore, while a considerable number of African Americans have worked their way into the American middle class, the percentage of black people that fall below the poverty line is still three times higher than it is for white people. Committing what lawmakers deem a criminal act might be a greater temptation for any group living under similar disadvantaged circumstances.

Finally, it must be noted that despite the 1960s legislation enacted in response to the modern Civil Rights Movement, racism directed at African Americans has hardly disappeared. This is just as true for law enforcement and the criminal justice system as it is for any other institution in American society. For example, while blacks comprise 14 per cent of the monthly drug users, they make up 37 per cent of the people arrested by the police for drug-related offenses. Across the nation, studies show that police are more likely to pull over and frisk blacks or Latinos than whites. In New York City, 80 per cent of the stops made by the police involved black and Latino people, and 85 per cent of those people were frisked. Additionally, after being arrested, African Americans in New York are 33 per cent more likely than whites to be detained while facing a felony trial.

The situation is even starker with respect to the nation's corrections system. As recent as 2010, the U.S. Sentencing Commission reported that African Americans received ten per cent longer sentences than white people for committing the same federal crimes. At the same time, black people were 21 per cent more likely to receive mandatory minimum sentences and 20 per cent more likely to be sentenced to prison for drug crimes compared to white defendants. The U.S. Bureau of Justice Statistics concluded that an African American male born in 2001 had a 32 per cent chance of going to jail in his lifetime. A Latino male had a 17 per cent chance, and a white male had only a 6 per cent chance.

Michelle Alexander, a civil rights litigator and legal scholar, addressed these disparities in 2010 in a book called *The New Jim Crow: Mass Incarceration in the Age of Colorblindness*. Alexander's central premise, from which the book derives its title, is that *"mass incarceration is, metaphorically, the New Jim Crow."* According to Alexander, the conventional historical narrative assets that discrimination mostly ended with the Civil Rights Movement of the 1960s. Instead, Alexander posits that the U.S. criminal justice system has become a tool for enforcing both traditional and new modes of repression. The result has been not only the highest rate of incarceration in the world, but also the disproportionate imprisonment of African American men. According to Alexander, if these trends continue, the United States will imprison one-third of its African American population. Ultimately, this has led Alexander to contend that mass incarceration is *"a stunningly comprehensive and well-disguised system of racialized social control that functions in a manner strikingly similar to Jim Crow."*

Many African Americans, including those living in America's more affluent suburbs, have multiple stories to tell of being pulled over by the police for *"Driving While Black."* Some families have experienced horrific violence and loss due to the racial disparities that continue to plague the U.S. criminal justice system. America still has two criminal justices systems, one for white people and another for black people. The perpetuation of American racism, and in particular, the greater likelihood that people of color will be stopped, arrested, detained, convicted, and incarcerated for longer periods of time, is another reason why the prison population in the United States has swelled.

Other Factors

In addition to the three factors mentioned above, there are a few other recent developments that one should consider. Starting in the 1960's, a movement began to deinstitutionalize those diagnosed with a mental illness. In the past, mentally ill people were locked up in institutional facilities, often against their will. After researchers published studies that described the abysmal conditions in these hospitals, which writers described in books like *One Flew Over the Cuckoo's Nest* (published in 1962), thousands of people suffering from mental illnesses were *"freed"* to wander the streets. Between the mid-1960s and 1980, the number of institutionalized mentally ill people in the United States dropped from a peak of 560,000 to just over 130,000. Many of these individuals were left destitute and would soon make up one third of the homeless population. Without adequate support, a significant portion of people with severe mental illness ended up incarcerated in correctional facilities, where most do not receive adequate care for their disorders.

A second consideration is the trend across the United States to hold elections for judges and prosecuting attorneys. In fact, the U.S. is the only country in the world where voters elect prosecutors, and in 22 states, judges run for their positions just like any other elected politician. While this movement may be more democratic because it provides more political power to the electorate, it also means that voters and campaign donors wield more influence over courtroom activities. Since running a tough-on-crime campaign often leads to positive political results, one consequence of this populist pattern has been longer sentences for those convicted of a crime, leading to larger prison populations.

Another factor stems from the legal and social barriers that impede successful reentry for people with criminal histories. In most states, employers may legally reject job seekers who check the application *"box"* that indicates a criminal record. This is also an obstacle for those seeking an apartment, an educational loan, or a host of public benefits. In addition, if someone's criminal record includes a conviction that is deemed a sex crime, he or she usually must register so that this information is available to the public. Regardless of how one views these policies, there is no doubt that one of the collateral consequences of these practices is a higher rate of recidivism. The harder it is for released inmates to reenter society, the more likely they will return to a life of crime.

One last development has been the rise of privately owned *"for profit"* prisons. Federal and state governments have a long history of contracting specific prison services to private firms, including medical services, food preparation, vocational training and inmate transportation. In the 1980s, prison overcrowding and rising costs became increasing problematic. In response, private businesses saw an opportunity for expansion, and their involvement in prisons increased from the simple contracting of services to the complete ownership and management of entire prisons. According to the U.S. Department of Justice, as of 2013, there were 133,000 state and federal prisoners housed in privately owned prisons, constituting 8.4 per cent of the overall prison population at that time. The advent of these privately owned prisons, which aim to increase profits and possess considerable lobbying clout, also likely contributed to rising incarceration rates.

Conclusion

Today, the American prison system is massive. Its estimated cost of $74 billion eclipses the GDP of 133 nations. The price of prisoners varies from state to state, but among the 40 states surveyed in a 2012 report by the Vera Institute of Justice, the average annual cost per inmate was $31,286. In New York, the average was just over $60,000. While this clearly adds to the burden of the American taxpayer, the human cost is exponentially higher. Most of America's 2.3 million inmates have families, adding considerably more to the list of people who are negatively affected. If mom or dad is in prison, he or she is not around to bring home a paycheck, see the kids off to school or attend a school soccer match. Nationally, 7.3 million children have at least one parent in jail or prison. Unfortunately, far too many of these kids follow in the footsteps of their parents by becoming imprisoned at some point in their lives, as children of incarcerated parents are five times more likely than their peers to commit crimes. And given our recidivism rate, in which roughly two-thirds of released prisoners are rearrested within three years, it seems that mass incarceration is failing to keep us safer.

In the long run, the United States would unquestionably benefit in a variety of ways if the prison population could be reduced. What is the best way to achieve this goal?

To answer that question, it might help to view the 2.3 million people locked away in jails and prisons as the symptom of a disease rather than its cause. The solution is not necessarily as simple as legalizing marijuana, dispensing shorter prison sentences or providing earlier opportunities for parole. While this may help in the short term, it only treats some of the most glaring factors. To effectively address the underlying causes, efforts to reduce poverty, provide better educational opportunities and eradicate racism will go much further to lower crime rates and decrease our prison population.

Chapter 10

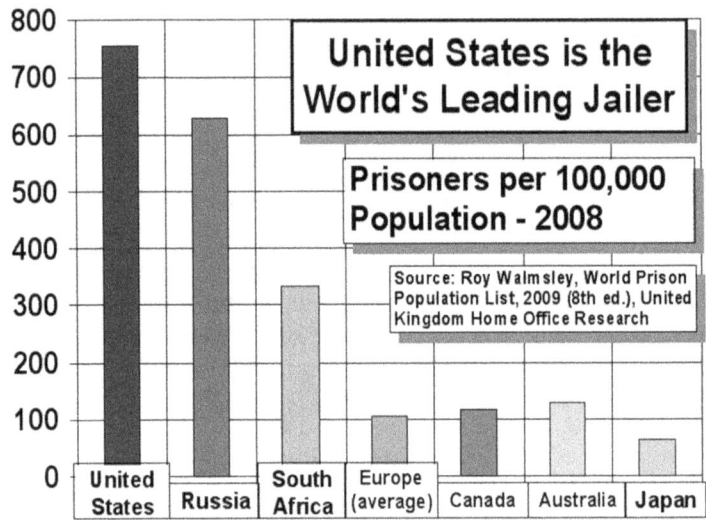

Incarceration rates worldwide
Courtesy of November Coalition(PD-author)
https://commons.wikimedia.org/wiki/File:Incarceration_rates_worldwide.gif

Sources and further reading:

Alexander, Michelle. *The New Jim Crow: Mass Incarceration in the Age of Colorblindness.* New York: The New Press, 2010.

Brandenburg, Bert. "Justice for Sale." *Politico.com.* September 1, 2014. https://www.politico.com/magazine/story/2014/09/elected-judges-110397_Page2.html#.WA6ka2QrJjil.

Chang, Cindy. "Louisiana is the World's Prison Capital." *Nola.com.* May 13, 2012. https://www.nola.com/crime/index.ssf/2012/05/louisiana_is_the_worlds_prison.html.

Costa, Chloe Della. "What are America's Prisons Costing Taxpayers?" *CheatSheet.com.* March 23, 2015. https://www.cheatsheet.com/personal-finance/what-are-americas-prisons-costing-you.html/?a=viewall.

Currie, Elliott. *Crime and Punishment in America.* New York: Picador, 2013.

"11 Facts About Racial Discrimination." *DoSomething.org.* Accessed October 14, 2016. https://www.dosomething.org/us/facts/11-facts-about-racial-discrimination.

"Facts About the Death Penalty." *Death Penalty Information Center.* October 6, 2016. https://www.deathpenaltyinfo.org/documents/FactSheet.pdf.

Godard, Thierry. "The Economics of the American Prison System." *SmartAsset.com.* March 23, 2016. https://www.smartasset.com/insights/the-economics-of-the-american-prison-system.

"History and Development of Corrections 1700-Present." *Preceden.com.* Accessed October 10, 2016. https://www.preceden.com/timelines/23091-history-and-development-of-corrections-1700-present.

"History of Angola Prison." *AngolaMusuem.org.* Accessed October 12, 2016. https://www.angolamuseum.org/history/history/.

Ingraham, Christopher. "There Are Now More Guns Than People in the United States." *WashingtonPost.com.* October 5, 2015. https://www.washingtonpost.com/news/wonk/wp/2015/10/05/guns-in-the-united-states-one-for-every-man-woman-and-child-and-then-some/.

Jaffe, Ina. "Cases Show Disparity of California's 3 Strikes Law." *NPR.org.* October 30, 2009. https://www.npr.org/templates/story/story.php?storyId=114301025.

Kaeble, Danielle, Lauren Glaze, Anastasios Tsoutis, and Todd Minton. "Correctional Populations in the United States, 2014." *U.S. Department of Justice.* January 21, 2016. https://www.bjs.gov/content/pub/pdf/cpus14.pdf.

Levitt, Steven D., and Stephen J. Dubner. *Freakonomics: A Rogue Economist Explores The Hidden Side of Everything.* New York: HarperCollins Publishers, 2006.

Lussenhop, Jessica. "Clinton Crime Bill: Why is it so Controversial?" *BBC.com.* April 18, 2016. https://www.bbc.com/news/world-us-canada-36020717.

"Mandela Rules on Prisoner Treatment Adopted in Landmark Revision of UN Standards." *Amnesty.org.* May 22, 2015. https://www.amnesty.org/en/press-releases/2015/05/Mandela-rules-on-prisoner-treatment-adopted-in-landmark-revision-of-un-standards-1/.

Mosely, E. "Incarcerated-Children of Parents in Prison Impacted." *Texas Department of Criminal Justice*. July 6, 2008. https://www.tdcj.state.tx.us/gokids/gokids_articles_children_impacted.html.

Pan, Deanna. "Timeline: Deinstitutionalization and its Consequences." *MotherJones. com*. April 29, 2013. https://www.motherjones.com/politics/2013/04/timeline-mental-health-america.

"The Price of Prisons: What Incarceration Costs Taxpayers." *Vera Institute of Justice*. July 20, 2012. https://archive.vera.org/sites/default/files/resources/downloads/price-of-prisons-updated-version-021914.pdf.

"The Prison Reform Movement." *Galegroup.com*. Accessed October 12, 2016. http://ic.galegroup.com/ic/uhic/ReferenceDetailsPage/ReferenceDetailsWindow?failOverType=&query=&prodId=UHIC&windowstate=normal&contentModules=&mode=view&displayGroupName=Reference&limiter=&currPage=&disableHighlighting=true&displayGroups=&sortBy=&search_within_results=&action=e&catId=&activityType=&scanId=&documentId=GALE%7CCX2587100021&userGroupName=k12_histrc&source=Bookmark&u=k12_histrc&jsid=f64c864b1e4768825efa8277309030de.

"Recidivism." *National Institute of Justice*. Accessed October 14, 2016. https://www. nij.gov/topics/corrections/recidivism/pages/welcome.aspx.

Ross, Philip. "Death Penalty in the US: Which States Still Practice Capital Punishment and What Methods They Use." *InternationalBusinessTimes.com*. January 15, 2015. https://www.ibtimes.com/death-penalty-us-which-states-still-practice-capital-punishment-what-methods-they-use-1785124.

Savali, Kristen West. "Killers Behind the Badge: NewsOne's Investigative Series onPolice Brutality in Black America." *NewsOne.com*. Accessed October 14, 2016. https://newsone.com/2023676/police-brutality-against-blacks/.

Sipes, Leonard A., Jr. "Violent and Property Crime in the US-Crime in America." *CrimeinAmerica.net*. Accessed October 14, 2016. https://www.crimeinamerica.net/crime-rates-united-states/.

"Timeline: Treatments for Mental Illness." *PBS.org*. Accessed October 24, 2016. https://www.pbs.org/wgbh/amex/nash/timeline/timeline2.html.

"Trends in U.S. Corrections." *TheSentencingProject.org*. Accessed October 10, 2016. https://www.sentencingproject.org/wp-content/uploads/2016/01/Trends-in-US-Corrections.pdf.

Turner, Laura Teddy. "What Has Caused an Increase in Prison Populations?" *Synonym.com*. Accessed October 13, 2016. https://www.classroom.synonym.com/caused-increase-prison-populations-7898.html.

"United States Index Crime Rate, 1933-1998." *Jrsa.org*. Accessed October 12, 2016. https://www.jrsa.org/projects/Historical.pdf.

Chapter 11

Why has the role of popular culture expanded in modern society?

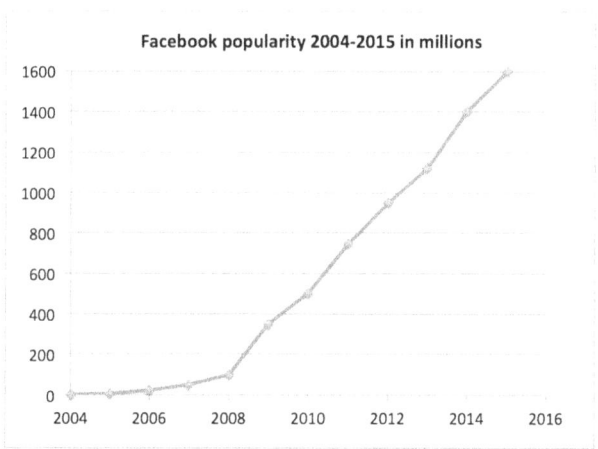

Courtesy of Tatiraju.rishabh(CC-BY-SA-3.0)
https://commons.wikimedia.org/wiki/File:Facebook_popularity.PNG

"Pop culture is a reflection of social change, not a cause of social change."

John Podhoretz

"People are sheep. TV is the shepherd."

Jess C. Scott

How does the average American spend his or her day? For those over the age of 15, the number one activity is still working and its related activities, which takes up 8.9 hours out of every 24. Sleeping comes in second at 7.7 hours. Next comes a little over five hours a day for leisure and sports.

Was this always the case? Many historians believe that by the early 19th century, most American workers adopted the practice of working from "*first light to dark*" – spending most of their free hours with work. Farmers were out in the fields shortly after sunrise, and by sunset, they were so exhausted they might fall asleep soon after dinner. There might be a few minutes to read, smoke a pipe or engage in a little conversation, but otherwise, six days of the week were thoroughly dominated by work and sleep.

Sundays were a different matter. After spending several hours in church during the morning, the average American might spend the afternoon playing or listening to live music, attending a country fair or participating in some kind of athletic competition. In addition, he or she might have spent the evening before at the theater, playing cards or attending a dance. In all likelihood, the average American probably did not have much more than a few hours per week to spend on leisure or sports activities and most of this was largely on Saturday nights and Sunday afternoons.

Contrast that life with how the average American spends his or her spare time in the present. According to a survey taken by the Bureau of Labor Statistics in 2014, 17 minutes each day is spent relaxing and thinking. The same number is also spent participating in sports and exercise. Reading takes up to 19 minutes, using a computer for games or some other kind of leisure consumes 27 minutes and 38 minutes are spent socializing and communicating. Then, a whopping two hours and 49 minutes are spent watching television.

Over the past two or three centuries, significant changes have occurred in how Americans use their time. As the hours spent at work have steadily receded, a time vacuum was created, and most of this was consumed by the rise of modern popular culture. The term *"popular"* simply refers to the masses, the largest segment of the population. The word culture, however, is a bit trickier to define.

Different meanings of the word culture

Anthropologically speaking, a culture is a system of shared beliefs, values, customs, behaviors and artifacts that the members of a society use to cope with the world and one another, and which are transmitted from one generation to another through some sort of learning. In the scientific study of the wide array of civilizations around the world, this definition has enormous value. Yet it is much too broad when applied to the subject of popular culture.

Culture can also be defined as the arts and other manifestations of human intellectual achievement created collectively. This is the sort of *"high culture"* performed at the ballet or the opera house, seen in an art museum, enjoyed at the symphony or viewed on the stage of a major Broadway production. For the most part, however, this type of culture is accessed and enjoyed by only those with the means to afford a pricey admission ticket. While this form of haughty culture has been around for thousands of years, it has always had limited access.

Finally, there is popular culture. By definition, popular culture is based on the tastes of ordinary people rather than on educated elite. Since it is quite possible for some human achievements to appeal to a broad spectrum of the populace, there is a wide overlap between the fine arts that dominate higher culture and the entertainment consumed by the masses. Anyone can enjoy music, whether it is listening to a performance of Brahms and Beethoven at the New York Philharmonic or watching the latest Jonas Brothers video on MTV. The same can be said for performance art, whether it involves of sitting in the front row of a Broadway production of *Hamilton* or munching popcorn while watching the most recent *Star Wars* movie at the local Cineplex. If something with entertainment value is offered to the public, it will qualify as some form of culture. The main delineating factor between higher culture and popular culture is the breadth of its appeal.

Pop culture has grown to include many forms. There is a multitude of musical genres, a long menu of Hollywood's latest releases at multi-screen movie theaters and 500+ channels available to anyone with a television hooked up to cable, satellite or the Internet. In addition, there is professional wrestling, the rodeo circuit, video games, comic books, dog shows, truck and tractor pulls, dance clubs and casino gambling. Pop culture sometimes includes the fine arts, but it also encompasses so much more. This was not always true. In fact, popular culture primarily began within the last two centuries.

The impact of the Industrial Revolution in the 1800s

Originating in Great Britain in the late 18th century, the Industrial Revolution produced one of the most significant changes in the history of the world. Machines began to replace the human hand in the production of products, making it possible for people to work less but have more. It began with the manufacturing of textiles and clothing, but soon spread to household goods, transportation and the production of food. Industrialization also spawned a wide array of new inventions, including radios, telephones, electric light bulbs, phonographs, movie projectors, automobiles and airplanes. In the relative blink of an eye, it drastically changed people's workplaces, homes and leisure time.

The commencement of the Industrial Revolution is closely linked to three major innovations. The first was the use of machines such as Richard Arkwright's water frame and James Hargreaves's spinning jenny that weaved cotton into clothing for mass consumption. Textiles proved to be the first industry of consequence in England's Industrial Revolution. The second development involved iron founding. Using coke made from charcoal, a new process was developed to produce the metal that became the building block of the new industries. Finally, the steam engine was invented to provide a necessary energy source in factories. Although there were others who helped pave the way, it was James Watt who in 1781 first patented a steam engine that produced a continuous rotary motion. Its original purpose was to pump water from coal mines, but eventually, the idea of harnessing the energy from expanding steam was not only used to power the machines in the emerging factories, but also the railroads and steamboats that revolutionized transportation in the 19th century.

In the short term, the Industrial Revolution created a nightmarish new life for millions of factory workers. Many who were used to the clean air and slower pace of agricultural work now labored up to 12 hours a day, six days a week in poorly ventilated factories. The work was grueling and monotonous, the pay was low, and if there was a debilitating accident on the job, the factory worker was more likely to receive a pink slip than any financial compensation. In addition, children as young as five or six worked in the factories, mills and mines, particularly since their small hands could sometimes do the work that adults could not do.

It took well over a century for these conditions to improve. This was largely due to the gradual success of labor unions that frequently had to experience violent strikes in order to improve their hours, pay, benefits and conditions. The elimination of property requirements in order to vote also provided the growing proletariat of factory workers with the political clout to achieve political reforms. Over a long stretch of time, this led to the elimination of child labor, the creation of Social Security pensions, a shorter workweek, workers' compensation and a minimum wage. The first wave of factory workers had to make considerable sacrifices so that later generations could have the luxury of being able to work less while still enjoying a higher standard of living.

The average manufacturing laborer put in about 66 hours a week in the 1850s. By 1900 that number had declined to fewer than 60, and by 1930, it had been further reduced to 50. It was under 40 by 1955. The pattern was clear. Machines were increasingly doing the work that had once been performed by hand, which meant that more consumer goods were being produced while requiring less human labor. This trend began in Great Britain, but it soon spread to France, Germany, Italy, Japan and especially the United States. There was also an explosion of new products that the average laborer could purchase with their growing incomes. Electricity lit up their homes, flush toilets and indoor plumbing improved their health and sanitation, and inventions like telephones, phonographs, movie projectors and radios provided new ways to spend their expanding free time.

By the early 1900s, the ranks of the middle classes were beginning to swell. One indicator that middle class status had been achieved was when mothers could stay home fulltime to raise their families, and children could spend their days attending school. More people lived in comfortable row houses or detached Victorian style homes. Due to further improvements in assembly line production that were pioneered by Henry Ford, millions started driving automobiles powered by the internal combustion engine. A significant percentage of the population lagged behind, particularly black people and other minorities, but for millions of Americans, the 20th century unfolded with nearly limitless potential. These colossal economic changes also brought about dramatic new lifestyle patterns.

Looking for new ways to spend their additional time and money, millions of Americans turned to sporting events. Baseball had been invented before the Civil War, and the first professional team was founded in Cincinnati in 1869. 776,000 fans attended major league baseball games in 1890. That number tripled by 1899 and almost tripled again ten years later. Even those who lived too far away to attend the games could follow their favorite teams in the newspapers that often sold for as little as a penny. By the 1920s, they could also follow baseball games on their radios. Other sports that quickly grew in popularity by the turn of the century included boxing, horseracing and college football. The revival of the modern Olympiad in 1896 immediately caught on in the United States, and eight years later, St. Louis was the first American city to host the games.

In addition to sporting events, popular culture by 1900 included a wide range of other forms of entertainment. Americans attended vaudeville shows and traveling circuses. They flocked to nickelodeons to view the latest movies, and with the advent of feature-length silent films, they put Hollywood on the map as the epicenter of big screen productions. Enormous department stores took root in every city, not just as places to shop but also to dine out and socialize. Spacious urban parks were laid out as places to picnic, exercise and explore by bicycle. People also built the first amusement parks during this time period. Between 1880 and the start of World War Two, Coney Island in New York was the largest amusement park in the United States, attracting several million visitors each year. On a larger scale, Americans traveled to dazzling world's fairs in cities like Chicago in 1893 and St. Louis in 1904.

The growing amount of free time and affluence generated by the Industrial Revolution only continued to expand in the 20th century. This led to an exponential growth in the number of ways that Americans could spend their time and money. More than anything else, this dramatic upsurge was augmented by the rise of modern technology. Always searching for new profit, America's capitalistic economic engine sought the latest applications of modern science to expand the options available in the realm of popular culture. Radio and movies soon gave way to the rise of television. Advances in highway construction offered the road trip as a vacation option to millions of American motorists. The first airplanes, which were used primarily to deliver the mail, started performing death-defying stunts in entertaining air shows. The merger of these trends and developments in the 20th century, fueled largely by the outburst of modern technology, laid the foundation for the popular culture that defines our contemporary world. More than any other decade, this direction was essentially set in the 1920s.

The Jazz Age

In many respects the decade that followed the First World War was filled with dynamic contradictions. Two decades of Progressive reform was followed by one of the most politically conservative periods in American history. Yet despite the pro-business policies of three consecutive Republican administrations, on a social level, millions of people were engaging in radically new lifestyle changes. For example, many women became *"flappers"* by lighting up cigarettes, shortening their hair, reducing the height of their dresses and dancing the Charleston to the latest jazz tunes. The same type of contradiction could be seen in the treatment of minorities. The Progressive Era had ended with the 19th Amendment that finally granted women the right to vote. In stark contrast, the 1920s was dominated by a dramatic rise in intolerance, including the Red Scare, immigration quotas and the revival of the Ku Klux Klan that saw roughly five million Americans become members.

During the 1920s, the number of Americans living in big cities surpassed the population residing on farms and in small towns. This urban-rural split starkly highlighted the contrast between the conservative religious traditions observed in the countryside, versus the more secular values of cities like New York, Philadelphia and Chicago. This tension bubbled to the surface during the trial of John Scopes in Dayton, Tennessee. Falling squarely in the middle of the decade, the Scopes *"Monkey Trial"* put a high school biology teacher in front of a jury for violating a state law that prohibited the teaching of anything that contradicted the Bible. Millions around the world followed the trial in newspapers and on the radio, particularly after William Jennings Bryan, the former presidential candidate, agreed to head the prosecution, while the legal titan Clarence Darrow arrived to lead the defense. In the end, Scopes was convicted and sentenced to pay a fine, which was dropped on appeal. Nonetheless, across the nation, people witnessed how the United States was pulling in two opposing directions during the 1920s.

It was in the midst of this tension that American manufacturing began to reach new heights. Led by relatively new industries like radio, film, electric appliances, airplanes and especially the automobile, the phenomenal economic growth helped to spawn the moniker of *"the Roaring Twenties."* Utilizing new techniques such as assembly line production, the average factory worker was producing 50 per cent more at the end of the decade than at its start. In order to sell these products, businesses employed new marketing strategies, such as advertising and installment buying. By the end of this decade, the American people gravitated towards the material values that characterize our modern world. With some glaring exceptions, such as farmers, minority groups and those working for *"sick industries"* like coal and textiles, the American people were making more money than ever before. They also had more free time in which to spend their additional resources. Our contemporary popular culture emerged from the 1920s, and despite the setbacks imposed by the Great Depression of the 1930s, the Roaring Twenties set the United States on a cultural trajectory that propelled the nation into the modern era.

Mass media and the emergence of our modern popular culture

More than anything else, the 20th century witnessed the astonishing acceleration of technological change. For example, a teacher in the 1960s who wanted to show a movie to his or her class would have to carefully thread a 16 mm film into a projector. By the late 1970s, that same teacher could show the same film on a videocassette recorder, also known as a VCR. In fact, the teacher might have recorded the movie the night before on videotape from his or her own television. By the 1990s, the teacher could show the same film via a digital videodisc, a DVD, which had better sound and picture quality. A decade later, the DVD could be more easily played on the teacher's laptop computer and then projected onto a Smart Board in front of the whole class. This was followed by the disappearance of the DVD altogether because Internet sites like YouTube or Netflix could stream the entire film onto the teacher's computer.

Even before the start of the 20th century, new advances in printing technology led to the advent of dime novels. The low cost of these paperbacks meant that millions of readers could be absorbed by the exaggerated stories of such western legends as Buffalo Bill Cody, Jesse James and Wyatt Earp. In fact, this early form of mass media helped to literally invent the genre of the Western, which would later make the leap from paperback books to film and television. Advances in printing technology also helped to bring hundreds of magazines and newspapers into the hands of millions of subscribers.

Following right behind dime novels came the rise of the film industry. Among Thomas Edison's one thousand plus inventions were the motion picture camera and the film projector. Commercially, the first movies emerged as short films viewed on nickelodeons that charged five cents for admission and flourished from 1905 to 1915. Following in their wake were the first feature length silent films, and by 1927, these were replaced by the first "*talkies*" that could synchronize the movies' sights and sounds. By the early 1920s, Hollywood had become the world's film capital. The California studios were producing virtually all the movies shown in the United States and received 80 per cent of the revenue from films shown abroad. During the 1920s, movie attendance soared. By the middle of the decade, 50 million people a week went to the movies, the equivalent of half the nation's population. In Chicago in 1929, theaters had enough seats for half of the city's population to attend a movie each day.

Another new technology that blossomed into a popular form of mass media was radio. Although most people associate the name of Guglielmo Marconi with its invention, there were many other people in the late 19th century that contributed theory and inventions into what became the radio. Originally conceived as a form of *"wireless telegraphy,"* radio evolved by the 1920s into the latest form of broadcast mass media. It not only brought news stories into millions of living rooms across the nation, but also entertained the masses with music, sports and original comedic and dramatic programming. Since some of the melodrama carried by radio into people's homes was sponsored by the soap industry, it led to the rise of the first so-called *"soap operas."* For the first time in our nation's history, people from coast to coast could listen to the same radio programming at the same time. Radio proved to be a powerful unifying cultural force in a large country marked by a wide range of regional diversity.

Coming next in this parade of new gadgets was the television. It was first available in crude experimental forms in the late 1920s, but these did not sell to the public. After World War Two, an improved form of black-and-white TV broadcasting became popular, and television sets were soon commonplace in homes across the nation. In 1950, nine per cent of the households in the United States owned at least one television. In just ten years, that percentage increased to a staggering 87 per cent. By 1978, 98 per cent of American homes possessed a TV. Along with this new form of popular entertainment came a glut of other devices and industries: VCRs, DVDs, coaxial cable, satellite transmission and Internet streaming devices. Three or four major television broadcasting networks were soon joined by several hundred more. Today, there are TV networks that specialize 24 hours a day on just sports, news, history, science, game shows, soap operas, travel, music and just about any other area that will attract enough viewers to earn a profit. Today, the average American home has just fewer than three television sets, and at least one of those TVs is on several hours per day. While smart phones, tablets and laptops may have a prominent place in the lives of most Americans, they still have not replaced the television. Technological advances have also provided TVs with increasingly larger but thinner screens, higher quality pictures and sound, and relatively cheaper prices.

This astonishing pace of technological change largely defines our modern era. The result is that there has been an endless flow of new devices and high tech toys that enable much of contemporary popular culture. Newspapers and radio helped to make Major League Baseball *"America's Sport"* in the first half of the 20th century. Television would do the same to elevate the three other big spectator sports: the National Hockey League (NHL), the National Basketball Association (NBA) and especially the National Football League (NFL). With the aid of technology, many people today also follow sports like soccer, golf, tennis, bowling, car racing (NASCAR) and professional wrestling.

The advent of high tech toys was not just for spectators but also for those who wanted to more actively participate in leisurely activities. Running, for example, took off in the 1970s as a means for exercise and recreation. At first, the only requirement was a pair of comfortable, padded shoes. Yet over the next forty years, dedicated runners could complete their workout inside on a mechanical treadmill, track distance through GPS technology and precisely count steps using a watch attached to their wrists. This rising emphasis on health and fitness soon reached the youth in the form of Little League Baseball, soccer leagues and a dazzling array of high school athletics.

Like many other forms of popular culture, the fitness craze has become a multi-billion dollar industry. In 2014, fitness centers generated approximately $27 billion per year. Additionally, the weight-loss industry earned roughly $20 billion per year. The combination of new technological equipment, the desire to earn unlimited profits and the growing appetite to achieve a higher level of fitness has also led to giant industries in everything from high-tech bicycles and weight equipment to membership in gyms and yoga studios. In 2016, 56 per cent of the population ages six and over participated in at least one high caloric burning activity. Over the last century or so, popular culture has expanded from the passivity of spectators to the engagement of active participation.

More than anything else, modern popular culture blossomed in every direction toward the end of the 20th century due to the revolution in mass media and new technology. It has produced a wide range of new *"toys"* to occupy people's time, and due to the accelerated pace of technological innovation, many people struggle to keep up with the rapid speed in which new products are introduced. In the workplace, novel machinery is increasingly taking the place of human labor. As computers and robotics push more people off the factory floor, the amount time available for individuals to engage in popular culture, whether as observers or spectators, has also increased. Finally, and most important, the technological revolution has significantly expanded the definition of popular culture. Relatively speaking, it was not long ago that when people spoke about popular culture, they were referring to such activities as viewing Hollywood movies, watching sitcoms on TV and attending baseball games. Today, that list would have to be expanded to accommodate such pursuits as rock climbing inside a gymnasium, playing video games, down hill skiing, contributing to blogging sites, running marathons, updating Facebook pages, playing chess on the Internet, taking online cooking classes, competing in fantasy sports and listening to entire books read from a smart phone.

Conclusion

Due to the nebulous nature of popular culture, it is difficult to pinpoint a simple explanation as to why it has expanded so much in modern society. For that matter, it is even a challenge to formulate a clear definition of popular culture that most people would accept. Popular culture might be defined as the activities and commercial products that reflect the tastes of the general masses. In addition, it is safe to say popular culture is not a new human endeavor. Prehistoric tribes may have spent their days hunting and gathering, but at night, they would still play games, tell stories and dance around campfires. What is relatively new, however, is how popular culture has expanded over the last two centuries. Why? Basically, there are three reasons.

First, the Industrial Revolution provided people with considerably more discretionary time. In 1790, when the population of the United States was just under four million people, 83 per cent of the labor force worked as farmers in order to feed the nation. By 1900, farmers made up just 38 per cent of the work force, and today, in a nation of 324 million people, farm and ranch families comprise just two per cent of the U.S. population. In 1800, it took 56 worker-hours to grow an acre of wheat. By 1970, it took just three. However, the yield per acre in that time period has more than doubled. Similar growth is generally found in the production of just about every other consumer product. Related to this pattern was the custom of employers providing vacation time and the growing respect accorded to the *"sacred weekend."* If someone's workday ended for at 5:00 pm, and no work was required on Saturdays and Sundays, the amount of free time available for the personal pursuit of popular culture dramatically expanded.

The second cause behind the recent growth of popular culture has been the exponential growth in the number of ways to spend this additional free time. New inventions, particularly in the field of mass media, combined with the creative explosion of recreational business schemes, have provided the masses with an almost limitless menu of activities. Take vacation travel, for instance. In the early 1800s, a family might travel in wagons or on the backs of horses for several days just to visit other family members a hundred miles away. Anything more was usually too prohibitive in terms of time, money and safety. Today, a family can board a commercial jetliner as the sun is setting, fall asleep in comfortable recliners and wake up the next morning on the other side of the planet. When not on vacation, that same family, at least those who have climbed into the ranks of the middle class, has a host of *"toys"* to fill their time. The most popular include big-screen televisions, personal computers, smart phones, and digital tablets. Connected through the Internet, people use these electronic devices to view entertainment, play games, communicate with each other and engage in a wide variety of social media. Contrast this with the books and simple board games that were among the few options available two hundred years ago.

Finally, a third cause behind the growing role of popular culture in modern society is also the most controversial. Between 1700 and 1740, an estimated 75 to 80 per cent of the American population regularly attended churches, which were being built at a feverish pace. Today, that number has declined to less than 20 per cent. What this reflects, among other things, is a basic change in society's values. In the past, many placed a higher premium on the pursuit of a respected vocation, the raising of a sizable family and the quest for spiritual salvation. There has been a seismic shift in values in recent times, and today, many people are more interested in secular pursuits and the acquisition of material wealth. Without passing moral judgment over this change, it is safe to say that our evolving values have contributed to the rise of popular culture.

In closing, however, one should consider a figure from the U.S. Bureau of Labor Statistics, which states that about 25 per cent of the American population volunteered for a benevolent organization of some kind at least once in the past year. Just because the vast majority of the American people have more discretionary money and time than ever before, it does not mean that they have forgotten their sense of compassion.

Sources and further reading:

"Agriculture." *Digital History.* Accessed November 3, 2016. https://www.digitalhistory.uh.edu/disp_textbook.cfm?smtID=11&psid=3837.

"Charts from the American Time Use Survey." *Bureau of Labor Statistics.* Accessed October 20, 2016. https://www.bls.gov/tus/charts/.

Chomsky, Noam. "Noam Chomsky Quotes." *Tumblr.com.* Accessed October 20, 2016. https://www.noam-chomsky.tumblr.com/post/16032419749/noam-chomsky-and-pop-culture.

D'Costa, Krystal. "How Many TV Sets Do You Have and Why Does it Matter?" *ScientificAmerican.com.* March 16, 2015. https://blogs.scientificamerican.com/anthropology-in-practice/how-many-tv-sets-do-you-have-mdash-and-why-does-it-matter/.

"Fast Facts About Agriculture." *American Farm Bureau Federation.* Accessed November 3, 2016. https://www.fb.org/newsroom/fastfacts/.

Hinckley, David. "Average American Watches 5 Hours of TV Per Day, Report Shows." *NYDailyNews.com.* March 5, 2014. https://www.nydailynews.com/lifestyle/average-american-watches-5-hours-tv-day-article-1.1711954.

"How Big is the Fitness Industry?" *Reference.com.* Accessed November 2, 2016. https://www.reference.com/health/big-fitness-industry-f9a122a4ac9e314#.

Immerso, Robert. *Coney Island: The People's Playground.* Piscataway: Rutgers University Press, 2002.

Kindelan, Megan. "How Americans Spend Their Time." *U.S. Department of Labor.* June 24, 2016. https://blog.dol.gov/2016/06/24/how-americans-spend-their-time/.

"The Ku Klux Klan in the 1920's." *PBS.org.* Accessed November 2, 2016. https://www.pbs.org/wgbh/americanexperience/features/general-article/flood.klan/.

Lebowitz, Shana. "Here's How the 40-Hour Workweek Became the Standard in America." *BusinessInsider.com.* October 24, 2015. https://www.businessinsider.com/history-of-the-40-hour-workweek-2015-10.

"Leisure Time on an Average Day." *Bureau of Labor Statistics.* Accessed October 20, 2016. https://www.bls.gov/TVS/CHARTS/LEISURE.HTM.

"1900-1909 Attendance." *BallparksofBaseball.com.* Accessed November 1, 2016. https://www.ballparksofbaseball.com/1900-09attendance.htm.

"Religion and the Founding of the American Republic." *Library of Congress.* Accessed November 3, 2016. https://www.lof.gov/exhibits/religion/rel02.html.

"The Rise of Hollywood and the Arrival of Sound." *DigitalHistory.edu.* Accessed November 26, 2016. https://www.digitalhistory.uh.edu/topic_display.cfm?tcid=124.

Scott, Jess C. *GoodReads.com.* Accessed October 20, 2016. https://www.goodreads.com/quotes/543974-people-are-sheep-tv-is-the-shepard.

Shattuck, Kelly. "7 Startling Facts: An Up Close Look at Church Attendance in America." *ChurchLeaders.com.* Accessed November 3, 2016.

https://www.churchleaders.com/pastors/pastor-articles/139575-7-startling-facts-an-up-close-look-at-church-attendance-in-america.html.

Solomon, Deborah. "The Legacy." *NewYorkTimes.com.* December 9, 2007. https://www.nytimes.com/2007/12/09/magazine/09wwwin-q4-t.html?_r=0.

"Television History-The First 75 Years." *TVHistory.TV.* Accessed November 2, 2016. https://www.tvhistory.tv/facts-stats.htm.

"2016 Participation Reports." *Physical Activity Council.* Accessed November 2, 2016. https://www.physicalactivitycouncil.com/pdfs/current.pdf.

"Volunteering in the United States, 2015." *Bureau of Labor Statistics.* February 25, 2016. https://www.bls.gov/news.release/volun.nr0.htm.

Whaples, Robert. "Hours of Work in U.S. History." *EH.Net.* August 14, 2001. http://eh.net/encyclopedia/hours-of-work-in-u-s-history/.

Chapter 12

Why is organized religion at the center of so many world conflicts?

Religious Circle
Courtesy of Szczepan1990(CC-BY-SA-3.0)
https://commons.wikimedia.org/wiki/File:RELIGIONES.png#mw-jump-to-licens

"Religious conflict can be the bloodiest and cruelest conflicts that turn people into fanatics."

Associate Supreme Court Justice William J. Brennan

"The need of the moment is not one religion, but mutual respect and tolerance of the devotees of the different religions."

Mahatma Gandhi

The troubles in Northern Ireland lasted for more than three decades. The incessant violence was largely waged between the Roman Catholic nationalist community that sought union with Ireland and the primarily Protestant unionist community who wanted to remain part of the United Kingdom. At its heart, the conflict revolved around the discrimination by the Protestant majority against the Catholic minority. Between 1969 and 2001, over 3500 people were killed by the

Republican and Loyalist paramilitary groups and by British and Irish security forces. The Belfast Agreement of 1998 brought about an uneasy peace, but so far, it has endured.

Also during the 1990s, a bloody war raged in the opposite corner of Europe. Following the breakup of Yugoslavia, the Socialist Republic of Bosnia and Herzegovina was proclaimed through a referendum for independence. This new nation consisted of three religious faiths: the mainly Muslim Bosniaks (44 per cent), the Orthodox Serbs (32.5 per cent) and the Catholic Croats (17 per cent). However, most of the Bosnian Serbs did not want to join this new multi-ethnic nation and decided to boycott the referendum. After the vote for independence, they linked up with the government of neighboring Serbia and mobilized their military forces. War soon spread across the country, accompanied by the ethnic cleansing of the Bosnian and Croat population. Since the war was characterized by bitter fighting, indiscriminate shelling of cities and towns, systematic mass rape and the massacre of civilians, it rose to the level of genocide. By the time peace was restored in 1995, it was estimated that 2.2 million people were displaced and approximately 100,000 people had been killed. This was the most devastating European conflict since the end of World War Two.

Meanwhile, a deeply rooted religious conflict continued to fester on the Asian subcontinent just over 3000 miles to the east. When India had finally acquired its independence from the British Empire in 1948, it came at the price of a partition of their land into two separate nations. The larger Hindu population gained India, while the Muslims, who had been entrenched in the area since the 7th century, received Pakistan. During the riots that paved the way for the partition, it is estimated that as many as 2,000,000 people were killed in the genocidal violence between the two religions. In addition, 14 million Hindus, Sikhs and Muslims were displaced, making this event the largest mass migration in human history. Since the partition, the two South Asian nations have been involved in four wars, including one undeclared war and many border skirmishes, particularly over a contested region called Kashmir. The religious tension between these two countries continues to this day, and considering that both possess nuclear weapons and their combined population numbers almost one and a half billion people, this is arguably the world's most serious ongoing religious conflict.

Over the past two centuries, the rise of modern science has greatly contributed to an increasing secularization of the world's population, particularly in the more developed nations of the West. The religiously unaffiliated are growing significantly in population. They are now the second largest religious group in North America and most of Europe. In the United States, they make up almost a quarter of the population. Therefore, it might be tempting to think that religion has lost its hold as a primary source of global conflict.   As the previous examples show, however, this is far from the truth. Instead, daily headlines are still focused on religious acts of terrorism, religious tribal conflicts across the African continent and millions of refugees seeking asylum from religious civil wars throughout much of the Middle East. One day, the news might focus on a suicidal bombing in Baghdad. The next day, it might shift to the most recent beheadings of Iraqi soldiers by ISIS. This in turn might be followed by news of the firebombing of a mosque in Tracy, California before the start of a daily prayer service. Despite perceptions to the contrary, organized religion continues to inspire bloodshed and violence across the planet. In order to understand the reasons behind this phenomenon, it is necessary to understand the past.

The One true God

Since the inception of the first organized religions, there has been conflict over worshipping the correct god or gods. In addition, people have fought, killed and died over such questions as which faith should control a certain city, who should lead a particular religion and even over what is required in order to achieve salvation upon one's death.

In ancient times, the Hebrews were credited with being the first monotheistic faith— that is the first to worship only one God. Since this meant by implication that all of the gods worshiped by all of the other religions were *"false gods,"* conflict quickly ensued. Since the Hebrews inhabited what is now the nation of Israel, located at the crossroads of Europe, Asia and Africa, there was a constant stream of invading armies. At different times, the ancient Hebrews were conquered by Assyrians, Babylonians, Greeks and Romans. When exposed to the sophisticated Hellenic culture of the Greeks after the invasion by Alexander the Great, many of the younger Hebrews were drawn toward Greek ideas concerning philosophy, science, government, and even athletic games. In other words, they became increasingly humanistic and less focused on the worship of their one Hebrew God. Over time, the situation exploded into a religious civil war eventually won by the Maccabees, the leaders of the more religious faction. Today, this victory is celebrated by the Jewish holiday of Hanukkah. Ironically, Hanukkah, the Jewish *"festival of lights,"* is intended to celebrate the principle of religious freedom. While it did free the Hebrews from the Hellenistic Seleucid Empire based in Syria to worship their one Hebrew God, it did not provide religious liberty to the more Hellenized Jews living in Judea.

About 250 years later, the same Hebrews began a revolt against their Roman oppressors. Refusing to accept the divinity of Caligula, the emperor of Rome, a group of religious Jews called Zealots initiated a rebellion in the year 66 C.E. against the Roman Empire that led to one of the greatest catastrophes in Jewish history. Its early success helped to swell the Zealot's numbers, but after 60,000 heavily armed and highly professional Roman troops arrived, the rebellion degenerated into a bloody slugfest. By the time it ended eight years later, Jerusalem had been sacked, most of the Temple had been destroyed and an estimated one million Jews were dead. The last of the Zealots retreated to the mountain fortress of Masada, but sensing that all was lost after a three-year Roman siege, 960 Hebrew men, women and children infamously chose to commit mass suicide rather than surrender.

The choice by early Christians to worship Jesus of Nazareth as their one God resulted in a similar fate at the hands of the Roman Empire. For centuries, the Romans hunted, tortured and executed the early Christians. It was only after the conversion to Christianity by the emperor Constantine that the Edict of Milan was issued in 313 C.E., decreeing tolerance for Christianity throughout the Roman Empire. Shortly afterward, Christianity became the official religion of the entire empire, giving it a platform to grow into the world's largest religion today. As of 2010, there were an estimated 2.2 billion Christians, nearly a third (30 per cent) of the 7.4 billion people on Earth. While separated into Roman Catholics, Eastern Orthodox and well over 200 different Protestant denominations, the issues dividing them have largely been over ceremonies, sacraments, the central authority of the Church and the steps necessary to achieve salvation. What they all share in common, however, is the belief that Jesus Christ is their one true God.

About 600 years later, the third major monotheistic religion entered the world stage. Revolving around the teachings and writings of the prophet Mohammed and built on a foundation previously established by Jews and Christians, Islam proclaimed Allah as the one true God. Spread by warfare and conquest, this new Muslim faith soon extended out of the deserts of Arabia to encompass a world that stretched from Spain and North Africa in the West through the Middle East to the Asian subcontinent and the modern-day nations of Indonesia and the Philippines. Today, there are 1.6 billion Muslims, almost 22 per cent of the global population. With a higher birth rate, it is estimated that Islam will equal Christianity in numbers by 2050 before eclipsing it 20 years later.

Throughout the Middle Ages, Christians and Muslims competed with each other for followers and the acquisition of territory. Most of the Jews that had been driven out of their ancient homeland by the Romans simply attempted to survive as a Diaspora living in distant lands. Always a numerical minority, they suffered through centuries of inquisitions, pogroms and other forms of virulent anti-Semitism, mostly at the hands of their Christian neighbors. It was not until the Holocaust took the lives of six million Jews between 1938 and 1945 that the United Nations saw fit to recreate the nation of Israel as a modern Jewish homeland. This decision, which may appear innocuous, has sparked a series of lethal wars and acts of terrorism ever since.

It was also during the Middle Ages when some of the Christian kingdoms in Europe, at the behest of the Pope in Rome, began a series of invasions to conquer the *"Holy Land"* and reclaim it from the Muslims. Known as the Crusades, these waves of invasions lasted for about 200 years, and in the end, proved to be a strategic failure. The one lasting positive outcome, however, is that the Crusades exposed thousands of European Christians to the more advanced civilization of the Middle

East, helping to spark an end to the Middle Ages and the start of a cultural revolution known as the Renaissance. For over 1500 years, the three monotheistic religions that came to control the West and most of the Middle East had been competing over who worshipped the one true God. In the 15th century, however, a cultural transformation that began in Italy and soon spread throughout the rest of Europe set off a chain reaction of developments that completely altered the role of religion in sparking the world's major conflicts.

Renaissance, Reformation and the conquest of the planet

For most people, the Italian Renaissance conjures up the names of famous artists like Leonardo da Vinci, Michelangelo and Raphael. However, the Renaissance involved much more than just the development of new innovations in the conception of paintings and sculptures. During the 15th and 16th centuries, a new perspective began to evolve in the minds of millions of Europeans. Rather than viewing the world through the lens of faith and religious salvation, an increasing number of people developed a more secular and scientific outlook on life. They began to think more about their lives on earth and how to maximize their worldly experiences rather than how to gain eternal salvation. This meant the gradual application of a more logical and critical approach, including their views concerning the Roman Catholic Church.

Seeing corrupt practices that had become endemic within the Church, such as the sale of indulgences by priests to absolve people for their sins, Martin Luther, a German monk and a professor of theology, challenged the Church to a debate when he nailed his Ninety-five Theses to the door of the Wittenberg Castle Church in 1517. Luther strongly disputed the claim that freedom from God's punishment for sin could be purchased with money. After being excommunicated by the Pope, Luther launched the Reformation by starting the first Protestant denomination, one that still bears his name.

As it turned out, the Lutherans were just the first in a long series of Protestant faiths that spun off from the Roman Catholic Church. Some, including the various Congregational, Reformed and Presbyterian churches, were based on the teachings of John Calvin, who preached that human salvation had already been predestined by an all-powerful God. Others wanted to provide individuals with a larger role in seeking their own spiritual redemption instead of relying upon the Pope and the Catholic Church's central authority to make salvation possible. Protestants believed that any individual, if properly educated to read and understand the Bible, could achieve his or her own salvation through the grace provided directly by Jesus Christ, rather than relying upon a priest to act as an intermediary.

The Protestant Reformation divided Europe in half. Much of the northern part of the continent turned to the Protestant ideology espoused by Luther and Calvin, while most of the southern areas remained largely Catholic, especially after the

Counter-Reformation reformed some of the Catholic Church's most questionable practices. The divide proved to be as much political and economic as it was religious. In 1618, a complicated war broke out that pitted Catholics against Protestants and lasted until 1648, thus earning the conflict's name, the Thirty Years' War. With eight million casualties, the Thirty Years War was the deadliest religious conflict in European history. Unlike most of the previous religious conflicts, however, this one was not fought over who worshipped the one true God. All of the people who fought and died on both sides were Christians who worshipped Jesus Christ as their lord and savior. The issues that divided the combatants had grown subtler and more complex.

Related to the cultural and religious changes swirling around Europe in the 15th and 16th centuries was the economic upheaval commonly called the Commercial Revolution. This transformation was relatively gradual and did not take place at the same time across the European continent. It involved the rise of profit-making enterprises to replace the feudalism that had dominated much of the Middle Ages.

Feudalism was an economic institution that had arisen to provide a sense of security and stability for people at a time when they could no longer count on the shelter of the Roman Empire. Feudal lords provided protection by building castles and employing small armies, and in return, the local peasants, known as serfs, agreed to work on the lord's manor. Serfs could not be bought or sold, but in most other respects, their lives were similar to that of slaves. A serf could not leave or travel without the lord's consent since they were tied down to the land. Working from sunrise to sunset every day except for the Sabbath, a serf could keep enough food to feed his family, but all of the other products of their labor went to the support of the manor.

During the Renaissance, feudalism, at least in Western Europe, was gradually replaced by the rise of manufacturing, trade and commerce. New methods to generate investment capital were developed, including business partnerships, banking and the sale of commercial stock. Cities and towns grew as more individuals began to seek profits and amass fortunes. In fact, it was the money earned by bankers and commercial enterprises in Italian city-states that financed and patronized the artistic achievements that characterized the Renaissance. Related to these economic developments were new inventions and scientific discoveries, including the building of more stable sailing ships, the invention of navigational instruments and the use of gunpowder in the firing of muskets and cannons.

By the late 15th century, the smaller political states in Western Europe had coalesced into larger, centrally organized nations. Wooden ships flying the flags of nations in Western Europe, including Portugal, Spain, France, Great Britain and the Netherlands, were soon claiming overseas colonies throughout North and South America. As a result, Christian churches were built from Newfoundland in Canada to Patagonia in Argentina. Within a few centuries, the religious traditions of the people indigenous to the Western Hemisphere had largely vanished in the wake of Christianity's spread.

By the late 19th century, the Western powers had achieved an even higher level of superiority in their political organization, military prowess and technological achievement. Motivated by the desire to find natural resources to feed their modern factories and to establish new markets for their machine-made goods, nations like Great Britain, France, Germany and the Netherlands settled colonies throughout Africa, the Middle East and parts of Asia. By the outset of the First World War in 1914, Africa had been carved up like an enormous pie with only Liberia and Ethiopia retaining a semblance of freedom. At its height, the British Empire held sway over 412 million people, 23 per cent of the world's population, and by 1920, it covered 24 per cent of the Earth's total land mass. This is where the saying developed that "*the sun never sets on the British Empire.*" Even the United States jumped into the imperialist race to take overseas colonies, claiming Guam, Puerto Rico and the Philippines from Spain after winning the 1898 Spanish-American War.

This worldwide spread of Western civilization naturally brought Christianity into closer contact with Eastern religions such as Hinduism and Buddhism. The potential for greater religious conflict was somewhat tempered, however, by the rise of another intellectual development in the West. Starting in the late 17th Century, British, French and American philosophers and scientists like Hobbes, Locke, Descartes, Newton, Voltaire, Montesquieu, Rousseau, Franklin and Jefferson began to focus the sharp lens of reason on just about everything around them. This movement, commonly known as the Enlightenment, applied its ideas to the physical laws of the universe, the ideal political state and the role of organized religion. In the realm of religion, the Enlightenment left behind at least two significant consequences.

First, building on the ashes produced by religious conflicts between Catholics and Protestants that were generated by the Reformation, the Enlightenment reinforced the principle of religious freedom. A measure of toleration first emerged in France by the issuing of the Edict of Nantes in 1598. In this document, King Henry IV granted substantial rights to the Calvinist Protestants, also known as Huguenots, in a nation that was predominantly Roman Catholic. One hundred years later, a freedom of worship law was passed in England as part of the passage of an English Bill of Rights.

In the 17th century, a primary reason why many so many English settlers made their way to the American colonies was to find the freedom to worship without fear of religious persecution. Puritans, Roman Catholics and Quakers originally established the colonies of Massachusetts, Maryland, and Pennsylvania, respectively, in order to find this cherished freedom. From the start, Rhode Island offered freedom of religion to all of its residents, which explains why the oldest Jewish synagogue in America can be found in Newport, Rhode Island. In 1777, as

America was waging its war for independence, Thomas Jefferson drafted the Virginia Statute for Religious Freedom. He was so proud of its later passage that it is one of only three accomplishments Jefferson instructed to be put in his epitaph (serving as the third president of the United States did not make the list). After the founders drafted the U.S. Constitution in 1787, its First Amendment began with "*Congress shall make no law respecting an establishment of religion, or prohibiting the free exercise thereof...*" If there had ever been a successful movement in history to minimize religious conflicts around the planet, this drive towards religious freedom that culminated in the passage of the First Amendment was just such an effort.

A second byproduct of the Enlightenment in regard to religion was the establishment of a new theology called Deism. This intellectual movement of the 17th and 18th centuries accepted the existence of a *"Supreme Creator"* on the basis of reason, but rejected any belief in a supernatural deity who interacts with humankind. The Deists tended to reject most of the tenets of organized religion since these were largely held on the basis of faith rather than reason. Therefore, with the possible exception of Unitarianism, there is no centrally organized Deist religion today. However, Deism has had a profound influence over the 1.1 billion people today that profess no religion, from atheists and agnostics to people with spiritual beliefs but no link to any organized religion. In fact, people with no religious affiliation make up the third-largest global faith-based group today, placing after Christians and Muslims and just before Hindus. Today, these secular humanists are largely found in the West and in communist China.

While an increasing percentage of the world's population has been gravitating towards secularism, the number of religious extremists at the opposite end of the continuum has been growing even faster. The increased interaction between these two polar religious extremes has been one of the principle causes behind many of today's religious conflicts.

The rise of religious extremism

Within every organized faith throughout history there has always been a continuum that runs between two opposing extremes. Generally, at one end sits the traditionalists who believe that every rule must be followed exactly and every word taken literally. At the opposing end of the spectrum are the liberals and reformers who want to keep their faith relevant to the changes taking place around them. In between are all other adherents, usually making up the majority of those who follow a particular religious faith.

Since the Holocaust decimated the number of Jews in the world, the Jewish population has been slowly returning to its pre-Holocaust level. Today, there are approximately 15 million Jews comprising about 0.2 per cent of the world's population. Compared to Christianity and Islam, the world's oldest monotheistic religion has always been infinitesimally small. For every Jewish person in the world, there are more than 100 Muslims and close to 150 Christians. Yet despite its diminutive size, there is an enormous gulf that separates Reform Jews at one end of the spectrum, from the Orthodox Jews on the other end. Orthodox Jews generally take every word of the Torah literally and are determined to strictly adhere to each of the 613 commandments they believe God expects them to follow. Conversely, while Reform Jews also tend to recognize themselves as the people who have been chosen by God to receive and follow the essential Ten Commandments, most have developed a much more secular lifestyle than the Orthodox. Naturally, there has always been a dynamic tension between these two extremes.

A similar spectrum can be found within the realm of Christianity. Amongst the 2.2 billion Christians in the world, one end of the continuum is occupied by liberal denominations like Congregationalists and Episcopalians. These groups are less bound to tradition and are much more willing to apply a broader interpretation to the Bible in order to place a stronger emphasis on such values as tolerance, social justice and the environmental stewardship of the Earth. At the opposing end of the spectrum sit the Pentecostal and Evangelical denominations that tend to take every word of the Bible as the literal truth spoken directly by God. By definition, all Christians believe that Jesus Christ is the lord and savior and that his death and subsequent resurrection made salvation possible for believers. Beyond this tenet, however, lurk a multitude of issues that have increasingly divided fundamentalists from more liberal denominations. As previously discussed, these have periodically sparked conflicts and even internecine wars within the worldwide community of Christians.

Islam has not fared much better when it comes to its internal strife. In addition to the expected split between traditional fundamentalists and those with a more liberal and open interpretation of the Koran, however, Muslims were split almost 1400 years ago by a more pragmatic issue. When the Islamic prophet Muhammad died in the year 632, there was a schism over who should take his place. The emotionally charged hostility between these two sects has continued to fester up to the present.

The Sunni branch believes the first four caliphs – Muhammad's successors – rightfully took his place as the leaders of the Muslims. They recognize the heirs of the four caliphs as their legitimate religious leaders. These heirs ruled continuously in the Arab world until the break-up of the Ottoman Empire following the end of the First World War. Shiites, in contrast, believe that only the heirs of the fourth caliph, Ali, are the legitimate successors of Muhammad. In 931, the Twelfth Imam disappeared. This proved to be a seminal event in the history of Shiite Muslims. They believed that they had suffered the loss of a divinely guided political leadership. Not until the 1978 ascendancy of Ayatollah Ruhollah Khomeini in Iran did they once again start to live under the authority of a unified religious figure.

The split may have begun over the simple issue of leadership, but as the centuries passed, a different set of traditions began to develop within the Shiite and Sunni communities. Approximately 85 to 90 per cent of the Muslims in the world are Sunni while only 10 to 15 per cent are Shiite. Sunnis are a majority in most Muslim communities. Nevertheless, there is a Shiite majority in Iraq, Iran, Azerbaijan and Bahrain, and they constitute a significant minority in Lebanon, Syria and Yemen. Both Shiite and Sunni branches are each further divided between the more modern and the more traditional.

Therefore, the 1.2 billion Muslims in today's world have fragmented into a host of potentially hostile factions. When combined with the geopolitical rivalries that dominate much of the Middle East, such as the ongoing animosity between Saudi Arabia and Iran, the Muslim world has become a cauldron of impending conflicts. With the modern Jewish state of Israel also in the epicenter of Islamic civilization, the situation has often been even more volatile. Sunnis versus Shiites; Israelis versus Muslim Palestinians; fundamentalists versus modernists – it should perhaps come as little surprise that millions of Muslims have gravitated toward extremist positions as they have felt forced to choose sides in the latest conflict. While this has fueled many of the conflagrations that burn across the planet, there are two additional reasons why religion continues to be at the center of so many of the world's conflicts.

Technology

So many recent developments in the modern world can be traced to the rapid rise of technological innovation. For thousands of years, different religions inhabited distinct parts of the world and had little contact with each other. There might be territorial disputes between two neighboring denominations, and some of these might span long periods of time and substantial areas of space, such as the Crusades 800 years ago. During the 18th century, however, the idea that Protestants living in the 13 English colonies might conduct a war inspired by religious differences in the far reaches of Iraq or Afghanistan would have seemed preposterous.

Fast-forward to September 11, 2001, and suddenly this notion became a reality. A group of Islamic fundamentalists calling themselves Al Qaeda, led by a leader named Osama Bin Laden and harbored by the Taliban, a group of Muslim extremists in Afghanistan, managed to hijack four commercial jetliners. By mid morning, they had flown two of them on suicide missions into the World Trade Center in New York City and an additional jetliner into the Pentagon, the massive building on the outskirts of Washington, D.C., which houses the U.S. Department of Defense. By the end of the day, nearly 3000 Americans had died, and the nation was spurred to begin its *"war on terrorism."* Over the next several years, American soldiers conducted this war against terrorism in the Middle Eastern nations of Afghanistan and Iraq.

What changed between 1776 and 2001? Looking beyond their primary motives for a moment, the technology had changed. In addition to the obvious, the jets that terrorists turned into lethal missiles that day, the Islamic fundamentalists also had access to many other forms of new technology that facilitated the planning and execution of their attack. Telephones and the Internet made it possible to communicate instantaneously. Satellites and television transmission made it possible to reach out to a massive audience. Jet travel made it possible to travel from Kabul to New York in less than a day. None of this was possible two hundred years earlier. In addition, the most recent technology has provided religious extremists with smart phones, access to social media, improvised explosive devises (IEDS) and hand-held rocket launchers.

At the risk of stating the obvious, one reason why religious extremists had struck so violently was because technology meant they could. Furthermore, while the new devices made it far easier for the attack to take place, the new technology was also linked, at least indirectly, with the motives behind the attack.

Living in a rapidly changing world

The rapid pace of technological change is only one of several features that characterize the modern world. Besides the abundance of material possessions and higher standard of living, the modern world, at least in the Western nations, is distinguished by a set of values that to a greater or lesser degree emphasize reason over faith, materialism over spirituality and progress over tradition. What is more, these modern values emanating from London, Paris, Berlin, New York and Hollywood, are progressively more secular in nature. Therefore, unlike the past, when religious conflicts involved issues like who worshipped the true God, territorial expansion or the path to salvation, today's conflicts are increasingly waged between the modern values of the secularized West and the traditional fundamentalism of the Middle and Far East.

The prime example of this clash occurred in Iran during the 1970s. The seeds for this mayhem were first planted in 1951 when Mohammad Mosaddegh was elected prime minister. He became enormously popular in Iran, especially after he nationalized the nation's petroleum industry and oil reserves. Two years later, as the Cold War was becoming increasingly tense, he was deposed in a coup d'état orchestrated by an Anglo-American covert operation that was concerned about growing ties between Iran and the Soviet Union. In his place, power returned to Iran's traditional monarch, Shah Mohammad Reza Pahlavi. Over the next several years, the Shah became progressively more autocratic. Employing arbitrary arrests and torture by his secret police, the SAVAK, he crushed all forms of political opposition. In addition, the Shah went to great lengths to modernize Iran and mold the nation into a largely secular state.

By the 1970s, the Shah's cozy relationship with the United States had fully opened the door to privately owned Western oil companies. Culturally, Iran had taken on the appearance of a modern, Western nation, with McDonalds restaurants, discothèques, and Hollywood-made movies. Millions of traditional Muslims quietly seethed with anger, awaiting an opportunity to rebel against the Shah and everything for which he stood. Waiting in the shadows to lead this revolt was Ruhollah Khomeini, an extremist Muslim cleric, who had been exiled to Paris because of his public denouncements of the Shah. As the 1970s drew to a close, a series of large-scale, increasingly violent anti-Shah protests swept Iran. Instability, including a wave of general strikes, crippled the nation's economy.

In January of 1979, the Shah left Iran for an *"extended vacation."* He never returned. All over Iran, Khomeini supporters tore down statues of the Shah. On February 1, Ayatollah Khomeini made a dramatic return from exile. Street battles raged across the nation between pro-Khomeini demonstrators and the supporters of the imperial regime. Two months later, the Ayatollah won a landslide victory in a national referendum. He declared an Islamic republic and was appointed Iran's political and religious leader for life. Turning their anger towards the United States and its secular Western culture, thousands of demonstrators gathered outside the American embassy in Tehran in early November. Burning American flags and hanging Uncle Sam in effigy, the protesters stormed the embassy building, where they took 52 hostages and held them until January 20, 1981.

Since then, Islamic extremism has rapidly spread to other nations throughout northern Africa and the Middle East. Prior to this development, most of the religious conflict in the Middle East had revolved around Israel. The birth of the modern state of Israel in 1948 spawned intermittent warfare between the Jewish state and its Arab neighbors. In addition, various Palestinian factions advocating the creation of an independent Palestinian state had employed terrorism against Israel as a weapon to fight against the Jewish state's massive, American-backed military. This conflict, however, had always been restricted to Israel and its immediate neighbors. Now for the first time, the conflict between Islamic extremism and Western modernism had spread far beyond the Arab-Israeli discord.

Ten years after the Iranian Revolution, Iraq invaded the adjacent nation of Kuwait. Led by its dictator, Saddam Hussein, the Iraqis were attempting to grab the rich oilfields of Kuwait, and quite possibly those of other Persian Gulf nations, including Saudi Arabia. Seeing this as an economic threat to the West, which had become increasingly dependent on Middle Eastern oil to quench its thirst for energy, the United States led a United Nations backed coalition of military forces to drive out the Iraqis. In the short term, the Persian Gulf War was an enormous success for the U.S. and its allies. Yet in the minds of millions of Islamic fundamentalists, the West was once again intruding into affairs in which it had no business.

The growing anger and resentment by Islamic extremists towards Western modernism has continued to mount ever since. Understanding they do not have the military resources to successfully win battles against Western powers that possess highly sophisticated weapons, the extremists have increasingly employed terrorism as their primary tool. This was seen not only on September 11, 2001, but in other terrorist attacks that have been launched all over the world, including London, Paris, Kabul and Baghdad. There are Islamic extremists today who operate in such far-flung spots as Nigeria, Pakistan and the Philippines. In addition, wherever there is a vacuum of power created by revolutions like the Arab Spring, which swept through North Africa and the Middle East beginning in 2010, Islamic extremists have rushed in to fill the void.

Nowhere has this been truer than in the border region between Iraq and Syria. Taking the name of ISIS, the Islamic State in Iraq and Syria, this coalition of radical Islamic extremists has carved out a *"caliphate"* across those two nations that as of 2014 controlled more than 34,000 square miles from the Mediterranean coast to an area just south of Baghdad. ISIS implemented Sharia Law, rooted in 8th century Islam, to establish a society that mirrors the region's distant past. In reaction to the endemic spread of Western secular values, ISIS has been known to kill dozens of people at a time, carrying out public executions, crucifixions and other noxious acts. Reaching out beyond their caliphate, ISIS has claimed responsibility for 90 attacks in 21 different nations, killing nearly 1,400 people. ISIS has made exceptional use of modern technology, including social media, to promote its reactionary politics and religious fundamentalism. According to a United Nations report, ISIS is believed to be holding up to 3,500 people as slaves.

At the present, ISIS is just one of several extremist groups that are embroiled in a wide range of religious conflicts. In many cases, what lies beneath the specific circumstances of each conflict is a group of religious traditionalists fighting to resist more modern values.

Conclusion

A popular adage currently circulating through social media states that *"the enemy is not Muslims or Christians or Judaism or Atheism… the real enemy is Extremism."* There are extremists within every religious sect and denomination. This has been true throughout human history. More often than not, these extremists lie at the heart of just about every religious conflict. The reasons they fight have varied throughout the ages. Who is worshipping the true God? Who should control a piece of *"holy land?"* What are the requirements to acquire the greatest objective humans have always sought: the achievement of everlasting life? These have largely been the reasons why religion has historically been behind so many world conflicts throughout history.

In more recent times, the rise of a secular outlook based on science and reason has incited a reaction from millions of people around the world that prefer to defend their traditional values and beliefs. It seems the more that some people gravitate towards materialism and modernism, the more the opposing side responds with a defensive reaction that often results in conflict. With new technology as part of the equation, these conflicts have also become easier to wage. In the short term, diplomacy, patience and understanding should be employed whenever possible in lieu of violence and bloodshed.

In the long term, it is difficult to predict who will prevail in the ongoing struggle between the forces of modernism and reason on one side, and those of tradition and faith on the other. A clear-cut victory by either side does not seem to be anywhere in sight.

Sources and further reading:

Brennan, William J. *BrainyQuote.com*. Accessed November 3, 2016. https://www.brainyquote.com/quotes/quotes/w/williamjb189779.html.

Bullard, Gabe. "The World's Newest Major Religion: No Religion." *National Geographic.com*. April 22, 2016. https://www.nationalgeographic.com/2016/04/160422-atheism-agnostic-secular-nones-rising-religion/.

Chappell, Bill. "World's Muslim Population Will Surpass Christians This Century, Pew Says." *NPR.org*. April 2, 2015. https://www.npr.org/sections/the-two-way/2015/04/02/397042004/muslim-population-will-surpass-christians-this-century-pew-says.

Eichner, Itamar. "Jewish Worldwide Population in 2015 is Nearly 16 Million." *YNetNews.com*. June 26, 2015. https://www.ynetnews.com/articles/0,7340,L-4673018,00.html.

"The Enemy is not Muslims or Christians or Judaism or Atheism." *OnSizzle.com*. Accessed December 2, 2016. https://www.onsizzle.com/i/the-enemy-is-not-muslims-or-christians-or-judaism-or-3600825.

Gandhi, Mahatma. "Religion of Mahatma Gandhi." *MahatmaGandhi.org*. Accessed November 3, 2016. https://www.mkgandhi.org/religionmk.htm.

Heneghan, Tom. " 'No Religion' is World's Third-Largest Religious Group After Christians, Muslims According to Pew Study." *HuffingtonPost.com*. December 19, 2012. https://www.huffingtonpost.com/2012/12/18/unaffiliated-third-largest-religious-group-after-christians-muslims_n_2323664.html.

"The Iranian Revolution." *BBC.co*. Accessed December 2, 2016. https://www.bbc.co.uk/2/shared/spl/hi/pop_ups/04/middle_east_the_iranian_revolution/html/1.stm.

"Isis Fast Facts." *CNN.com*. November 1, 2016. https://www.cnn.com/2014/08/08/world/isis-fast-facts/.

"John Calvin." *Biography.com*. Accessed November 30, 2016. https://www.biography.com/people/john-calvin-9235788.

Luscombe, Stephen. "The British Empire." *BritishEmpire.co*. Accessed November 30, 2016. https://www.britishempire.co.uk.

"Martin Luther." *Biography.com*. Accessed November 30, 2016. https://www.biography.com/people/martin-luther-9389283#synopsis.

"Muslim Population: 1941 Census." *JanaSangh.com*. Accessed November 10, 2016. https://www.janasangh.com/jsart.aspx?stid=364.

Rathod, Sara. "2015 Saw a Record Number of Attacks on US Mosques." *MotherJones.com*. June 20, 2016. https://www.motherjones.com/politics/2016/06/islamophobia-rise-new-report-says.

"Religiously-based Civil Unrest and Warfare." *ReligiousTolerance.org*. Accessed November 10, 2016. https://www.religioustolerance.org/curr_war.htm.

"Thirty Years' War." *History.com*. Accessed November 30, 2016. https://www.history.com/topics/thirty-years-war.

"Timeline: Faith in America." *PBS.org.* Accessed November 30, 2016. https://www.pbs.org/godinamerica/timeline/.

"Timeline of Islam." *PBS.org.* Accessed November 30, 2016. https://www.pbs.org/wgbh/pages/frontilne/teach/muslims/timeline.html.

"Welcome to Deism!" *Deism.com.* Accessed November 30, 2016. https://www.deism.com/deism_defined.htm.

"What are the Most Liberal Denominations in North America?" *WordPress.com.* August 22, 2009. https://www.transientandpermanent.wordpress.com/2009/08/22/what-are-the-most-liberal-denominations-in-north-america/.

"What is the Difference Between Sunni and Shiite Muslims-and Why Does it Matter?" *HistoryNewsNetwork.org.* Accessed December 1, 2016. https://www.historynewsnetwork.org/article/934.

Chapter 13

Why has there never been a World War Three?

Operation Castle Thermonuclear Test
Courtesy of the United States Department of Energy(PD-US-DOE)
https://commons.wikimedia.org/wiki/File:Operation_Castle_-_Romeo_001.jpg

"I know not with what weapons World War III will be fought, but World War IV will be fought with sticks and stones."

Albert Einstein

The residents of the Japanese city of Hiroshima woke up on August 6, 1945 thinking that this day would be no different from any other. The sky was clear and promised good weather. Many residents of Hiroshima had grown complacent over the past several months because few American bombs had fallen on their city compared to the devastation that had rained down on so many other Japanese cities, including Tokyo. They did not have any idea at the time that their city had been selected for something much more devastating.

At 8:16 in the morning, an American B-29 bomber flown by Paul Tibbets dropped a single bomb over the city. This was the first time in history a nation dropped an atomic bomb on a populated target. The bomb was known as *"Little Boy"* because of its narrow shape. It was a uranium gun-type bomb that exploded several hundred feet above the ground with about 13 kilotons of force. At the time of the bombing, Hiroshima was home to almost 300,000 civilians as well as 43,000 soldiers. Between 90,000 and 166,000 people are believed to have died from the bomb in the four-month period following the explosion.

Most of the people that died on August 6, 1945 lost their lives either from the blast-generated winds that leveled hundreds of building or from the intense heat that in many cases simply vaporized them and left nothing behind but dark shadows on the pavement. The U.S. Department of Energy has estimated that after five years, there were perhaps 200,000 or more fatalities that resulted from the bombing. The bomb's effects, including burns, radiation sickness and cancer, had killed them directly or indirectly.

One survivor, medical doctor Michihiko Hachiya, stated, *"Nothing remained except a few buildings of reinforced concrete. For acres and acres the city was like a desert except for scattered piles of brick and roof tile."* A grocer who survived stated, *"The appearance of people was...well, they all had skin blackened by burns... They had no hair because their hair was burned, and at a glance you couldn't tell whether you were looking at them from in front or in back... Many of them died along the road – I can still picture them in my mind – like walking ghosts... They didn't look like people of this world."* A Protestant minister who also survived stated, *"The feeling I had was that everyone was dead. The whole city was destroyed... I thought this was the end of Hiroshima – of Japan – of humankind... This was God's judgment on man."*

Three days later, another atomic bomb was dropped on the Japanese city of Nagasaki. Called *"Fat Man"* because of its rounder shape, and imploding an enriched plutonium core, it caused similar death and destruction. Shortly afterwards, the Japanese agreed to an unconditional surrender and the Second World War finally came to an end.

Some have defended the decision to use these two atomic bombs, the only ones ever dropped on populated targets, on the grounds that the Japanese had repeatedly demonstrated they would not surrender and that an invasion of the Japanese islands would have been far costlier than the use of the bombs. How could President Harry Truman explain to the families of the American servicemen who would have died in a prolonged war that he had the means to end it earlier? In the eyes of most Americans, the Japanese had started the war with their surprise attack on Pearl Harbor, and by the end of the war, the rules regarding the targeting of civilians had clearly changed.

Nevertheless, the U.S. decision to drop the atomic bombs on Hiroshima and Nagasaki had unleashed the Nuclear Age upon the world. After the conclusion of World War Two in 1945, it could now be guaranteed that a third world war would be completely annihilating. Yet over the past 70 years, there has been no world war. While there have been limited conflicts fought with conventional weapons waged all over the planet, and some of these have generated huge numbers of casualties, none have evolved into a third world war. Why has there never been a World War Three?

The First World War

While warfare has always been an endemic part of history, the concept of world war is relatively new. By definition, a world war involves many combatants, not just two, and is generally fought over a large portion of the planet. Throughout most of history, the world's population was considerably smaller than it is today. Without modern means of communication and transportation, contact between civilizations was minimal. Neighboring civilizations frequently fought wars with each other for control of territory, but this never expanded into a world war.

The first approximation of a world war occurred in the early 17th century. Lasting from 1618 to 1648, the aptly named Thirty Years' War involved several nations, divided Protestants from Roman Catholics and was waged all over the European continent. One hundred and fifty years later, the Napoleonic Wars, in which several nations formed a coalition to maintain the balance of power with the French behemoth, could also be considered a world war. However, it took the advent of modern technology, when nations had weapons that could kill in numbers never seen before, to create what history has labeled as World War One. Amazingly, this titanic clash that involved over thirty nations and spanned virtually the entire planet was triggered by a single assassination.

The Archduke Franz Ferdinand of Austria, heir to the Austro-Hungarian throne, and his wife Sophie, Duchess of Hohenberg, were shot and killed on June 28, 1914. They had been riding in an open convertible in Sarajevo, a city in the neighboring country of Serbia. Their assassin was Gavrilo Princip, a Bosnian Serb and a member of the Black Hand secret society. His political objective had been to break off Austria-Hungary's South Slav provinces so they could be combined into a larger Yugoslavia. If it became a new nation, Yugoslavia would unite several ethnic and religious groups along the western coast of the Balkan Peninsula.

Because of its rocky and mountainous terrain, combined with an incredibly jagged coastline, the geography of the Balkan Peninsula had always served more to divide the region than to act as a unifying force. This was largely the reason why ancient Greek city-states like Athens and Sparta spent more time killing each other than uniting into a powerful Greek Empire. In modern times, the peninsula had been divided up by Bulgarians, Macedonians, Serbs, Montenegrins, Croats, Bosnians, Slovenes and of course, Greeks. In addition, Roman Catholic and Eastern Orthodox churches along with Islamic mosques could be found throughout the region. Accordingly, the Balkan Peninsula had a long history of military conflict.

The situation grew even more volatile when the spread of nationalism took root in the Balkans. This patriotic emotion was infectious. It created a strong desire among people to either build up a nation's strength or create a new country if one did not already exist. The Austro-Hungarian Empire felt its effects. Since the Empire had formed by unifying a number of different ethnic groups, nationalism motivated its monarchs to do everything in their power to keep it from coming unglued. To the south, nationalism had prompted the diminutive nation of Serbia to seek expansion by bringing in the Serbian regions within the Austro-Hungarian Empire. Nationalism had created an explosive situation between these two nations. The Archduke had chosen to visit Sarajevo on a diplomatic mission intended to reduce the tension. Instead, his assassination led to a declaration of war within 48 hours after his death.

In a different time period, the Austro-Hungarian Empire would have waged war against the Serbs and probably won a decisive victory within a few months. The rest of the world would have paid little attention and the war would receive only a paragraph or two within most history textbooks. The world in 1914, however, was more than ready to go to war. It had been 99 years since the defeat of Napoleon Bonaparte, and there had not been a major war in Europe during the century that followed. Entire generations had come and gone without even seeing what a modern war looked like. European military experts actually traveled to the United States to observe its Civil War battles just to witness how the advent of new weapons had changed the nature of warfare.

In addition to the rising spirit of nationalism, Europe had also experienced a significant increase in tension due to the heightened competition resulting from imperialistic races to take colonies throughout Africa and Asia. This in turn led to an escalating arms race and the formation of military alliances. The entire continent had become a powder keg of political tension. What happened in the 31 days following the assassination of the Archduke and his wife has been carefully chronicled in Barbara W. Tuchman's Pulitzer-Prize winning book, *The Guns of August*. In this classic opus, she explained how most of the European nations fell into the First World War like a straight line of dominoes falling when the first is knocked over. When President John F. Kennedy had to find a way to compel the Soviets to remove their nuclear missiles from Cuba in 1962 without starting a world war in the process, it probably helped that he had recently read this book.

Within days after the assassination in 1914, Russia began to mobilize for war due to its alliance with Serbia. The Germans did the same because of their concord with Austria-Hungary. Since France was allied with Russia, the French were the next to join the fray. When the Germans invaded neutral Belgium in order to take a shortcut on the road to Paris, the British declared war to support the people of Belgium. In just a month, a small bushfire had grown into a huge conflagration. Most of the soldiers that marched off to war in the summer of 1914 thought they would be home by Christmas with medals pinned to their chests and stories about their victories to tell their grandchildren. The First World War, however, lasted for over four years and took the lives of 17 million people, of which seven million were civilians.

When the United States made the decision to finally enter the war in April of 1917, President Woodrow Wilson called it *"the war to end all wars."* He became obsessed with his plan to create a League of Nations after the war so that future international conflicts could be settled diplomatically. In the spring months following Germany's agreement to an armistice, the good news for President Wilson was that the Versailles Treaty, which officially ended the war, included a provision to create his League. The bad news was that it also included a number of harsh, punitive measures that stripped Germany of land, colonies and money, and which also imposed severe restrictions on the size of its military. The German people were livid. In the minds of millions of Germans, they yearned for any opportunity to get even.

Meanwhile, the next twenty years placed the world on a trajectory headed straight toward another world war. When President Wilson brought the Versailles Treaty back to the U.S. Senate for ratification, many of the senators baulked at its severe terms while others wanted to return the United States back to its longstanding tradition of isolationism. In the end, they failed to ratify the treaty, and as a result, the United States, which had emerged from the war as potentially the strongest and richest nation in the world, turned its back on the chance to assume an international leadership role.

Next came the start of a pacifist movement that spread from Great Britain to the United States. In the minds of the people that joined this movement, the First World War had wasted the lives of millions for no legitimate reason. In fact, many came to believe the war had been started to fill the coffers of some of the world's largest corporations. One result of this movement was that the British, and to a lesser extent, the French, looked the other way when fascist leaders like Adolph Hitler came to power in Germany and began to rearm their nations in open violation of the Versailles Treaty. The influence of this pacifist movement can even be seen in the passage of the Kellogg-Briand Pact, a 1928 international agreement where the signatory states promised not to use war to resolve "*disputes or conflicts of whatever nature or of whatever origin they may be, which may arise among them.*" Today, most historians get a wry laugh over these nations signing a treaty halfway between the First and Second World Wars that attempted to outlaw war.

Looking back from the present, one interpretation of the two world wars is that there was really just one long war interrupted by a 20-year intermission. Between 1918 and 1939, the Germans simply prepared to get even. In 1933, they put Adolph Hitler in power knowing his proclivity for extreme nationalism would propel the Reich towards another war. Almost immediately, Hitler began to rebuild Germany's immense military machine. In addition, he secured strong alliances with two other fascist nations that were also headed on a path towards military aggression: Italy and Japan. During the 1930s, all three of these *"Axis"* nations took provocative steps leading in the direction of war.

Japan was first, when it invaded Manchuria in 1931 and pursued an all-out assault on China. The Italians walked out of the League of Nations, while that increasingly impotent organization condemned them for their invasion of Ethiopia. Meanwhile, no one lifted a finger when Hitler rearmed the Rhineland along the French border or annexed Austria, all of which openly violated the terms of the Versailles Treaty. In 1938, Great Britain and France followed a policy of appeasement when they acquiesced to Hitler's demands for the Sudetenland region of Czechoslovakia. It was only after he invaded Poland on September 1, 1939, that they finally declared war on Nazi Germany. By then it was too late to prevent the start of the Second World War.

The worst war of all time

The Second World War lasted from 1939 to 1945. Unlike the first, new weapons and new strategy actually helped to reduce the number of casualties on the battlefield. In World War One, each army dug deep trenches where their soldiers could live for weeks or even months at a time. Occasionally, one army climbed out of its trench and scurried across *"No Man's Land"* into the teeth of enemy machine gun fire. The results were incredibly lethal and usually futile. As a result, the battles lasted a long time, resulting in many fatalities.

When the Nazis launched their attack on Poland in 1939, they unleashed a new form of warfare called *"Blitzkrieg"* or Lightning War. Using dive-bombers to rake over enemy trenches from the air and Panzer tank divisions to roll over them on the ground, the battles ended much faster, and as a result, there were fewer casualties. The capture of Poland took less than six weeks. The following spring, when Hitler launched an all-out blitz on France, he captured Paris and defeated France by June. In the four long years of World War One, the Germans had failed to achieve this goal.

Yet while troop movements in the Second World War were faster and less deadly, the deliberate effort to kill civilians made the war malignantly murderous. In China, up to twenty million people died, the vast majority of who were civilians. Many were brutally raped and killed, although the largest number died from starvation. When the Nazis invaded the Soviet Union in the summer of 1941, their intent was to take as much *"living space"* as they could for their *"Aryan master race."* Since the Russian people were in their way, the plan called for the Soviets to be used as slave labor or to be exterminated. By the end of the war, over 25 million Russians were dead. More than one out of every eight Soviets did not survive the war.

World War Two also included the Holocaust. In order to decontaminate the *"master race"* of all human impurities, the Nazis first created concentration camps, followed by the construction of six major death camps in Poland. These were designed to systematically exterminate people in the fastest, cheapest and most efficient manner possible. Trains ran around the clock to bring homosexual people, political opponents, people with mental and physical disabilities, criminals, Romani people and Jewish people to these camps for extermination. Some of those who were younger and stronger were temporarily spared to work as slave labor in the camps. The rest were immediately sent to their death. In most cases, they died from the noxious gas that filled chambers disguised as showers. In the end, 12 million people were murdered in the Holocaust. Roughly half of those people were Jewish.

It should be acknowledged that not all of the civilians who died in the Second World War were killed at the hands of the Axis Powers. The British Royal Air Force and the U.S. Air Force rained death from the skies over most German and Japanese cities during the war. Up to 600,000 Germans and as many as 500,000 Japanese civilians died as a result of Allied bombings. In Dresden, Germany, 25,000 died in a single night. In Hamburg, it was 45,000. The incendiary bombs dropped by the United States on Tokyo killed over 100,000 people. Finally, in order to bring a swift end to the war against the Japanese, the world's first atomic bombs were dropped on the cities of Hiroshima and Nagasaki. These two bombs quickly took the lives of approximately another 200,000 people, as well as many more thousands in the ensuing years.

In total, the Second World War claimed the lives of over 60 million people. In a world with a population of 2.3 billion in 1940, this number means that three out of every 100 people alive at the time died in the war. No other war in the history of the world has been so deadly or destructive. With this in mind, it might be tempting to believe that the nightmare of World War Two had sobered up the planet and convinced humankind that there must never be a World War Three. This idea might be further reinforced by the knowledge that a third world war would almost certainly involve the use of nuclear warheads. However, the reality is not so simple.

The Cold War

Even before the Second World War ended in 1945, there was growing tension between the two most powerful allied nations, the United States and the Soviet Union. The seeds for their mutual distrust had been planted in 1917 when communism transformed Russia, with its autocratic czar, into the Union of Soviet Socialist Republics (USSR). This triggered a growing suspicion within the United States of a worldwide communist conspiracy. After all, Karl Marx had aimed *The Communist Manifesto* at the international community, not just the laborers of a single country. After the Communists executed the czar and his family, they firmly established their power under the leadership of Vladimir Lenin and then attempted to systematically transform the entire economy into a classless society.

In response, the United States sent troops to support the White Army in their futile efforts to resist the takeover by the communist Red Army. Based in part on Karl Marx's prediction that communist revolutions would occur in the most industrially advanced nations, there was a mounting fear that a revolution might occur in the United States. As a result, a Red Scare swept the U.S. as suspected American communists were harassed and arrested in open violation of their constitutional rights. Accordingly, from its inception, there was a mutual mistrust between the USSR and the United States. The only reason why they fought together as allies in the Second World War was because Nazi Germany had invaded the Soviet Union in the summer of 1941, six months before the Japanese attacked the United States at Pearl Harbor.

In the closing years of World War Two, both President Franklin Roosevelt and President Harry Truman met with Soviet Premier Joseph Stalin to plan a strategy against Hitler and discuss a blueprint for rebuilding the postwar world. It soon became increasingly evident that Stalin had no intention of withdrawing the Red Army from Eastern European nations like Poland, Czechoslovakia, Hungary or the eastern part of Germany. Instead, he worked to prop up communist governments in each of those nations. In the eyes of Western leaders, the Soviets were exploiting the end of the war as an opportunity to spread communism. On the other hand, the Soviets, who had seen their land invaded by the French in the Napoleonic Wars, the Germans in World War One and the Nazis in the Second World War, wanted a more secure border to their west. Spreading communism to create buffer states in Eastern Europe would advance this goal.

At the conclusion of the Second World War, the American gross domestic product was roughly comparable to that of the rest of the world combined. The U.S. was also the only nation in the world that possessed the atomic bomb. Since the Axis nations had been vanquished and the Soviets were still seen as an ally, the vast majority of the 16 million Americans wearing military uniforms at the end of the war were allowed to resume civilian life. However, because most of the Soviet Red Army remained intact, the Soviets suddenly possessed the world's largest military.

Based on their respective assets, the US and the USSR emerged from the war in 1945 as the world's two *"superpowers."* With conflicting goals, they each took steps toward preparing for a military conflict with each other. Fortunately, despite many close calls, this tension never erupted into World War Three. Although the Americans and the Soviets each supported puppet states in locations like Korea and Vietnam where *"hot wars"* did break out, they never fought each other face-to-face. Instead, they vigorously competed with each other over the next half-century in what came to be known as the Cold War.

The Cold War was waged all over the planet. The two superpowers competed to see who could be the first to put a satellite into orbit (the Soviets in 1957) and who would be the first to put a man on the moon (the Americans in 1969). Every four years, they competed to see who could win the most medals in the Olympic games. Of much graver importance, they engaged in a costly military arms race. Spies operated in both nations, and it was largely through espionage that the Soviets were able to successfully test their first nuclear bomb in 1949. From that point on, the two superpowers competed with each other to build the largest and most powerful nuclear arsenals. By the 1950s, hydrogen super bombs based on nuclear fusion had replaced smaller atomic bombs that had utilized the technology of nuclear fission. It took the explosion of an atomic bomb just to detonate a hydrogen super bomb. By 1961, the Soviet Union tested a 50-megaton hydrogen bomb that was 3,800 times more powerful than the bomb dropped on Hiroshima.

In addition to the race to build stronger and larger stockpiles of weapons, the two superpowers also competed with each other over the technology to deliver warheads. By the 1960s, both sides possessed intercontinental ballistic missiles (ICBMs) that could reach each other's cities in less than an hour. Each missile carried multiple warheads capable of hitting multiple targets. For the United States, the Triad strategy was based on the idea that nuclear weapons could be delivered into the USSR in three different methods. Strategic bombers were the slowest, but they were the most accurate and could potentially be recalled. Missiles launched from underground silos were the easiest to maintain, but they were stationary targets. Finally, missiles launched from submarines like America's Trident sub could be hidden under the ocean's surface for months at a time. In theory, one Trident submarine carried enough firepower to destroy anywhere from 1,000 to almost 5000 *"Hiroshimas."*

This race to annihilate each other in the 1950s was based on the idea that it was possible to fight and win a nuclear war. This was one reason why the United States began to construct interstate highways during this decade as a means to transport missiles and other military hardware as quickly as possible from coast to coast. The height of interstate overpasses was even set to allow passage of a truck towing a nuclear missile. This was also why so many people built bomb shelters in their homes and why schools practiced atomic bomb drills. In the 1950s, many people, including President Eisenhower, naively believed it was possible to fight and win World War Three with the use of nuclear weapons. It took 13 chilling days in October of 1962 to awaken people to the reality that this must never happen.

Cuba and the rise of M.A.D.

The most terrifying crisis of the entire Cold War began when President Kennedy was informed that U-2 spy planes had taken photographs of missile silos that the Soviets were constructing in Cuba. A few years earlier, a communist revolution had taken place on that island nation, which is situated only 90 miles from the Florida coastline. President Kennedy had given the green light to a poorly executed plan to invade Cuba at the Bay of Pigs the previous year. When this attack failed, Cuba's communist dictator, Fidel Castro, felt the need to align closer with the USSR and agreed to the construction of Soviet missile sites on Cuban soil. Because of its extremely close proximity to the United States, President Kennedy believed that he had no choice but to demand the removal of all nuclear missiles sites from Cuba.

As the United States mobilized for the potential start of World War Three, tens of millions of Americans gasped in horror when the President came on nation-wide television to explain the details of the Cuban Missile Crisis. The U.S. had thrown up a naval blockade around the Caribbean island and the world held its breath to see who would blink first. At the last moment, Soviet vessels carrying missiles to Cuba backed down and headed for home. Meanwhile, because there were already missile sites in Cuba, a number of Kennedy's military advisors urged him to bomb and even invade the island nation. The President was more prudent and chose to explore other options. In the end, diplomacy saved the world. When the U.S. promised to leave Cuba alone and refrain from replacing outdated missiles in Turkey, the Soviets agreed to withdraw all nuclear missiles from Cuba.

As the planet breathed a collective sigh of relief, the countries made reforms to reduce the risk of another Cuban Missile Crisis. A special telephone line was installed between the White House and the Kremlin to facilitate easier communications between the leaders of the two super powers. They also signed treaties to minimize the proliferation of nuclear weaponry and ban the testing of atomic bombs above ground. Two years later, Nikita Khrushchev, the man who had been the Soviet Premier during the Cuban Missile Crisis, was removed from power. Most crucially, many of the leaders in both superpowers came to the realization that no one could win a nuclear war. To think otherwise was sheer madness.

From this realization came the principle of M.A.D., "*mutually assured destruction.*" If one nation ever pressed the button to launch its nuclear missiles, it would immediately invite a retaliatory response. Hundreds, maybe thousands of warheads would destroy just about every city, not just in the United States and the Soviet Union, but in their allied countries as well. This means Canada, Australia, Japan and most of Europe would also be obliterated. The casualty figures could climb into the billions. In addition, there would be so much radiation released around the planet that the entire earth would become uninhabitable to humans for thousands of years.

By the 1980s, scientists like Carl Sagan helped popularize the theoretical vision of a *"nuclear winter"* that would follow the detonation of hundreds of atomic warheads. They theorized that after the sky blazed with the radiance of a thousand suns, and billions of lives burned to ash and shadow, there would be nuclear firestorms that would incinerate not only cities but also farms and forests. This would lead to torrents of smoke ascending into the atmosphere and entombing the planet in billowing, black clouds of ash. The result would be noontime darkness, plummeting temperatures and the eventual death of all life on the planet.

When the Second World War ended in 1945, there were many circumspect people around the world who wanted to learn from the lessons of history and build a new world order without the possibility of a Third World War. This was a primary motivation behind the creation of the United Nations. However, what was more powerful than this idealistic dream, where issues would be settled through diplomacy rather than war, was the nightmarish fear of what the world would look like after a thermonuclear conflict. The terror of a nuclear retaliatory strike created an enormous deterrent for countries to ever take the first step towards World War Three.

Conclusion

The prospect of a Third World War did not completely disappear after the Cuban Missile Crisis. The Cold War continued for another 27 years. The late 1960s and the early 1970s witnessed a *"thaw"* in the Cold War as President Nixon established a period known as Détente, after he visited Communist China, normalized relations with the Chinese and signed the first Strategic Arms Limitation Treaty (SALT I) with the Soviet Union. Nevertheless, like a roller coaster ride, the improved relations between the United States and the USSR regressed in the late 1970s after Soviet tanks entered Afghanistan to protect a communist puppet regime. In 1980, the United States and its allies boycotted the summer Olympic games in Moscow, and four years later, the Soviet Union and its Eastern Europeans allies did the same for the games held in Los Angeles.

In 1983, President Ronald Reagan stated in a speech that the Soviets were *"the focus of evil in the modern world."* He accelerated the nuclear arms race and pushed for a new defensive strategy called the Strategic Defense Initiative (SDI) that came to be better known as *"Star Wars."* His goal of creating a defensive shield based on lasers that could be fired from satellites and aimed at Soviet ICBMs before they entered U.S. air space never materialized. Nonetheless, the possibility of its development increased tension between the two superpowers.

It was only after the USSR chose a reformer named Mikhail Gorbachev to be Premier that free elections were held in the Soviet Union, and the Communists were finally voted out of power. This in turn led to the dissolution of the Soviet Union into 15 separate republics, the spread of open market economies to the nations of Eastern Europe, the reunification of Germany and the negotiation of major reductions in nuclear warheads. By 1990, the Cold War was over. The United States was left standing as the one remaining superpower, and the threat of a third world war was considerably diminished.

Back in 1947, the members of *The Bulletin of the Atomic Scientists* Science and Security Board created "*The Doomsday Clock*" to represent how close the world was to global disaster. Its symbolic clock face represents a countdown to a worldwide catastrophe such as nuclear war or a major climate change. The closer the clock gets to midnight, the closer the scientists believe the world is to global Armageddon. At the most frightening times, the clock has come within two minutes of midnight. It stood at ten minutes before midnight in 1990, shortly after the fall of the Berlin Wall. The following year, after the signing of the first Strategic Arms Reduction Treaty (START I) and the dissolution of the Soviet Union that December, the clock was pushed back to 17 minutes. This was the furthest it has been since its creation. Today, however, it currently stands at just three minutes to midnight. Why so close?

First, Russia may not be the leader of the communist world any longer, but recent tensions have arisen between the United States and Russia reminiscent of the worst days of the Cold War. Modern-day conflicts in Ukraine and Syria have been accompanied by threats between Russian and American leaders. In the 2016 presidential election, the CIA and the FBI revealed evidence that Vladimir Putin and the Russians had hacked into emails in order to disrupt the American election and help Donald Trump win the presidency. Russian jets have buzzed frightfully close to American aircraft, and at one point, the director of a state-run Russian news agency made statements about turning the United States into radioactive ash. Although Washington and Moscow continue to adhere to most existing nuclear arms control agreements, they have also engaged in programs to modernize their nuclear arsenals.

Second, there is the specter of worldwide terrorism. Although it is undeniably tragic when suicide bombings and shootings take place in France, Belgium and the United States, not to mention Iraq, Pakistan and Nigeria, these have all been carried out with conventional weapons. What happens if terrorist groups like Al Qaida or ISIS gain possession of an atomic bomb? In light of the global instability generated by the carnage occurring in places like Syria and Ukraine, it unfortunately may be only a matter of time before weapons of mass destruction fall into the hands of dangerous groups.

Third, there are the other nations that have acquired nuclear weapons. In addition to the United States and Russia, Great Britain, France and China possess atomic bombs. India and Pakistan do as well, and considering the smoldering hostility between these two bordering nations, only M.A.D. has kept them from using short-range nuclear missiles on each other's cities. Many believe that Israel likely has atomic weapons, although this has never been publicly admitted; but if a nation like Iran were to acquire a nuclear bomb, there is little doubt that Israel would attempt to rattle the nuclear saber in its own defense. Then there is the rogue state of North Korea. Isolated and led by a man that could at best be described as a loose cannon, the testing of nuclear bombs and missiles by the Korean Hermit Kingdom sends chills down the spines of people living in Seoul, Tokyo and every city in between.

Why has there never been a World War Three? Up to the present, the answer lies primarily in the fear of mutually assured destruction. There have been close calls, but so far, the wars fought since 1945 have been limited to regional conflicts waged with conventional weapons. In fact, the one constructive feature of the unleashing of nuclear weapons from their Pandora's Box has been the powerful deterrence to their use. New weapons throughout history, from muskets and cannons to machine guns and submarines, have generally been utilized on the battlefield immediately. Only nuclear weapons, with their potential to obliterate all human civilization, have not been used since their initial appearance when they leveled the cities of Hiroshima and Nagasaki at the end of World War Two. Nonetheless, the question that history cannot answer is whether the delicate balance established by M.A.D will endure to permanently prevent the start of a World War Three.

Sources and further reading:

"Cuban Missile Crisis." *History.com.* Accessed December 13, 2016. https://www.history.com/topics/cold-war/cuban-missile-crisis.

Einstein, Albert. *Goodreads.com.* Accessed December 2, 2016. https://www.goodreads.com/quotes/14977-i-know-not-with-what-weapons-world-war-iii-will.

Gaddis, John Lewis. *The Cold War: A New History.* New York: Penguin Books, 2005.

"Kellogg-Briand Pact 1928." *The Avalon Project.* Accessed December 5, 2016. https://www.avalon.law.yale.edu/20th_century/kbpact.asp.

Lamb, Robert. "What Would Nuclear Winter Be Like?" *HowStuffWorks.com.* January 13, 2009. https://www.science.howstuffworks.com/nuclear-winter.htm.

Marx, Karl, and Frederick Engels. *The Communist Manifesto.* Oxford: Benediction Classics, 2016.

Mecklin, John, ed. "It is Still 3 Minutes to Midnight." *Bulletin of the Atomic Scientists.* Accessed December 16, 2016. https://www.thebulletin.org/sites/default/files/2016%20doomsday%20clock%20statement%20-%20final%5B5%5D.pdf.

Pandey, Avaneesh. "Hydrogen Bomb Vs. Atomic Bomb: Fusion-Powered Weapon More Destructive Than Fission-Powered Counterpart." *InternationalBusinessTimes.com.* January 6, 2016. https://www.ibtimes.com/hydrogen-bomb-vs-atomic-bomb-fusion-powered-weapon-more-destructive-fission-powered-2251137.

Reagan, Ronald. "Evil Empire Speech." *NationalCenter.org.* Accessed December 15, 2016. https://www.nationalcenter.org/ReaganEvilEmpire1983.html.

Sagan, Carl. "The Nuclear Winter." *Colorado.edu.* Accessed December 12, 2016. https://www.colorado.edu/AmStudies/lewis/ecology/nuclearwinter.pdf.

"Timeline." *Bulletin of the Atomic Scientists.* Accessed December 16, 2016. https://www.thebulletin.org/timeline.

"Trident Submarine and Missile System." *JonahHouse.org.* Accessed December 14, 2016. https://www.jonahhouse.org/archive/Disarm_Now_Plowshares/factsheet.htm.

Tuchman, Barbara W. *The Guns of August.* New York: Random House, 1990.

Chapter 14

Why has terrorism become increasingly prevalent in the modern world?

Flag of the Islamic State
Courtesy of Wikimedia Commons (PD ineligible (flags)
https://commons.wikimedia.org/wiki/File:Flag_of_Islamic_State_of_Iraq.svg

"At this point of the crusade against the Islamic State, it is very important that attacks take place in every country that entered into the alliance against the Islamic States, especially the U.S., U.K., France, Australia, and Germany. Rather, the citizens of crusader nations should be targeted wherever they can be found."

Al-Adnani in the October 2014 edition of Dabiq, the ISIS online magazine

49 people died in Orlando, Florida. 35 were killed in Brussels, Belgium. A few months earlier, 14 were murdered in San Bernardino, California. Less than three weeks before that event, 137 died in Paris, France. These were just the acts of terrorism that were placed in the spotlight by the Western media over a period of less than nine months between the end of 2015 and the first half of 2016. There were many others, including a raid in Nigeria that took the lives of 65 people and an attack in Pakistan that killed another 70. It seems that hardly a day goes by without a headline focused on a suicide bombing, shooting spree, commercial airliner blown out of the sky or some other act of terrorism. A shooting can take place in a

mall, school or movie theater, and the first question people always ask is whether it was an act of terrorism.

There is no denying that the modern world is plagued by terrorism. On one level, this is a relatively simple phenomenon. A person or a small group can acquire the deadliest weapons available and attempt to kill as many people as possible. The perpetrators usually do not know their victims and give them little thought. Escaping the scene of violence sometimes occurs, but more often than not, the terrorists are just as content to die committing their act of terrorism.

Terrorism is difficult to define because the term is so politically and emotionally charged. There is no universal agreement on the boundaries that separate terrorism from other acts that might fall into the realm of crime, government repression or even civil war. There is some consensus today that acts of terrorism involve the use of violence or the threat of violence in order to pursue a political, religious or ideological change. Most would also agree that while there is certainly immediate violence in any act of terrorism, the long term goal of terrorists is to publicize their cause to the widest possible audience. On a moral level, terrorists generally believe that an attack against innocent victims is an acceptable consequence in order to achieve their larger goals.

Acts of terrorism have become so ubiquitous that only the ones with a large number of victims usually garner front-page headlines. The others tend to get buried deeper within the newspapers. Most acts of terrorism today are usually linked to global organizations: ISIS, Al Qaida, Boko Haram, the Taliban, Al-Shabaab. When linked to one of these groups, the FBI refers to their deeds as acts of international terrorism. When committed by homegrown individuals, they are labeled acts of domestic terrorism. Of course, many of the actions by lone wolf terrorists may have been inspired or directed by outside organizations. Some of the more familiar acts of domestic terrorism include the Oklahoma City truck bombing in 1995 that took the lives of 168 people and the Boston Marathon bombing in 2013 that killed three civilians and injured an estimated 264 others.

Most people beyond the age of 40 or so can recall a time when acts of terrorism did not seem to occur on a daily basis. When they did, only two organizations were generally mentioned: the IRA (Irish Republican Army), which employed terrorism against Great Britain over the contested control of Northern Ireland, and the PLO (The Palestine Liberation Organization), which aimed its violence at Israel and its allies. In both cases, while most people viewed the use of terrorism as morally repugnant, it occurred because Irish Catholics in Northern Ireland and Palestinians in the Middle East saw themselves as *"victims"* with no hope of achieving their goals on an open battlefield.

What has changed? Why are there so many groups and organizations today that employ terrorism, and why is there the popular perception that many of these radiate out of the Middle East? In addition, the Islamic religion, at least those practitioners who are labeled as *"radicals"* or *"fundamentalists,"* often seem to be at the epicenter of many terrorist acts. How can this be explained? In the modern world today, why has the use of terrorism become increasingly prevalent?

A matter of perspective

A heated debate often ensues whenever certain crimes are labeled acts of terrorism. A political goal of some kind must underlie a terrorist act, but in many cases, this is not easily found. A mass shooting may lead to multiple fatalities, but without some sort of political motive, it remains just that: a terrible crime. Two students murdered 12 other students and a teacher in a Colorado high school in 1999, but whatever their motive, it was never seen as political. In 2012, when 12 other victims were murdered in a movie theater in Aurora, Colorado, the shooter pleaded not guilty by reason of insanity. Once again, there was no political motive. The same could be said for the 20 school children and six adults murdered in Sandy Hook Elementary School in Newtown, Connecticut, in 2012. All of these events led to tragic consequences and impassioned debates about the need for gun control. But were they acts of terrorism? The racially motivated shooting that took place at the Emanuel African Methodist Episcopal Church in Charleston, South Carolina, which took the lives of nine African Americans in 2015, was clearly a hate crime, but does it qualify as an act of terrorism? Determining whether there was a political motivation is often more difficult than it might seem.

A significant factor that complicates the issue further involves point of view. Omar Mateen took a pistol and an AR-15 assault-style rifle into the Pulse nightclub in Orlando, Florida, on the night of June 11, 2016, and killed 49 people. This is the worst mass shooting in U.S. history. Since the Pulse was a gay nightclub, the shooting could certainly be considered a hate crime. Since Mateen had declared his allegiance to ISIS, it could also be called an act of terrorism. In addition, since he was born in the U.S. and because he acted alone, the crime has been labeled an act of domestic terrorism. So far, classifying this crime appears simple. It becomes more complicated, however, if one considers how extremist Muslims in the Middle East perceived Mateen's actions. To members of ISIS and their sympathizers, Mateen was not a terrorist. He was a hero.

In 1859, the abolitionist John Brown led an attack on the federal arsenal at Harpers Ferry, Virginia, (now located in West Virginia). His intent was to capture the weapons stored there and use them to incite a slave uprising in the surrounding area. Had he been successful, there is a strong possibility that it would have caused the deaths of many people, including women and children. After all, Brown was certainly familiar with the earlier Nat Turner slave rebellion of 1831, also in Virginia, which killed approximately 60 white people. To Brown, it did not matter. To him, the higher cause of ending slavery justified the loss of life that might result from his actions. As it turned out, the attack was vanquished and

John Brown was captured, tried, convicted and hanged. Applying modern terminology, some would probably call John Brown a domestic terrorist. On the other hand, many northerners at the time considered him a martyr and a hero. In the past, just like today, terrorism is a relative term.

Why resort to terrorism?

Regardless of how it is labeled, the question might arise as to why anyone would be willing to commit an act of terrorism. The potential victims in and around Harpers Ferry were similar to the people murdered in the Pulse nightclub in that they were all anonymous victims unknown to the perpetrator of the crime. A moral line was clearly crossed in both cases. How can this be justified? The answer lies in the balance people are willing to strike between the value of a desired goal on one hand and the price they are willing to pay to achieve that goal on the other. Throughout the past and right up to the present, there is no consensus on how to achieve that balance.

Martin Luther King's birthday is celebrated today as a national holiday, and one reason why was his use of non-violent methods. Dr. King was the antithesis of a terrorist. But what about Malcolm X? Malcolm fought for many of the same goals as Martin Luther King, but he was more willing to employ violent methods to achieve them. Malcolm X once said, *"Be peaceful, be courteous, obey the law, respect everyone; but if someone puts his hand on you, send him to the cemetery."* On another occasion he said, *"If ballots won't work, bullets will."* Since Malcolm never acted on these sentiments, he should not be considered a terrorist. It can be argued, however, that his rhetoric certainly implied that its use would be justified by the higher cause of achieving racial equality. It is unlikely that the nation as a whole will ever celebrate the birthday of Malcolm X, but more than fifty years after his assassination in 1965 Malcolm is still viewed positively by many. In a YouGov survey conducted in 2015, 26 per cent of whites had a favorable opinion of Malcolm X, while 41 per cent had a negative view. Among black Americans, however, 67 per cent had a favorable opinion, while only six per cent had a negative outlook. The willingness to employ different forms of violence, including terrorism, is often demonstrated by those who consider themselves victims.

Why resort to terrorism? The answer lies partly in the maxim that *"the end justifies the means."* In other words, there may have to be some loss of life in order to advance a higher cause. Of course, not everyone believes in this precept, but many people do. By definition, a terrorist is *always* fighting for what he or she feels is a justified reason. While it is natural to consider the actions of terrorists as cowardly because they aim to harm innocent victims, their defenders would contend that they are merely resorting to the only means available.

Guerilla tactics

Throughout history, whenever a smaller group pursues a cause with zeal and passion against a larger enemy that cannot be defeated on an open battlefield, they have frequently resorted to guerilla tactics. These strategies strongly resemble terrorism in that methods are frequently employed that are morally questionable. Like the terrorist, the guerilla warrior is usually an extremist that embraces the belief that the end justifies the means. In fact, it can sometimes be quite difficult differentiating between the two. Overall, guerilla warriors are more focused on reducing the military prowess of their enemy by employing hit-and-run tactics, and they are not as willing to sacrifice their lives in suicide bombings. In modern times, however, the two approaches have become almost synonymous and the use of both has significantly been on the rise.

The term *"guerilla warfare"* did not appear until the early 19th century when it was used to describe the *"irregular war"* carried on by Spanish peasants and shepherds against Napoleon's occupying French Empire. South Carolinians employed it during the Revolutionary War, as did Haitians in their successful bid to gain independence from Napoleonic France. It was utilized by various indigenous tribes in North America who attempted to preserve their autonomy and by the Irish in their long pursuit for freedom from Great Britain. After the Philippines had been ostensibly *"liberated"* from Spain in the Spanish-American War of 1898, the United States found itself the target of guerilla tactics. Filipino partisans employed these tactics for three years after learning that America intended to keep the Philippines as a U.S. colony. While the United States eventually won this struggle, it proved to be far deadlier than the original war with Spain. As many as 250,000 Filipino civilians died during these three years, mostly from disease. The United States had also been treated to a preview of what the years 1964 to 1973 would later bring in the jungles of Vietnam.

In an age where superpowers can use nuclear weapons to pulverize an enemy, guerilla tactics, like terrorism, have been effectively used in the face of overwhelming odds. Yet while the term *"guerilla warfare"* is only about 200 years old, the methods themselves have been employed much longer. In fact, they first surfaced about 2000 years ago.

The Hebrew revolt

During a two hundred year period in history known as the Pax Romana, when Rome governed an area encompassing approximately 20 per cent of the world's population, there was virtually no other nation that could compete with the Roman military, so few even tried. The result was one of the longest sustained periods of global peace the world has ever known.

One glaring exception was the Hebrew revolt. Since the Romans had first incorporated Israel into their empire in 63 BCE., their rule had grown increasingly oppressive. Iniquitous taxes, coupled with the Roman decision to appoint the Jewish High Priest, led to a rebellion by Hebrew zealots that lasted for more than six decades. It was largely fueled by the belief that any means were justified to attain political and religious liberty. The resistance markedly increased during the reign of the erratic emperor Caligula, who in the year 39 declared himself to be a god and ordered his statue to be erected in every temple throughout the Roman world. The Jewish people, who had built their faith around the fervent belief that there could only be one true God, refused to heed this command. They refused to defile their Temple with a statue of Rome's latest deity.

From this point, matters only went from bad to worse. By the year 66 C.E., a combination of financial exploitation, Rome's palpable contempt for Judaism and the brazen partiality the Romans extended to the gentiles living in Israel started an open revolt. Initially successful, Rome soon brought in a sledgehammer in the form of 60,000 heavily armed troops to crush the insurrection. The first attack was launched against the Galilee in the north, the Jewish state's most radicalized area. The Zealots were soundly defeated, and an estimated 100,000 Jews were killed or sold into slavery.

The Romans next turned their attention to the city of Jerusalem. In a manner reminiscent of the current infighting in nations like Iraq and Syria between Shiite and Sunni Muslims, the Jews within Jerusalem began to turn on one another. The more fanatical Zealots engaged in a suicidal civil war with the more moderate factions. For example, one of the Zealot bands burned the entire food supply that had been stockpiled to feed the city during a multiyear siege, apparently with the hope that the destruction of this "security blanket" would force everyone to participate in the revolt against the Romans. If modern terminology were to be applied, this act of arson would certainly be considered a form of terrorism.

During the summer of the year 70 C.E., the Romans breached the walls of Jerusalem and launched a storm of violence and death. Shortly afterwards, they destroyed the Second Temple and dispersed many of the remaining Jews into the Diaspora period that lasted up until the creation of the modern state of Israel in 1948. Nevertheless, some Zealot bands continued to harass the Romans by using guerilla hit-and-run tactics. Finally, the last of the Zealots holed themselves up on the mountain fortress of Masada. A siege then ensued that lasted about three years. When the Romans used thousands of Jewish slaves to construct a massive ramp and battering ram to take the fortress, they found inside its ramparts the bodies of 960 people who had committed an act of mass suicide. It is estimated that as many as one million Jews died in the Great Revolt against Rome, making it the most deadly event in Jewish history prior to the Holocaust.

Toward the end of the 19th century, the Zionist Movement emerged in Europe amongst modern Jews who sought to reclaim the land that had been lost to the

Romans 1900 years earlier. At first, these Jews quietly purchased land and homes in their biblical land of Zion, a region under the political thumb of the Ottoman Turkish Empire. After the nightmare of the Holocaust, however, the gentle stream of Jewish immigrants turned into a torrential flood. Guerilla tactics and terrorism then reappeared in the Middle East as some Jewish immigrants utilized them in order acquire their modern state of Israel. Since then, Israel's enemies have employed them, particularly the Palestinian people who felt cheated out of a nation of their own. This ongoing conflict, characterized by guerilla warfare and terrorism, dominated much of the 20th century.

The 20th century

The advent of modern weaponry in the 20th century has enabled terrorists and guerilla forces to achieve greater success than in previous centuries. While the use of these methods had been somewhat sporadic in the past, they have appeared on a more regular basis over the last century, particularly as nationalism created further causes for which people have been willing to fight, kill and die.

One method that gained popularity in the 19th and 20th centuries has been the assassination of a world leader. By 1901, three American presidents had been assassinated, although only Abraham Lincoln's murder was clearly connected to a political cause. In 1881, the Russian czar, Alexander II was also assassinated. The murder of the Archduke Franz Ferdinand and his wife, Sophie, as their motorcade maneuvered through the streets of Sarajevo on June 28, 1914, ignited the First World War.

After the conclusion of World War Two in 1945, the use of terrorism and guerilla tactics has continued to increase. While the United States and USSR began the Cold War, a growing movement spread amongst many of the indigenous people in Africa and Asia to drive out their Western colonizers and secure independent nations of their own. After all, many people around the planet viewed the defeat of the Axis powers as a victory for freedom and democracy, and the residents that made up the Western colonial empires wanted their share of liberty. Since defeating a Western power on an open battlefield was a daunting challenge, guerilla tactics were employed in an anti-colonial effort that led to the creation of such new nations as Indonesia (from the Netherlands in 1949), Algeria (from France in 1962) and Angola from (Portugal in 1974). Vietnam used these tactics twice, first against France in 1954 and then against the United States between 1964 and 1973.

The modern state of Israel

As for terrorism, it made its first post-World-War-Two appearance in Israel. At the time, the region was called Palestine, the name given to the area by the Romans. Since the end of World War One, it had been under the control of the British.

Contrary to what some might believe, the first terrorists in Israel were Zionist Jews, not Islamic Arabs.

Prior to World War One, the land known today as Israel was part of the Ottoman Turkish Empire. Since the Turks had fought on the losing side during the war, the victorious Allies agreed to divide the Middle Eastern land acquired from the Ottoman Empire into two mandates: one controlled by England and the other by France. This agreement placed Palestine under British control. Both Arabs and Zionist Jews were disappointed that they were not given a nation of their own.

After the Holocaust, there was a great outpouring of global sympathy for the Jewish people, and the movement to create a modern Jewish state started to gain momentum. Nonetheless, since the British emerged from the war with a determination to retain the remnants of what had once been an enormous empire, they stubbornly clung to their Middle Eastern mandates. The fact that the Middle East was abundantly rich in petroleum also influenced this decision. The growing population of Jewish Holocaust survivors infiltrating Palestine spurred tension, as the Zionists became increasingly determined to drive out the British and create a modern Jewish state.

The Zionists recognized they had no hope of defeating the British military on an open battlefield. Therefore, some of the more extremist groups turned to terrorism. The Irgun was a Zionist paramilitary organization that had been operating in Palestine since 1931. On July 22, 1946, the Irgun was responsible for the terrorist bombing of the British administrative headquarters for Palestine in Jerusalem's King David Hotel. 91 people of various nationalities were killed and 46 more were injured. Two years later, after the newly created United Nations voted to partition the region between the Jews and the Arab Palestinians, the Irgun participated in another terrorist act. On April 9, 1948, 120 Zionist paramilitary soldiers attacked Deir Yassin, a Palestinian Arab village of roughly 600 people near Jerusalem. The offensive was motivated by the desire to retaliate against the blockade of Jerusalem by Palestinian Arab forces during the civil war that preceded the end of British rule in Palestine. During and after the battle for the village, 107 Palestinians were killed, including women and children. Some were shot while others were killed from hand grenades thrown into their homes.

Israeli independence officially came on May 14, 1948. Just three years after the conclusion of the Holocaust, however, the Jews were once again forced to fight for their lives and their survival. Armies from several surrounding Arab nations invaded the new Jewish state. With financial and military support from the United States, however, the Israelis were not only successful at defending themselves, but managed to considerably enlarge their nation, particularly after the Six Day War in 1967. Positions had changed, and Israel's opponents began to believe that it could not be defeated on an open battlefield. Therefore, many of the Palestinians who either lived within Israel, in neighboring Arab nations or on lands taken by Israel since the original partition felt they were a people deprived of their own nation.

Following the pattern that had been established in the past, including by Zionist groups like the Irgun, some of the Palestinians and their allies waged terrorism as a means to achieve their goals. Their targets not only included Israelis but also their American and European allies. The result has been over 65 years of terrorism and counter-terrorism, as well as several brief wars.

To this day, it is nearly impossible to tell the story of Israel's creation and its ongoing survival without stirring up a hornet's nest of controversy. Yet while the storm that has revolved around the state of Israel since its creation in 1948 is a big source of terrorism in the Middle East, it is not the only one.

Iran

In 1979, a revolution occurred in the land of the ancient Persians that still reverberates to this day. Mohammad Reza Pahlavi, better known as the Shah of Iran, was overthrown by a combination of leftist and Islamic organizations along with a large number of Iranian students. The Shah had originally taken power in a 1953 coup d'état that toppled a democratically elected Prime Minister. This was accomplished with support from the United States and Great Britain who wanted a *"friend"* in power that would open up Iranian oil fields for Western development, and who could be trusted not to cozy up to communist leaders in the Soviet Union. Over the next 26 years, the Shah repressed all political opposition. Social and political protest was often met with censorship, surveillance, harassment, illegal detention and torture. Moreover, the Shah had opened Iran up to the infiltration of modern culture. Western films, music and clothing styles became increasingly endemic. There was mounting pressure to provide women with the greater equality that had recently been acquired in Western society and to remove the burkas that concealed their bodies and faces. In little more than a generation, Iran had changed from a traditional, conservative, and rural society to one that was industrial, modern and urban. Now the traditionalists wanted their country back.

The Shah was overthrown while receiving treatment for cancer in the United States. When the U.S. refused to turn the Shah over for trial, the revolutionaries turned their hostility on anything American. Uncle Sam was burned in effigy, the stars and stripes were openly incinerated in the streets of Tehran and massive mobs took control of the U.S. embassy and held 52 Americans hostage. The anger and resentment had been building for decades. Some of it originated from the intrusion of Cold War politics into Iran back in 1953 and part stemmed from America's steady support for Israel. The lion's share, however, radiated from the growing chasm between Western culture and traditional Islamic values.

For the United States, the Iranian Hostage Crisis was 444 days of fruitless frustration. Diplomatic efforts and economic pressure were ineffective, and a military rescue mission proved to be a disaster. Any stronger military efforts by the President Carter administration would probably have led to the deaths of the

American hostages. One of the strongest superpowers the world has ever known was helpless in the face of this act of terrorism. To add insult to injury against the president they had been dueling with for well over a year, the Iranians finally released the hostages on the day that Ronald Reagan was sworn in to replace Jimmy Carter. The Iranians chose to release the hostages on their own terms. This was a turning point. For the next 35 years, Islamic fundamentalism, determined to defend Muslim traditions and values, was bolstered by this early victory.

Ten years later, when the Iraqi leader, Saddam Hussein, invaded the neighboring nation of Kuwait in order to take over that nation's rich oil fields, the United States once again stepped into an intricate web of Middle Eastern geopolitics. In the short term, the Persian Gulf War proved to be an unmitigated success. The United States, leading a coalition of military forces with the backing of the United Nations, easily liberated Kuwait and drove the Iraqi forces back towards Baghdad. This Western victory influenced the strategies of many Islamic fundamentalists from North Africa to the Arabian Peninsula east to Afghanistan and Pakistan. A perception was reinforced that the United States and its Western allies would militarily fight in the Middle East to maintain its hegemony and guard its economic interests. More importantly, American tanks, jets and missiles had demonstrated they could not be defeated in these open deserts; radical Islamic forces believed they were left with just one other option.

Radical Islamic terrorism

Depending on how one defines terrorism, this modus operandi has recently been igniting wildfires all over the planet. Some of the violence has been fueled by nationalism, like the destructive acts directed at the Russians in Chechnya or against the Turks by the ethnic Kurds. Some have been the byproduct of civil wars in places like Sudan, Ukraine and Syria. Within the realm of organized religion, extremist views have been most likely to surface amongst those who follow the more dogmatic forms of worship, including Orthodox Judaism and Fundamental Christianity.

While Jews have employed terrorism and guerilla tactics in defense of Israel, and Christians have conducted holy inquisitions and religious crusades throughout the centuries, the use of terrorism by radical Islamic fundamentalists has recently dominated the headlines. Some of this may likely be the byproduct of the inherent bias of the Western media. Nevertheless, Islam is increasingly connected in some way to manifestations of terrorism in the modern world. How can this be explained?

According to Shadi Hamid, in his book *Islamic Exceptionalism*, "Islam, in both theory and practice is 'exceptional' in how it relates to politics. Because of its outsize role in law and governance, Islam has been – and will continue to be – resistant to secularization." He claims that this is not necessarily good or bad per se, *"it just is,* and we need to understand and respect it, even if it runs counter to our own hopes and preferences."

Hamid cites a historical cause behind this phenomenon. Unlike Jesus, the Prophet Muhammad was a theologian, preacher, warrior and politician all at once. He emerged as the leader of a new state and spent much of his adult life capturing, holding and governing new territory. From the outset, religious, political and military functions were entangled within one man. To many, Islam held appeal due to its simplicity. Agree to receive Allah as the one true God and Muhammad as his greatest and final prophet, and the rest was relatively easy. By accepting this tenet, along with praying five times a day, giving to charity, making a once-in-a-life-time pilgrimage to Mecca and honoring the holy month of Ramadan, any person who sought spiritual fulfillment could become a Muslim. In addition, those who agreed to follow the values and traditions of this new faith that developed from the Arabian deserts 1400 years ago could expect instant acceptance through the gates of paradise upon their deaths. This was simple, easily understood and exceedingly appealing to the millions who came into contact with the jihad, or holy war, which spread Islam from the Arabian Peninsula to the far reaches of Spain and Northern Africa in the west, and to India and Indonesia in the east.

In the 12th and 13th centuries, the Christian kingdoms of Europe launched their own military campaigns intended to recapture the *"Holy Land"* from the Muslims. These Crusades unleashed brutal violence that rival the beheadings and killings committed by ISIS today. Throughout history, religious fervor has ignited cruel wars, guerilla campaigns and acts of terrorism. However, a crucial distinction is noted in Hamid's thesis. While millions died during the two centuries of the Crusades, there is no basis for this violence in the teachings of Jesus. The earliest Christians died as martyrs victimized by Roman violence. The value placed by these early Christians on peace and love gradually appealed to many people throughout the Roman world. In this sense, there is a key difference in the origins between the world's two largest religious faiths.

Additionally, there is the Quran. While secularization in the West requires the separation of religion, specifically the Bible, from governmental policy, this has often proven to be more difficult to achieve in Islamic countries. According to Hamid, the Quran is not merely the words of God. For Muslims, it is *"God's direct and literal speech."* The Quran's divine authorship not only places it at the center of Islamic theology, but also political policy, cultural traditions and daily life. While most Muslims do not take the words of the Quran literally, for the radical fundamentalists, there is not much flexibility in its language. They are passionately committed to defending its precepts and traditions.

To a large extent, searching for the roots of radical Islamic terrorism in the history of the Muslim faith involves gross generalizations peppered with bias, controversy and the acknowledgement that there are many exceptions to the rule. The vast majority of Muslims today value peace as much as anyone else and abhor the violence caused by radicals. Furthermore, the use of American missiles launched by unmanned drones in the skies over Islamic nations like Pakistan and Yemen is arguably as morally reprehensible as the methods employed by some radical Islamic terrorists.

However, the last thirty-five years has increasingly been defined by the growing chasm between modern Western culture and traditional Islamic values. To confront the expanding Western civilization, Muslim fundamentalists have constructed a theological fortress. They reject pop culture, feminism and the emphasis placed by the West on the ownership of possessions. There are currently 1.6 billion Muslims in the world, representing just fewer than 22 per cent of the planet's population. When placed on a spectrum, most might be labeled as moderate or even liberal in how they have adopted Western culture, technology and values. Yet a growing number seem to be shifting to the opposite end of the spectrum.

The role of modern technology

New technology has also had a considerable impact on terrorism. For example, one hundred years ago, there were no commercial flights available to be hijacked; yet this has become a tool of many terrorists. Jets can provide potential hostages, they can be commandeered to fly into targets or they can simply be blown out of the sky. In this regard, the Japanese kamikaze pilots established a tactic for modern terrorists to follow. Their willingness to blow themselves up if it meant damaging or destroying an American warship established a precedent for the suicide bombers of today.

There is also more weaponry available today than ever before. Automatic weapons are relatively cheap and easily available. Rising industrialization explains part of this growth, but some of this phenomenon is also due to America's legacy of arming the enemies of our enemies, even if it means those weapons have come back to haunt us. The United States government was willing to share military technology with the Mujahideen in Afghanistan when they were fighting against the Soviets during the late 1970s, but the Taliban then used some of those same weapons against American troops after the attacks on September 11, 2001. Within the United States, the laxity in policy regarding access to automatic weapons has also been a contributing factor.

Besides guns, new technology has also introduced electronic timers and a wide range of explosive devices that are accessible to those who possess the will. When Timothy McVeigh blew up the Alfred P. Murrah Federal Building in Oklahoma City, he placed a bomb in the back of a rented Ryder truck. It consisted of 5,000 pounds of ammonium nitrate and nitromethane. This may sound beyond the reach of most Americans, but he merely had to acquire an agricultural fertilizer and a certain type of fuel oil. If this pattern continues, it is likely only a matter of time before a terrorist acquires some kind of weapon of mass destruction.

Finally, computer technology, the Internet, cellular phones and the rise of social media have also spurred the proliferation of terrorism. This technology has facilitated the communication and education of modern terrorists. It explains the growing dissemination of radical ideology into every corner of the world. Omar Mateen was born an American citizen, but he received his propaganda and political education from ISIS over the Internet. He was successful at killing so many people in a relatively short period of time because of his access to a sophisticated automatic weapon, and he pledged his allegiance to ISIS during the mass shooting over his smart phone. The World Wide Web has made the planet a smaller place, and this alone is a major factor in explaining the growing prevalence of terrorism in the modern world.

Conclusion

For much of modern history, there have been groups willing to utilize guerilla tactics and terrorism. All that was required was a combination of three ingredients. The first element is a strongly held conviction, usually one originating from a powerful force such as nationalism or religious faith. The second is a set of circumstances where this conviction cannot be attained on an open battlefield. The third is a willingness to accept the moral tenet that a political or ideological principle justifies violent methods.

Terrorism and guerilla tactics have been around in some form for thousands of years. Why has their use expanded so much in the past few decades? First, its successful use in the past, which led to the creation of new nations like the United States, Haiti and Israel, has set a precedent for its use today. Second is the growing willingness by radical Islamic factions to use terrorism in defense of their religious and cultural values. Finally, the rise of modern technology to facilitate its use also plays a large role. Others might disagree with this analysis, but however one chooses to answer the question, the roots of any explanation for why terrorism has become so prevalent in the present extends deep into the past.

What can be done to alleviate this growing problem? There are obviously no simple answers. However, throughout history, any nation confronted with an impending war had two options: prepare to fight or turn to diplomacy. The same is true today. The United States and other Western nations can use their economic wealth and military muscle to try to defeat terrorists. This might mean giving up more privacy and freedom in the name of tighter security. On the other hand, these nations might consider *"diplomatically negotiating"* with terrorists in order to address their motives. Both approaches have their drawbacks, and unfortunately, neither is guaranteed to solve the problem anytime in the near future.

Sources and further reading:

Boot, Max. *Invisible Armies: An Epic History of Guerrilla Warfare.* New York: Liveright Publishing, 2013.

Cullen, Dave. *Columbine.* New York: Hachette Book Group, 2009.

Ellis, Ralph, Ashley Fantz, Faith Karimi, and Eliot C. McLaughlin. "Orlando Shooting: 49 Killed, Shooter Pledged ISIS Allegiance." *CNN.com.* June 13, 2016. http://cnn.com/2016/06/12/us/Orlando-nightclub-shooting/.

Hamid, Shadi. *Islamic Exceptionalism: How the Struggle Over Islam is Reshaping the World.* New York: St. Martin's Press, 2016.

"Iranian Hostage Crisis." *PBS.org.* Accessed June 16, 2016. http://www.pbs.org/wgbh/americanexperience/features/general-article/carter-hostage-crisis/.

Jeralyn. "ISIS Releases Dabiq No.4: Yazidis, Sotloff and Attacks on the West." *TalkLeft.com.* October 12, 2014. http://www.talkleft.com/story/2014/10/12/17018/365/wariniraq/ISIS-Releases-Dabiq-No-4-Yazidis-Sotloff-and Attacks-on-the-West.

Law, Randall. *Terrorism: A History.* Cambridge: Polity Press, 2009.

LoGiurato, Brett, and Harry Blodget. "Boston Massacre: The Full Story of How Two Deranged Young Men Terrorized an American City." *BusinessInsider.com.* April 29, 2013. http://www.businessinsider.com/boston-bombings-2013-4.

"Malcolm X Remembered Favorably by Blacks But Not by Whites." *YouGov.com.* February 21, 2015. http://www.today.yougov.com/news/2015/02/21/malcolm-x/.

"Oklahoma City Bombings." *History.com.* Accessed June 14, 2016. http://www.history.com/topics/Oklahoma-city-bombing.

O'Toole, G.J.A. *The Spanish War: An American Epic 1898.* New York: W.W. Nortonand Company, 1984.

Steffen, Jordan, and John Ingold. "James Holmes Sentenced to Life in Prison in the Aurora Theater Shooting." *DenverPost.com.* August 7, 2015. http://www.denverpost. com/2015/08/07/james-holmes-sentenced-to-life-in-prison-in-the-aurora-theater-shooting/.

Telushkin, Joseph. *Jewish Literacy.* New York: Harper Collins Publishers, 2008.

Vogel, Steve, Sari Horwitz, and David A. Fahrenthold. "Sandy Hook Elementary Shooting Leaves 28 Dead, Law Enforcement Sources Say." *WashingtonPost.com.* December 14, 2012. http://www.washingtonpost.com/politics/sandy-hook-elementary-school-shooting-leaves-students-staff-dead/2012/12/14/24334570-461e-11e2-8e70-e1993528-222d_story.html.

Chapter 15

Why has the pace of technological change grown so fast in recent times?

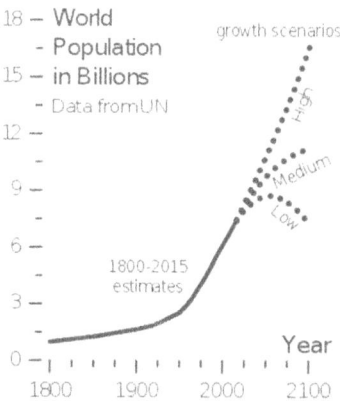

World population estimates from 1800 to 2100, based on "high", "medium" and "low" United Nations projections in 2015 and UN historical estimates for pre-1950 data
Courtesy of Bdm25 (CC-BY-SA-4.0)
https://commons.wikimedia.org/wiki/File:World_population_v3.svg

"Technology made large populations possible; large populations now make technology indispensible."

Joseph Wood Krutch (American writer, critic and naturalist)

"If we continue to develop our technology without wisdom or prudence, our servant may prove to be our executioner."

Omar Bradley (General, U.S. Military)

"Cars will soon have the Internet on the dashboard. I worry that this will distract me from my texting."

Andy Borowitz (American writer, comedian, satirist and actor)

The global average life expectancy since 1900 has more than doubled and is now approaching 70 years. People in the nations today with the lowest life expectancies live longer than people did in the countries with the highest life expectancies in 1800. Over the course of human history, this is possibly the most noteworthy change in the quality of life enjoyed by the human species. Virtually no one today would like to revert to the days when the average human was lucky to reach his or her 30th birthday. This development is almost exclusively the result of the rise in science, industry and technology.

In addition, there is no denying that life is more comfortable in the present than it was in the past. Not long ago, people would have to continually feed wood or coal into a furnace or fireplace just to keep from freezing to death in many quarters of the planet. Prior to the 1950s, there was no escape into an air-conditioned home or apartment when a heat wave hit. In 1936, a heat wave took the lives of over 5000 Americans. When a heat wave struck India as recently as 2015, where many people still do not have access to air conditioning, there were 2500 fatalities. Air conditioning has even had a profound influence on modern demographics. For example, the population of the Las Vegas metropolitan area recently pushed past two million residents. In 1950, the number was fewer than 50,000. With an average high temperature in July of 106 degrees, would this phenomenal growth have ever taken place without air conditioning?

Modern technology has generated physical comforts that surround every moment of our daily lives. In developed countries, electric lighting, toilets that flush and clean drinking water have become so ubiquitous that few people give much thought to how much comfort these technological advances provide. Anyone who has ever experienced modern surgery or even the filling of a dental cavity might take for granted the use of anesthesia.

Thanks to modern technology, the advent of automobiles and commercial aviation has revolutionized transportation. A journey from Independence, Missouri to Oregon City, Oregon on the Oregon Trail would have taken about six months in the 1840s. Today, it would take less than six hours by airplane. The prevalence of automobiles has not only made it possible to live significantly further from places of employment, but has completely transformed the average vacation experience. The result has been a significant rise in the average person's freedom of movement.

Similar changes have resulted in the field of communications. Samuel Morse developed the first telegraph in 1832, and twelve years later the message, "*What hath God wrought,*" was sent over a telegraph line from the U.S. Capital to a railroad station in Baltimore. After much trouble and expense, a transatlantic cable was successfully laid by 1858 so that President James Buchanan and Queen Victoria could exchange formal introductory and complementary messages. Today, they could speak to each other's visual images instantaneously by way of smart phones and the Internet. The rise of computers and digital technology has completely revolutionized how information is disseminated. The world is at our fingertips, though many of the younger generations who have grown up with this technology take it for granted.

Throughout most of human history, people were on their own when it came to entertainment. Evenings might be spent singing songs or telling stories, but there was not much else. Although the printing press was invented in the mid-15th century, it was not until the end of the 19th century that advances in printing technology brought the cost of books down to an affordable level. Since then, there has been an explosion in entertainment options available to most people via new technology including radio, film, television and the Internet. Not long ago, the only way to enjoy music was to listen to a live performance. Today, music is available anywhere and anytime online.

The development of new technology has made our lives longer, more comfortable and more entertaining. For most of that time, these advances came about in a slow, sporadic manner. It has only been over the past two centuries that the pace of new inventions began to accelerate. On March 10, 1876, Alexander Graham Bell transmitted the first coherent complete sentence over his recently invented telephone: the famous, "*Mr. Watson, come here; I want you.*" However, it was not until 1920 that the first telephones were commercialized, and it took until 1946 for them to be used in 50 per cent of U.S. homes. On the other hand, smart phones, as they are known today, did not exist a decade ago, and three decades earlier, no one owned a computer. By 2013, 83.8 per cent of U.S. households reported computer ownership and 68 per cent of adults own a smart phone as of this writing.

According to American author, computer scientist, inventor and futurist Ray Kurzweil in his book, *The Singularity is Near: When Humans Transcend Biology*, the pace of technological change has been continuously accelerating. He writes that the cause behind this expansion has been an idea he dubbed the Law of Accelerating Returns. According to this law, the pace of technological progress – especially information technology – speeds up exponentially over time. Because each generation of technology improves over the last, the rate of progress from version to version speeds up. Kurzweil wrote in 2001 that every decade our rate of progress was doubling. "*We won't experience 100 years of progress in the 21st century – it will be more like 20,000 years of progress (at today's rate).*"

15 years later, the progress made in the first part of the 21st century has been stunning: the global adoption of the Internet, smart phones, ever-more agile robots, and artificial intelligence that learns. The first human genome was sequenced in 2004 at a cost of hundreds of millions of dollars. Now, machines can sequence 18,000 annually for $1,000 a genome. For better or worse, an avalanche of new technology is emerging every year. It has become a prime characteristic of modern life. Younger generations adapt faster and take many of the new innovations that come out each year in stride. For many older people, the quickened velocity is overwhelming. Why has the pace of technological change grown so fast

in recent times? To answer that question, it is once again necessary to dive into the past.

The birth of modernity – Three revolutions

The modern world is largely the byproduct of three revolutions that have occurred over the past five hundred years. The first coincided with the cultural rebirth of knowledge and civilization in Western Europe collectively known as the Renaissance. The Middle Ages, 1,000 years of relative drudgery and stagnation that commenced with the fall of the Roman Empire in Western Europe during the 6th century, slowly and unevenly came to an end. Many Europeans, who had previously known only superstition and ignorance, began to take an interest in literacy, knowledge and reason. The Age of Faith was gradually replaced by a desire to rediscover the knowledge and achievements of the ancient Greeks and Romans. Michelangelo painted the ceiling of the Sistine Chapel, Johannes Gutenberg invented the printing press and William Shakespeare wrote his famous sonnets and tragedies.

Along with this cultural transformation came an economic revolution. Feudalism, which had dominated the Middle Ages, gradually declined and was replaced by a new economy that emphasized the private ownership of property, the rise of commerce and the advent of the profit incentive. Under the tenets of feudalism, wealthy lords had owned most of the land and provided protection in the form of castle fortresses and small armies. In return, the local peasants known as serfs worked the lord's land, shared the annual harvest with the lord's family and were not free to leave or travel without the lord's consent.

After Europeans learned about gunpowder from the Chinese, they used it in cannons to blast holes through the walls of the lord's castles. As the power of feudal lords waned, European monarchs expanded their hold on the loyalty of the people. The rise of larger and more powerful nation-states provided their citizens with greater freedom to choose other options beyond life as a serf. Many moved to growing towns and turned to manufacturing, trade and commerce as new avenues toward greater wealth. The Church had generally frowned upon the accumulation of wealth during the Middle Ages, but with the Protestant Reformation that accompanied the European Renaissance, economic success that resulted from the pursuit of a *"calling"* was seen as a sign of salvation.

At the heart of this economic transformation was the rise of the profit incentive. It did not matter whether wealth was generated by the production of goods or through their exchange by way of trade or commerce; the desire for unlimited riches became the world's economic driving force. The Commercial Revolution that arose to take the place of feudalism created a financial incentive for individuals to explore any legitimate way to earn greater wealth. Coinciding with the rise of the profit incentive was the emergence of the patent system. Since governments now issued patents to protect the intellectual property of inventors, the desire to earn unlimited wealth created a powerful incentive to invent any new product that would appeal to a large market. There was now a compelling reason for people to develop new technology.

For more people to engage in manufacturing, trade and commerce, there needed to be a way for fewer people to grow more food. The second revolution, one that took place in the field of agriculture, accomplished this goal. Between the mid-17th century and the late 19th century, an unprecedented increase in agricultural production took place in Great Britain. Up to 1770, agricultural output grew faster than the population, and thereafter, productivity remained among the highest in the world. The increase in the food supply contributed to the rapid growth in the British population, from 5.5 million in 1700 to over nine million by 1801. During this period, there was a decline in the agricultural share of the labor force, adding to the number of urban workers on which industrialization depended.

Leading the way in the expansion of new farming methods was the move in crop rotation to turnips and clover in place of leaving fields fallow. This move enabled the soil to be replenished with nutrients in a more timely and effective manner. Accompanied by the Enclosure Movement, where wealthy farmers bought and combined smaller plots of land into larger, more efficiently run farms, the Agricultural Revolution continued to gain momentum. There were soon new advances in fertilization, irrigation, herbicides, pesticides and a wide range of new farm machinery. The demographic results of these rather innocuous changes were astonishing. Over 200 years ago, 90 per cent of the U.S. population lived on farms and produced their own food to eat. Today, only two per cent of the population is engaged in the production of food. This created the human muscle necessary to power the third and most important of the recent revolutions.

In simple terms, the Industrial Revolution involved the use of machines, factories and new technology to manufacture most of the consumer goods that used to be produced by hand. Once again, Great Britain led the way, starting with inventions to weave cotton thread into various articles of clothing. By the late 18th century, English textile mills were blazing a path towards new methods of industrial production. Although Great Britain did not occupy much space on a world map, the British Isles possessed the right combination of natural resources; particularly coal and iron ore, along with a growing labor force, an abundance of investment capital spawned from overseas trade, a supportive government and an efficient transportation network. Industrialization soon spread to nations on the European continent, such as France, Italy and particularly Germany. It also leaped over the oceans to such places as Canada, Japan and the United States. By the dawn of the 20th century, the Americans passed the British to develop the most industrially advanced economy on the planet. The American Industrial Revolution provided the United States with a gross domestic product that still leads the world.

During this revolution, national governments in nations like Great Britain and the United States largely allowed individual entrepreneurs to build their mills, mines and factories without much regulation. This laissez-faire approach was one of the definitive principles of the modern free enterprise or capitalist economic model first expounded upon by the English philosopher Adam Smith in his hallmark treatise, *The Wealth of Nations*, published in 1776. Yet while the government granted maximum freedom to capitalists to earn unlimited profits unhindered by regulations or taxes, this did not prevent governments from providing cheap land, low interest loans and other forms of support to the rising industries of their nations. One of the chief forms of support came from the protection afforded by the granting of patents.

Knowing that it would be relatively easy to secure a patent from the government for a new form of technology, inventors understood that a new product that would appeal to a broad market could lead to unprecedented wealth. This created a huge financial incentive to invent. As a result, there was an explosion of new patents granted in the 19th century. Thomas Edison, the inventor of the phonograph, the motion picture camera and most significantly, the light bulb, single-handedly received almost 1,100 patents. In 1800, the U.S. Patent Office dispensed 41 utility patents for new inventions. Since westward expansion offered alternatives to working in a factory, American industrial growth was slower in the years leading up to the Civil War. Therefore, the number of patents issued in 1850 had grown to only 884. Twenty years later it had climbed to 12,157 and by 1915, the number had reached 43,117.

Many of the new inventions went straight into the factories and mines to increase the speed and efficiency of production. In particular, Henry Ford used some of these inventions when he designed the first moving assembly line to produce his Model T automobile. Beginning in 1913, Ford began using a system that broke the car's assembly into 84 distinct steps and trained his workers to do just one at a time as the chassis traveled from station to station on a moving assembly belt. His innovation reduced the time it took to build an automobile from more than 12 hours to just two hours and thirty minutes. This meant significantly lower production costs, an appreciably lower sticker price on the car, and ultimately, a rising standard of living for the American populace. Henry Ford elevated the Industrial Revolution to a level where people could work significantly less and have significantly more.

Less than thirty years later, the life-and-death struggle of the Second World War created a fresh incentive for the development of new technology. In the race to incorporate science to build new weapons like radar, rockets and atomic bombs, both sides in the war pushed to meld two separate worlds into one. Through the late 1930s, university professors generally included purely theoretical scientists who possessed little interest in practical matters. Working in their small laboratories and *"ivory towers,"* they labored to expand our scientific understanding of the universe. Meanwhile, technicians and engineers with significantly less formal education dominated the world of applied science. Their accomplishments and discoveries owed more to careful observation and trial-and-error experimentation than to theoretical science. Thanks to World War Two, these two worlds were joined for the first time in history on a massive scale. The result was a newly created hybrid that drastically changed our world.

The rise of big science

On one side of the Second World War were fascist nations, particularly Nazi Germany, that were fueled by unlimited nationalistic ambitions and were bent on world domination. In order to achieve his goal of greater lebensraum, literally meaning *"living space,"* for his Aryan *"master race,"* Adolph Hitler would do anything necessary to win the war. This is why the Germans connected their theoretical scientists with technicians in massive projects to pioneer such enterprises as unmanned rockets, jet engines and nuclear bombs. The Allies, particularly the British and the Americans, did the same.

During the war, the Allies developed radar technology to detect the presence of Axis bombers and to win the war in the air. Sonar was created to do the same with the threat of Nazi submarines. The effort to break the Nazi Enigma code led Alan Turing, an English mathematician, logician and cryptographer, to create what became the world's first modern computer. However, by far the biggest collaboration between the worlds of science and technology began with the simple writing of a letter from physicist Albert Einstein to President Franklin D. Roosevelt. In this letter, Einstein informed the president about the ramifications of applying atomic theory to the practical logistics of constructing a super bomb. When President Roosevelt realized that the Germans could potentially use this bomb to win the war, he ordered the creation of what later came to be known as the Manhattan Project.

This top-secret project began modestly in 1939, but soon grew to employ more than 130,000 people and cost nearly $2 billion (about $26 billion in today's money). Over 90 per cent of the cost was for building factories and producing the fissile materials, with less than ten per cent going to the development and production of the weapon. Research and production took place at more than 30 sites scattered across the United States, the United Kingdom and Canada. Theoretical scientists were brought out of their laboratories and lecture halls on campuses such as the University of Chicago, Columbia University and the University of California, Berkley to work hand in hand with technicians and mechanics to build the world's first atomic bomb. While Nazi scientists had made some progress, it was the United States that first successfully tested a nuclear bomb on July 16, 1945 in the deserts of New Mexico. Three weeks later, one of these bombs was dropped on the Japanese city of Hiroshima.

It took the financial resources and the power of the national government to create the Big Science that effectively ended the Second World War. However, the intense rivalry that emerged after the war between the two most powerful Allies helped to make Big Science even bigger. The Cold War between the United States and the Soviet Union ran from the end of World War Two until almost 1990. Although these two superpowers never fought face to face, they competed with each other in a range of endeavors across the world map. They each backed opposing sides in limited conflicts in such places as China, Korea, Cuba, Berlin and Vietnam. The Soviet Union looked for opportunities to expand its communist way of life, possibly to insure greater national security, while the United States saw itself as the bulwark to the international threat of communism.

The competition between the U.S. and the USSR led both superpowers to build up Big Science in the name of national defense. Smaller atomic bombs needed to be detonated just to explode the exponentially larger hydrogen super bombs. Jet bombers gave way to intercontinental ballistic missiles, submarines packing nuclear warheads overtook battleships and spy satellites replaced spy planes. After 1945, roughly one quarter of all men and women trained in science and engineering in the West – and perhaps more in the Soviet Union – were employed full-time in the production of weapons to kill other humans.

Big Science combined the practically unlimited resources of national governments with those of massive corporations (in the United States) to enable the two superpowers to compete in a Space Race starting in the 1950s. In 1957, the Soviets used a long-range rocket developed in their nuclear weapons program to launch Sputnik, the world's first unmanned satellite, into orbit. Four years later, they sent the first cosmonaut circling the globe. Breaking from President Eisenhower's opposition to an expensive space program, President Kennedy, who was elected in 1960, made an all-out U.S. commitment to catch up with the Soviets and land a manned spacecraft on the moon "*before the decade was out.*" Harnessing pure science, applied technology and up to five billion dollars a year, the Apollo Space Program achieved its ambitious objective in 1969. Four more moon landings followed by 1972.

Since then, Big Science has only grown bigger. It has become practically impossible to distinguish between the pure scientist and the practical technician. Today, the small university laboratories and the tidy workshops have been replaced by enormous facilities funded by the government, multi-billion dollar corporations, or a combination of the two. In some respects, the rise of Big Science is at least somewhat synonymous with what President Dwight D. Eisenhower warned about in the closing days of his presidency when he cautioned that the growing *"Military-Industrial Complex"* would create or exaggerate global conflicts in order to be self-sustaining.

There is no question that the community of scientists has been growing at an unprecedented rate. Of all the scientists who have ever lived, nine out of ten are still alive today. The number of scientists has been doubling every 15 years for the past three centuries. There were, therefore, about four times as many scientists in 1975 as there were in 1945, just as there were a million times as many scientists in 1945 as there were in 1670. These scientists have, of course, increased the levels of their specialization. No one today can possibly master a broad field like physics or medicine. Instead, an area like physics is constantly dividing and subdividing into new specialties and sub disciplines. In addition, most of these specialists now work as parts of large teams, which renders it increasingly difficult to assign individual credit for any new advance or invention.

In many respects, Big Science has grown into a giant bureaucratic behemoth with an insatiable appetite. It churns out new inventions and new technology at an ever-accelerating rate. While the products of Big Science have given us longer and more comfortable lives, it must be acknowledged that this has come at a price. At some point in the near or distant future, people may look back and ask if it was worth the cost. This topic will be explored at greater length in the next chapter.

Conclusion

After years of rumors and speculation, Apple released the first iPhone to the public on January 9, 2007. By the end of July 2016, over a billion had been sold. While Apple leads the industry, there are obviously other smart phones on the market. By 2017, over a third of the world's population is projected to own a smart phone, an estimated total of almost 2.6 billion smart phone users in the world. The ubiquity of smart phones might be attributed to their many functional uses, but the rapid rate at which new smart phones with new functions come out every year has other background causes.

The first involves growing markets. Technology played a significant causal role in the world's population growth, and so long as the population continues to grow, there will be more people to purchase more iPhones. Apple, Samsung and the other makers of smart phones know this, so they will continue to manufacture and sell their products. In addition, a more crowded planet will inevitably crave new technology that will serve the needs of the growing masses. More powerful computers, the latest smart phones, new social media sites and other forms of technology still on the drawing boards will be necessary to improve, or at least maintain, the standard of living for the tens of millions crammed into the crowded metropolises of Tokyo, London or Kolkata. As Joseph Wood Krutch said: *"Technology made large populations possible; large populations now make technology indispensible."*

The other factor behind the rapid pace of recent technological change is purely economic. The profit incentive is as powerful today as at any time in the past. In fact, the rise of new technology has made the growth of multinational corporations that trade and market their goods all over the planet easier than ever before. The Apple Corporation may be based in California's Silicon Valley, but the iPhone's components come from all over the globe, most of the assembly takes place in China and they are sold in virtually every nation.

The profit incentive that resulted from the Commercial Revolution five hundred years ago created a motivation for the increasingly rapid pace of new technology. The expanding population of the planet brought about by the Agricultural and Industrial Revolutions produced an increasingly larger group of people from whom to earn these profits. The rise of Big Science starting in the Second World War enabled a more efficient process by which to generate new technology. Combined, these forces help to explain much about our modern world, including its growing addiction to new technology.

Sources and further reading:

"Alexander Graham Bell." *History.com.* Accessed December 30, 2016. https://www.history.com/topics/inventions/Alexander-graham-bell.

Berman, Alison E., and Jason Dorrier. "Technology Feels Like It's Accelerating-Because it Actually Is." *SingularityHub.com.* March 22, 2016. https://www.singularityhub.com/2016/03/22/technology-feels-like-its-accelerating-because-it-actually-is/.

Borowitz, Andy. *AZQuotes.com.* Accessed December 29, 2016. https://www.azquotes.com/quote/988542.

Bradley, Omar. *BrainyQuote.com.* Accessed December 29, 2016. https://www.brainyquote.com/quotes/quotes/o/omarbrad131387.html.

Brynjolfsson, Erik, and Andrew McAfee. *The Second Machine Age: Work, Progress, and Prosperity in a Time of Brilliant Technologies.* New York: W.W. Norton & Company, Inc., 2014.

"Comparing Agriculture of the Past With Today." *AnimalSmart.org.* Accessed January 2, 2017. https://www.animalsmart.org/animals-and-the-environment/comparing-agriculture-of-the-past-with-today.

Costello, Sam. "How Many iPhones Have Been Sold Worldwide?" *Lifewire.com.* November 3, 2016. https://www.lifewire.com/how-many-iphones-have-been-sold-1999500.

File, Thom, and Camille Ryan. "Computer and Internet Use in the United States: 2013." *Census.gov.* November 2014. https://www.census.gov/history/pdf/2013computeruse.pdf.

"First Transatlantic Telegraph Cable Completed." *History.com.* Accessed December 29, 2016. https://www.history.com/this-day-in-history/first-transatlantic-telegraph-cable-completed.

"Ford's Assembly Line Starts Rolling." *History.com.* Accessed January 2, 2017. https://www.history.com/this-day-in-history/fords-assembly-line-starts-rolling.

Jacobson, Rebecca. "8 Things You Didn't Know About Alan Turing." *PBS.org.* November 28, 2014. https://www.pbs.org/newshour/updates/8-things-didn't-know-alan-turing.

Krutch, Joseph Wood. *GoodReads.com.* Accessed December 29, 2016. https://www.goodreads.com/quotes/93735-technology-made-large-populations-possible-large-populations-now-make-technology.

Kurzweil, Ray. *The Singularity is Near: When Humans Transcend Biology.* New York: The Penguin Group, 2005.

"The Manhattan Project." *USHistory.org.* Accessed January 2, 2017. https://www.ushistory.org/us/51f.asp.

McKay, John P., Bennett D. Hill, and John Buckler. *A History of Western Society.* New York: Houghton Mifflin Company, 1991.

Mediati, Nick. "Pew Survey Shows 68 Per cent of Adults Now Own a Smartphone."

PCWorld.com. November 1, 2015. https://www.pcworld.com/article/2999631/phones/pew-survey-shows-68-percent-of-americans-now-own-a-smartphone.html.

Moschella, David. "The Pace of Technology Change is Not Accelerating." *Leadingedgeforum.com*. September 2, 2015. https://www.leadingedgeforum.com/publication/the-pace-of-technology-change-is-not-accelerating-25021/.

Overton, Mark. "Agricultural Revolution in England 1500-1850." *BBC.com*. Accessed January 2, 2017. https://www.bbc.co.uk/history/british/empire_seapower/agricultural_revolution_01.shtml.

Roser, Max. "Life Expectancy." *OurWorldInData.org*. Accessed December 29, 2016. https://www.ourworldindata.org/life-expectancy/.

Smith, Adam. *The Wealth of Nations*. New York: Random House, 1994.

Stearns, Peter N. *The Industrial Revolution in World History*. Boulder: Westview Press, 2013.

"U.S. Patent Activity: Calendar Years 1790 to the Present." *United States Patent Office*. Accessed January 2, 2017. https://www.uspto.gov/web/offices/ac/ido/oeip/taf/h_counts.

Chapter 16

Why does industrial progress threaten the future of our planet?

Workers using high-pressure, hot water washing to clean an oiled shoreline after the Exxon Valdez Oil spill in 1989.
Courtesy of the U.S. National Oceanic and Atmospheric Administration (PD-US NOAA)
https://commons.wikimedia.org/wiki/File:OilCleanupAfterValdezSpill.jpg

> *"Only within the moment of time represented by the present century has one species – man – acquired significant power to alter the nature of the world."*
>
> Rachel Carson, Silent Spring

In the central part of India lies a city with just under 1.8 million people. It is considered one of India's greenest cities because of its proximity to two lakes. On the banks of the upper lake sits a national park that is the home to tigers, lions and leopards. On the night of December 2, 1984, piercing shrieks of horror suddenly disturbed the relative quiet throughout several neighborhoods in this city. Something was silently causing people to cough, gasp and die.

An accident had occurred at the Union Carbide plant that made its home in this city. The chemical factory released at least 30 tons of a highly toxic gas called methyl isocyanate, as well as other poisonous gases. Because shantytowns surrounded the pesticide plant, more than 600,000 people were exposed to the deadly gas cloud that night. The gases stayed close to the ground, causing victims' throats and eyes to burn and inducing nausea. Estimates of the death toll varied from

3,800 to as many as 16,000, but government figures now estimate that 15,000 were killed over the years. Toxic materials still remain, and more than 30 years later, many women exposed to the gas have given birth to children with physical and mental disabilities. Human rights groups say thousands of tons of hazardous waste remain buried underground, and the government has conceded that the area is still contaminated.

The name of the city is Bhopal and it has become synonymous with the lethal devastation that modern industry has inflicted upon the planet. Other names that have recently become emblematic for environmental desolation include the *Exxon Valdez*, Chernobyl and Love Canal. While these individual disasters have been cropping up with increasing frequency, the worst harm is more insidious. Every day of every year, the impact of over 7 billion humans scrambling to live the longest and most comfortable lives possible slowly pollutes rivers and streams, poisons the soil and the air and even impacts the planet's temperature and weather patterns.

According to the latest findings, modern humans appeared approximately 160,000 years ago. For the first 159,500 years, the environmental consequences of human activity were minimal. In a few areas, forests were cut down for firewood, certain fish and animal populations were reduced in the search for food and the fertility of soil was reduced due to over-farming. However, the rise of industry and new technology over the last five centuries has wrought greater damage to the planet than all of the previous years combined. In addition, despite the significant gains, such as longer life spans and a more comfortable standard of living, there is much debate over the survivability of the long-term consequences.

Humans live longer today than ever before. On the whole, people also work less but enjoy considerably more goods and services than any generation in the past. This is the result of the industrial progress that began a few centuries ago when a handful of English weavers invented new machines to spin cotton into thread and thread into fabrics. The ensuing revolution sparked changes that went beyond any of their imaginations. Only recently, however, have people begun to acknowledge the cost of this progress. In the long-term, how much of a threat does industrial advancement pose to the future of the planet? Once again, the past must be examined in order to answer this question.

The revolution that gave birth to the modern world

Before 1720, life in England was relatively simple. The Industrial Revolution was still decades away, and Britain was predominantly rural like most of the European continent. However, agricultural output was already at least double that of any other European nation, largely due to the recent changes in crop rotation and fertilization. Consequently, Britain was exporting more grain than it was importing, productivity and real wages were inching upward, and people's lives were improving materially.

Until 1720, England's population growth had been held in check by periodic harvest failures and by diseases such as influenza, smallpox, dysentery and typhus. The increase in agricultural production, however, along with other improvements in the overall standard of living, enlarged the British population by more than 70 per cent by 1800. France still had more than three times England's population, but Britain led in world commerce. In addition, the English had planted viable colonies in the New World and were benefitting financially from a new economic system called mercantilism, which expanded government support for any enterprise aimed at generating greater national wealth.

In the late 17th century, England experienced the Glorious Revolution that transferred political power from the monarchy to elected members of Parliament. London became an epicenter of government, commerce and culture, and its population soon grew to over one million people. The Enlightenment, with its emphasis on science and reason, soon captured the minds of England's leading intellectuals. For the English, these were times of increased literacy, as personal correspondence and other forms of writing were on the rise. Book production had increased along with newspaper distribution. During the 18th century, England's literacy rate rose from 45 to 63 per cent. There was a new vitality in English life, and although few recognized it at the time, Great Britain was on the verge of a momentous change.

In retrospect, the factors necessary to begin an Industrial Revolution are well understood: investment capital, natural resources, a growing population to provide a labor force and expanding markets, efficient transportation and a supportive government that fosters the inventiveness of the people. It just so happened that England possessed all of these features in the 18th century. It took a simple spark to ignite these elements and place Great Britain on the path towards becoming the world's first industrialized nation.

That spark was the textile industry. In the past, textiles had been largely made in people's homes, giving rise to the term *"cottage industry."* Merchants often provided the raw materials and basic equipment, and after a period of time, they picked up the finished product. Workers set their own schedules under this system, which proved difficult for merchants to regulate and resulted in numerous inefficiencies. This began to change in the 1700s when a series of innovations, encouraged by the financial protection afforded by government-issued patents, led to ever-increasing productivity that required less human energy. For example, around 1764, James Hargreaves invented the spinning jenny (*"jenny"* was an early abbreviation of the word *"engine"*). This machine enabled an individual to produce multiple spools of threads simultaneously. By the time of Hargreaves' death in 1778, there were over 20,000 of these machines in use across the nation. English inventor Edmund Cartwright developed another key innovation in textiles during the 1780s: the power loom, which mechanized the process of weaving cloth.

While the earliest textile mills were located on the banks of rivers and streams to derive power from the moving water, the invention of the steam engine made it possible to build these mills anywhere. Coal, which was plentiful in the British Isles, was used to boil water, and the power of the expanding steam became the energy source of the early Industrial Revolution. A number of inventors, motivated by the desire to secure a patent that would protect their intellectual property and allow them to earn more wealth, contributed the ideas that led to the first steam engines. Originally designed to pump water out of mines, steam engines soon powered ships and railroads as well as mills and factories.

One invention soon led to another, fueled by the exponential issuance of patents, and by the end of the 1800s, Great Britain led the world in industrial production. The machines and new technology that dominated the burgeoning English factories now manufactured products that had been previously produced by hand in the shops of skilled craftsmen. Although the English passed laws to protect their industrial trade secrets, men like Samuel Slater covertly took their industrial knowledge with them when immigrating to the United States. Slater set foot in New York in late 1789 having memorized the details of Britain's innovative machines. He went on to build America's first water-powered cotton spinning mill in Pawtucket, Rhode Island, and today is considered to be the *"father of the American factory system."*

While the Industrial Revolution began in Great Britain, it soon appealed to other nations around the world. After all, it not only held the promise of generating vast profits, but of utilizing machines to produce more goods and services with considerably less human labor. While not recognized at the time, the Industrial Revolution also had the benefit of being accompanied by a host of new advances in science and technology that generated cleaner drinking water, better sanitation and new medical advances. These collectively extended people's life spans. In Great Britain, the average life span climbed from about 35 before the start of the Industrial Revolution to 40 in 1800, 48 in 1900, 65 in 1950 and over 80 as of this writing.

Countries with the right combination of capital, natural resources and labor soon followed in England's wake. Nations like France, the Netherlands, Italy, Germany and the Scandinavian countries were well on their way toward full industrial development by the end of the 19th century. Japan also attempted to industrialize when it was rattled out of its self-proclaimed isolation by the intrusion of Commodore Matthew Perry and his U.S. naval ships in 1853. Within 35 years, the Industrial Revolution had so transformed Japan into a modern economic and military power that the Japanese established colonies of their own.

Then there was the United States. The Americans possessed significantly more land and natural resources than their mother country. With a high birth rate and a steady influx of immigrants, the population of the United States exceeded that of Great Britain by 1840. The U.S. also had plenty of navigable rivers for transportation, and where necessary, massive projects to construct canals and railroads were soon underway. Thanks to early ventures in trade, commerce and manufacturing, as well as agriculture, there was ample investment capital available in the States. Finally, the government in Washington, D.C., was happy to provide utility patents to inventors and other forms of economic encouragement and support.

So why did the United States lag behind in industrial growth during the first half of the 19th century? First, the spread of slavery throughout the American South encouraged the growth of a plantation economy that drained investment capital from any kind of new manufacturing. The invention of the cotton gin by Eli Whitney in 1793 had made cotton so much easier and cheaper to grow that a modest movement to bring an end to slavery in the South soon boomeranged.

The second answer lies largely in America's enormous land mass. As long as the frontier continued to attract millions of pioneers to settle in the west, the cost of labor to work in eastern factories was prohibitive. Why work long hours for relatively low pay and under deplorable conditions when the American West called to the populace to establish farms, mines, ranches, and in the case of the South, cotton plantations? It was not until the end of the Civil War in 1865 that America was ready to fully industrialize. By then, huge waves of immigration provided enough cheap labor to construct the Transcontinental Railroad, to work in Andrew Carnegie's steel plants, to build John D. Rockefeller's oil derricks and to work in thousands of other mines, mills and factories. Although few recognized it at the time, the United States had become the richest and most industrialized nation in the world by the dawn of the 20th century.

At the time of publication, it feels like many Americans and other people living in industrially developed nations take their advanced lifestyles for granted. They likely are not aware of how much longer they will live on average than people did just a century before. They enjoy their automobiles, televisions, computers and other *"toys"* that add comfort and entertainment to their lives, but many view the possession of these material goods as almost a fundamental right. They might see a factory's smokestacks belching out dark fumes, sit in congested traffic jams or occasionally wince at the smell of a nearby landfill, but most see this as the price of creating high-paying jobs and enjoying a higher standard of living.

This might not be able to continue indefinitely. While it is impossible to predict the future with a high degree of certainty, there are many reasons to be concerned. The fact that other nations like China, India, Indonesia, Brazil, Pakistan, Nigeria and Bangladesh, seven of the world's ten most populated countries, are striving to catch up with the West through their own technological development, means the threats that emanate from industrial progress will likely worsen in the near future. What are those threats, and why do they menace the future of our planet?

The looming peril

Industrial development, Big Science, new technology. For better or worse, these forces have shaped our modern lives. Some of the negative changes they have effected are not immediately apparent. For example, people spend more time inside with their televisions, computers and hand-held devices. While they benefit from the expanded access to knowledge and enjoy their many entertainment options, they are also quietly experiencing an epidemic in obesity due partially to their decline in physical activity. In 1990, obese adults made up less than 15 per cent of the population in most U.S. states. By 2010, 36 states had obesity rates of 25 per cent or higher, and 12 of those had obesity rates of 30 per cent or higher. Today, nationwide, roughly two out of three American adults are overweight or obese (69 per cent) and one out of three is obese (36 per cent).

Another consequence has involved changes in the workplace. Before the Industrial Revolution, Americans may have worked harder and died at an earlier age, but the majority worked outside on their own land and according to their own schedules. Now, millions spend hours every day commuting in stressful traffic jams just to punch a clock, work on an assembly line or in a cubicle, and then wonder if their employer even knows their names. Rising industrialization has also been accompanied by rising urbanization; therefore, millions of people live in more claustrophobic conditions than ever before. The less personal environment that has come to characterize where millions of people live and work has been linked, in scientific studies, to rising stress, depression and other mental disorders.

The flood of new technology that cascaded from the Industrial Revolution has also had more obvious consequences. For example, while the advances in public health, modern medicine and vaccinations led to drastic reductions in countries' death rates, it generally took generations to convince people to lower their birth rates. The result was an explosion in population. Japan, for instance, had already begun to industrialize in 1890 when it had a population of about 40 million people. Fifty years later, when Japan was on the brink of launching its attack on the United States at Pearl Harbor, its population had grown to 73 million people. The same pattern has been repeated across the planet. After a few generations have passed, the birthrate declines and the rate of population growth stabilizes. In fact, Japan's population has recently begun to shrink. However, because so much of the world has yet to fully undergo the process of industrialization, the world's overall population is continuing to spike upward.

The planet housed just fewer than one billion people in 1800. It grew to 1.65 billion by 1900, 2.5 billion by 1950 and over 6 billion in 2000. Today, the world's population stands at over 7 billion and is predicted to grow to over 9.7 billion by 2050. Trying to establish a point where the world is considered overpopulated will most certainly spawn debates, but until the planet's population growth plateaus, the population explosion must be considered an enormous price to pay for a longer and more comfortable life. In addition, the varying rates of industrial development between the nations of the world have only accentuated the economic differences between nations that have fully industrialized and those still undergoing the process.

A quick side-by-side comparison between the United States and India will reinforce this point. The U.S. possesses three times as much land as India but has only about a fourth of its population. More importantly, despite its recent industrial development and the consequential economic gains, India's gross domestic product per capita is still only about one tenth that of the United States. Americans have considerably more space and ten times as much wealth. Simple geography will explain the first disparity, but the second can be largely attributed to America's Industrial Revolution and its subsequent access to new technology.

Meanwhile, the industrially developed nations continue to amass greater wealth. Many of these western countries were blessed from the start with fertile land, rich natural resources and numerous factors that led to the accumulation of investment capital. With this sizable head start in industrial progress, combined with the dramatic increases in population taking place in the less developed nations, the gap between the rich countries of the world and the less economically developed is bound to increase long before it begins to close. Indirectly, this is likely to contribute to increased military conflicts, terrorism, political instability and the physical movement of millions of refugees. According to the United Nations, there were over 65 million people forcefully displaced from their homes by the end of 2015. After an increase of five million last year alone, stemming largely from the political implosion of Syria, the number of refugees in the world has reached the highest level ever recorded.

The scariest consequence

Another negative outcome of the rise of new technology involves its application to the battlefield. If there is one grim maxim that holds true whenever nations go to war, it is that there is no limit to the human capacity to invent new ways to kill each other. Military experts in Europe throughout the 19th century were particularly vexed by the fact that there was no major war fought on their continent after the defeat of Napoleon in 1815. As a result, they had no chance to try out some of the latest technology in combat situations. Therefore, several traveled to the United States to personally witness the American Civil War.

They were not disappointed. Many got a chance to see the first repeating rifles, the first submarines, the first hot air balloons used for military reconnaissance, the first hand-cranked machine guns, the first iron-plated ships powered by steam engines and the first military use of telegraph lines and railroads. By 1965, when the U.S. Civil War ended, 620,000 Americans had died on battlefields, about two per cent of the total population. This number exceeds the total number of Americans who had died in all wars prior to the Vietnam War in the 1960s. While much of this can be attributed to the fact that every fatality on both sides of the war was an American, the advent of the new weapons also contributed to the Civil War's extreme mortality rates.

By the onset of the First World War fifty years later, the Industrial Revolution that had created the Machine Age naturally gave rise to the advent of the machine gun. This weapon dominated the prolonged and lethal battles of this catastrophic conflict because armies huddled in trenches for weeks and even months at a time to avoid their deadly fire. World War One also included the first use of airplanes, tanks and poisonous gas. Even the then-recent invention of barbed wire was used on the battlefields to slow down enemy attacks.

By the end of the war in 1918, the total number of deaths was close to 18 million. Roughly 11 million were military personnel and the other 7 million were civilians. Never before in history had the world encountered this kind of bloodshed and carnage. Warfare had been around for thousands of years prior to the start of the 20th century. The difference now was not the lust for war; it was the new weapons used in this war that were the byproduct of the Industrial Revolution.

Twenty years later, the Second World War went on to generate a litany of additional new weapons based on the latest technology. If there was any good news, it was that the new uses found for tanks and military aircraft helped to shorten the battles and reduce the number of battlefield casualties. Unfortunately, the introduction of new weapons reduced the adherence to the traditional rules of warfare. It became more acceptable to wage total war against civilian populations.

A sneak preview of this was seen in the Spanish Civil War that occurred between 1936 and 1939. In support of Francisco Franco and his Nationalist forces, the Italians and particularly the Nazi Germans indiscriminately dropped bombs on Spanish villages and towns. Available information suggests that there were about 500,000 deaths from all causes during the Spanish Civil War. Of these, only about 200,000 died from combat-related causes.

During the Blitz, also known as the Battle of Britain, when the Nazis rained bombs down on British cities night after night, it is estimated that more than 40,000 civilians were killed. The English, along with their American allies, got plenty of revenge. Before the war ended, around 600,000 German civilians died in the Allies' wartime raids, including 76,000 German children. In July 1943, during a single night in Hamburg, 45,000 people perished in the vast firestorm.

Further, from January 1944, until August 1945, the United States dropped 157,000 tons of bombs on Japanese cities. On one night, March 9-10, 1945, U.S.

warplanes dropped 2,000 tons of incendiary bombs on Tokyo over the course of 48 hours. Almost 16 square miles in and around the Japanese capital were incinerated, and between 80,000 and 130,000 civilians were killed in the worst single firestorm in recorded history. It is estimated that at least 333,000 Japanese civilians were killed in total, including 80,000 in the August 6 Hiroshima atomic bomb attack and 40,000 more in Nagasaki three days later. Other estimates are considerably higher. Fifteen million of the 72 million Japanese were left homeless.

In addition, because of the racism endemic in the German and Japanese invasions during the Second World War, civilians were deliberately targeted, in many cases, simply because they were in the way. This helps to explain why 20 million Chinese were killed during the war, along with more than 24 million Soviets. Twelve million people were killed by Nazi gas chambers during the Holocaust, half of which were Jewish. All told, 60 million people were killed in the Second World War. Seventy-five per cent were civilians. The motives to kill have always been present throughout history, but modern technology made the killing far easier. Even the systematic methods employed by the Nazis in the Holocaust involved the use of Zyklon B gas, something reminiscent of the efficiency found in German factories.

The acceleration of military technology, which culminated in the detonation of the world's first atomic bombs on Hiroshima and Nagasaki, went on to generate a massive nuclear arms race during the Cold War that followed. This was a horrifying development that only seemed to grow worse over the next few decades. The dark and ugly nuclear arms race, however, had at least one silver lining.

Throughout history, whenever nations had engaged in arms races, they almost always ended up using the weapons they had been stockpiling. However, in this case, the weapons in question were simply too terrifying. The assembly of tens of thousands of nuclear warheads aimed by the United States and the Soviet Union at each other helped, ultimately, to dissuade their use. The fear of igniting a nuclear Armageddon effectively deterred the start of World War Three. The concept of M.A.D. (Mutually Assured Destruction) managed to prevent a global thermonuclear conflict, at least during the Cold War.

It should be noted that as of this writing, nine nations – the United States, Russia, the United Kingdom, France, China, India, Pakistan, Israel and North Korea – collectively possess approximately 16,300 nuclear weapons. This is less than the total possessed by the United States and the Soviet Union during the height of the Cold War, but it is still far more than necessary to destroy most human civilization on the planet.

While traditional antagonists like the United States and Russia, or for that matter, India and Pakistan, have respected the principles imposed by M.A.D., that may not be the case with a rogue nation like North Korea, where the decision to use nuclear weapons might be in the hands of a single man with questionable sanity. Israel has made it clear that it will use nuclear weapons to protect itself, something that could become a real possibility if Iran ever achieves its goal of building an atomic bomb. Finally, there is always the threat that a terrorist group like ISIS could build or acquire an atomic weapon. Thanks to the advent of nuclear weapons, along with the accompanying technology designed to deliver them, the world is still far from being considered a safe place.

One more threat

Barring the start of a third world war, the most negative consequence of the world's industrial and technological development is glaringly apparent. For the last two hundred years, the planet has witnessed the environmental decimation of its soil, water and air. In the quest to build longer and more comfortable lives, industrial development has led to the never-ending mining of natural resources, the cutting down of forests, the building of factories that belch toxins into the atmosphere and the ground water, the burning of fossil fuels for heating and transportation and the discarding of refuse into overflowing landfills. Toxic pollution today affects more than 200 million people worldwide. In some of the worst polluted places, babies are born with birth defects, children have lost 30 to 40 IQ points, and life expectancy may be as low as 45 years because of cancers and other diseases attributed to human-made pollution.

While all forms of industrial pollution can do irreparable damage to the planet, air pollution may be the most lethal. The first major source of air pollution was the burning of coal, which came into large-scale use during the Industrial Revolution. The resulting smog and soot had a serious impact on the health of residents living in growing urban centers. In 1952, pollutants from factories and home fireplaces mixed with air condensation to kill at least 4,000 people in London over the course of several days. A few years earlier, in 1948, severe industrial pollution created deadly smog that asphyxiated 20 people in Donora, Pennsylvania, and made 7,000 more people sick. Acid rain, first discovered in the 1850s, was another problem resulting from the burning of coal. The release of human-produced sulfur and nitrogen compounds into the atmosphere has negatively impacted plants, fish and the soil.

The effects of air pollution on human health vary widely depending on the pollutant, but if the contaminant is highly toxic, the effects can be widespread and devastating. Chemicals and chlorofluorocarbon pollutants created by industry and agriculture have had a negative impact on the ozone layer. Such deterioration of the ozone allows large amounts of ultraviolet B rays to reach Earth, which can then cause skin cancer and cataracts. According to the World Health Organization, air pollution causes about seven million deaths annually. That is one in eight deaths worldwide.

Another major problem associated with industrial progress is deforestation. In addition to the insatiable demand for trees to supply paper and building materials, forests are frequently leveled to create more farming to support the planet's growing population. Forests are quickly disappearing, particularly in developing nations in Africa, Central and South America. One and a half acres of rainforests are lost every second. Humans have already chopped down about 50 per cent of the rainforests that once existed on the planet, and at the current rate of destruction, the rainforests will be completely destroyed in the next 40 years. Not only does this mean fewer trees, less cleansing oxygen, and the displacement of wildlife, but deforestation also contributes to global warming, the number one threat to the Earth's long term future.

What makes the pollution of the planet's oceans and waterways so insidious is that much of the effluence that enters the water ends up in our bodies. Just like air, water has been under assault from numerous types of pollution. For centuries, humans unknowingly contaminated sources of drinking water with raw sewage, which led to diseases such as cholera and typhus. Even today, over one billion people worldwide lack access to safe water and every 15 seconds somewhere on the planet, a child dies from water-related diseases.

Water pollution increased in conjunction with the Industrial Revolution, when factories began releasing pollutants directly into rivers and streams. In 1969, chemical waste released into Ohio's Cuyahoga River caused it to burst into flames. The waterway became a symbol of how industrial pollution was destroying the nation's natural resources. In 2007, CNN estimated that up to 500 million tons of heavy metals, solvents and toxic sludge were released into the global water supply every year. In the developing world, it is estimated that as much as 70 per cent of industrial waste is dumped untreated into the rivers and lakes.

Water sources are also contaminated by rain runoff from such surfaces as oil-slick roads, construction areas, mining operations, dumpsites and livestock wastes from farm operations. Leaky septic tanks, pesticides and fertilizers are among other sources that contaminate groundwater. Over half the American people rely on groundwater for drinking. In addition, groundwater is heavily used for crop irrigation. Many of the advances recently made in public health and modern medicine have been counterbalanced by the many contaminants that enter our bodies via the water we drink.

The rise of the modern environmental movement in the 1960s helped to bring about the passage of the Clean Water Act in 1972. Various other pieces of anti-pollution legislation have followed since that time, and today, the U.S. has relatively clean, safe drinking water compared with much of the world. Nevertheless, water pollution is still a problem. Over 40 per cent of American waterways are considered unsafe for swimming and fishing. Additionally, water resources face an ongoing threat from man-made environmental disasters such as the 1989 *Exxon Valdez* oil spill, during which approximately 11 million gallons of crude oil were accidentally dumped into the sea off Alaska's Prince William Sound. The disaster, which created a 3,000-square-mile oil slick, instantly killed hundreds of thousands of birds, fish and other wildlife and devastated the area for years afterward. Even more oil spilled into the Gulf of Mexico in 2010 after the British Petroleum Deepwater Horizon oil derrick exploded and unleashed over 125 million gallons of petroleum into the Gulf of Mexico.

The industrial progress contributing to the warming of the planet has grown into a major political issue. In the name of protecting industry and the jobs created by manufacturing, there are still high-level politicians that deny the reality of global warming and climate change. This only exacerbates the problem. The reality is that the polar ice caps are melting, and this will cause sea levels to rise. According the National Resources Defense Council, average temperatures in the Arctic region are rising twice as fast as they are elsewhere and the ice is melting and rupturing. NASA satellite images reveal that the area of our permanent ice cover is shrinking at a rate of nine per cent every decade. At that rate, the Arctic could be totally ice-free in the summer season by the end of the century. The excess water will have to go somewhere. Coastal cities across the planet will soon feel its effects.

Conclusion

Why does industrial progress threaten the future of the planet? Despite much of the discouraging evidence discussed in this chapter, there are at least three reasons why the future may not be entirely doomed. The first is M.A.D. Industrial progress has created such nightmarish weapons that only a complete lunatic would ever seriously consider using them. While this remains a distinct possibility, and while conventional warfare has hardly disappeared, M.A.D. has enormous potential to prevent the devastation of a third world war.

Second, the awareness of the deleterious impact of industrial progress on the environment is nothing new. In the 19th century, Henry David Thoreau and John Muir made philosophical contributions to a growing awareness in the United States that our natural world might be in jeopardy. A century ago, conservationists like Gifford Pinchot and President Theodore Roosevelt helped to spearhead a movement that led to the creation of the U.S. Forest Service and the National Park Service. Then in the 1960s, Rachel Carson wrote her historic book, *Silent Spring*. Published in 1962, this book documented the detrimental effects on the environment of the indiscriminate use of pesticides. It helped to start a modern environmental movement that continues to this day.   As a result of this movement, there have been laws passed to restrict air and water pollution, a mounting effort to recycle plastic, paper, aluminum and other products that typically end up in landfills and global agreements to slow down the rate of climate change. These efforts have also given rise to expanding industries in the field of renewable energy.

The third reason for cautious optimism is the enormous potential for the cause of the environmental threats to become part of the solution. In the ongoing debate over pollution and other environmental concerns, many people cite newer technologies as the potential savior to the problems generated by the older technology. After all, the catalytic converter helped to reduce the toxins released from the exhaust pipes of billions of automobiles, and new technology in areas like solar and wind power might eventually replace our dependency on fossil fuels. Ultimately, the question in the future will be whether the development of this new green technology can exceed the pace of the ongoing damage to the environment that has resulted from industrial progress.

Sources and further reading:

"An Epidemic of Obesity: U.S. Obesity Trends." *Harvard School of Public Health.* Accessed January 2, 2016. https://www.hsph.harvard.edu/nutritionsource/an-epidemic-of-obesity/.

Boren, Zachary Davies. "Battle of Britain 75th Anniversary: The Staggering Numbers Behind the Four-Month War Over UK's Skies." *Independent.com.* July 10, 2015. https://www.independent.co.uk/news/uk/home-news/battle-of-britain-75th-anniversary-the-staggering-numbers-behind-the-four-month-war-over-uks-skies-10380910.html.

Bradfor, Alina. "Pollution Facts and Types of Pollution." *LiveScience.com.* March 10, 2015. https://www.livescience.com/22728-pollution-facts.html.

"Britain in the Mid-1700's." *FSmitha.com.* Accessed January 5, 2017. https://www.fsmitha.com/h3/h29-fr.htm.

"By the Numbers: World-Wide Deaths." *NationalWW2Museum.org.* Accessed January 5, 2017. https://www.nationalww2museum.org/learn/education/for-the-students/ww2-history/ww2-by-the-numbers/world-wide-deaths.html?referrer=https://www.google.com/.

Carson, Rachel. *Silent Spring.* New York: First Mariner Books, 2002.

"Civil War Casualties." *CivilWar.org.* Accessed January 5, 2017. https://www.civilwar.org./education/civil-war-casualties.html?referrer=https://www.google.com/.

"Civil War Technology." *History.com.* Accessed January 2, 2017. https://www.history.com./topics/American-civil-war/civil-war-technology.

"Commodore Perry and Japan(1853-1854)." *Columbia.edu.* Accessed January 5, 2017. https://www.afe.asia.columbia.edu/special/japan_1750_perry.htm.

Cookson, Clive. "Discovery of Earliest Homo Sapien Skulls Backs 'Out of Africa' Theory." *BradshawFoundation.com.* Accessed January 5, 2017. https://www.bradshawfoundation.com./herto_skulls.php.

"The Cuban Missile Crisis Comes to an End." *History.com.* Accessed January 5, 2017. https://www.history.com/this-day-in-history/the-cuban-missile-crisis-comes-to-an-end.

"Deadly WWII U.S. Firebombing Raids on Japanese Cities Largely Ignored." *Japan Times.com.* March 10, 2015. https://www.japantimes.co.jp/news/2015/03/10/national/deadly-wwii-u-s-firebombing-raids-on-japanese-cities-largely-ignored/#.WHDmoGQrJjl.

"Firebombing of Tokyo." *History.com.* Accessed January 5, 2017. https://www.history.com/this-day-in-history/firebombing-of-tokyo.

"Gassing Operations." *UnitedStatesHolocaustMuseum.org.* Accessed January 5, 2017. https://www.ushmm.org/wic/en/article.php?moduleId=10005220.

Harding, Luke. "Germany's Forgotten Victims." *TheGuardian.com.* October 22, 2003. https://www.theguardian.com/world/2003/oct/22/worlddispatch.germany.

Hobsbawm, Eric. *Industry and Empire: The Birth of the Industrial Revolution.* New York: The New Press, 1999.

"Japan: Historical Demographical Data of the Whole Country." *PopulationStatistics. info.* Accessed January 2, 2017.
https://www.populstat.info/Asia/japanc.htm.

Lambert, Tim. "A Brief History of Life Expectancy in Britain." *LocalHistories.org.* Accessed January 5, 2017. https://www.localhistories.org/life.html.

Macias, Amanda. "Nine Nations Have Nukes-Here's How Many Each Country Has." *BusinessInsider.com.* June 17, 2014.
https://www.businessinsider.com/nine-nations-have-nukes-heres-how-many-each-country-has-2014-6.

Painter, Sally. "Seven Biggest Environmental Threats." *LovetoKnow.com.* Accessed January 5, 2017.
https://www.greenliving.lovetoknow.com/Seven_Biggest_Environmental_Threats.

"Population Growth." *WorldBank.org.* Accessed January 2, 2017.
https://www.data.worldbank.org/indicator/SP.POP.GROW.

Quayle, Dan. *Snopes.com.* Accessed January 2, 2017.
https://www.snopes.com/politics/quotes/quayle.asp.

"Samuel Slater." *PBS.org.* Accessed January 5, 2017.
https://www.pbs.org/wgbh/theymadeamerica/whomade/slater_hi.html.

"Spanish Civil War Breaks Out." *History.com.* Accessed January 5, 2017.
https://www.history.com/this-day-in-history/spanish-civil-war-breaks-out.

Taylor, Alan. "Bhopal: The World's Worst Industrial Disaster, 30 Years Later." *The Atlantic.com.* December 2, 2014.
https://www.theatlantic.com/photo/2014/12/bhopal-the-worlds-worst-industrial-disaster-30-years-later/100864/.

"Water and Air Pollution." *History.com.* Accessed January 17, 2017.
https://www.history.com/topics/water-and-air-pollution.

Yeung, Peter. "Refugee Crisis: Record 65 Million People Forced to Flee Homes, UN Says." *Independent.com.* June 20, 2016.
https://www.independent.co.uk/news/world/europe/refugee-crisis-migrants-world-day-un-a7090986.html.

Zimmer, Lori. "7 Biggest Threats to the Environment-Why We Still Need Earth Day." *Inhabitat.com.* April 21, 2012. https://www.inhabitat.com/7-biggest-threats-to-the-environment-why-we-still-need-earth-day/.

Conclusion

Portrait of Herodotus, Roman copy of a Greek original of the early 4th century BCE From the area of Porta Metronia, Rome. Courtesy of Marie-Lan Nguyen
https://commons.wikimedia.org/wiki/File:Herodutus_Massimo_Inv124478.jpg

Most historians know that Herodotus was the *"father of history."* This ancient Greek lived in the 5th century BCE and was a contemporary of Socrates. The famous Roman orator, Cicero, first referred him to as *"The Father of History"* because he was the first historian to break from the Homeric traditions and treat subjects as the focus of empirical investigations. Herodotus developed the modus operandi of collecting materials and primary sources, and then critically arranging them in a historical narrative.

Since the days of Herodotus, numerous issues have confronted the discipline of history. How should historians separate the meaningful facts about the past from the trivial? Is everyone's past important, or should the focus stem from the historian's own cultural background? How should deleterious bias be detected and how is it best addressed? What should happen if the primary source record is incomplete or contradictory? Should historians only attempt to chronicle what has happened in the past, or should they also make an effort to interpret its meaning for guidance into the future? Historians have been wrestling with these issues, among others, for thousands of years.

In addition, there is another important function of the historian, although for some, it has come to be resented. Not only should historians study the past in order to make it meaningful to the present, they are also charged with the task of teaching it to the public. On most university campuses, history professors spend approximately half their time on research and the other half teaching classes. Many prefer their academic research to the responsibility of educating students, but both are vitally important.

We are a stronger democracy if the wider electorate is well versed in the story of its past. The role of the history educator frequently overlaps with that of the pure historian, and in many ways, it is just as important. Unfortunately, it often takes a backseat to the academic *"creation"* of history. It has also frequently become bogged down in the chronological regurgitation of the past as written by traditional historians. The end result is millions of adults like my sister Debby, who may possess collegiate degrees but are frustrated by their lack of understanding regarding the past.

There is no single best way to teach history. However, one that is frequently overlooked is the inquiry approach driven by curiosity and relevant questions. Rather than trying to master an elongated timeline filled with an infinite number of details, it might make more sense, especially for adults that have already completed their formal education, to start with questions and then dive into the past to find the answers. In this respect, *Relearning History* was written not to provide an all-encompassing summary of the past, but to model a process for answering questions that originate from the present.

The creation of a chronological narrative summarizing the past was the goal of Herodotus and most historians ever since. This is of limited value, however, to most adults who simply want to better understand the current world and make more informed decisions as citizens of a democracy. Humanity's past is filled with magical and inspiring stories, but in the end, it must serve as a resource, a colossal database, that should be explored to more meaningfully grasp the issues relevant to both the present and future. It all begins with questions.

Acknowledgements

As stated at the outset, the idea for this book originated from a conversation with my sister, Debby Jacobson, who had the courage to admit that her social studies education had left her with more questions than answers.

A huge shout out must also go to my son, Jack, who took a particular interest in this book from its inception. Jack proofread each chapter as it was written, provided invaluable content suggestions and patiently spent many hours on the phone each week reviewing useful suggestions and corrections. In addition, he probably spent more time editing the book once it was completed than I did in writing the first draft.

Finally, this book, like almost every other achievement in my adult life, is the product of a partnership that began 38 years ago. My wife, Dana, spent countless hours proofreading, checking sources and filling in details, and without her help, this book would never have made it to press.

Index

1

13th Amendment, 107, 111
14th Amendment, 18, 107
15th Amendment, 111
19th Amendment, 142

A

Abolition Movement, 111
Agnew, Spiro, 24
Akin, Todd, 25
Al Qaeda, 158
Alcatraz, 124
Alexander, Michelle, 131
Angola State Penitentiary, 124
Anti-Federalists, 30
Apollo Space Program, 200
Arkwright, Richard, 139
Articles of Confederation, 16
atomic bombs, 166, 174
authoritarianism, 40

B

baby-boomers, 126
Battle of Britain, 212
Bell, Alexander Graham, 195
Big Science, 200, 201, 202
Bill of Rights, 17, 18, 42
Bin Laden, Osama, 158
Black Lives Matter Movement, 109
Black Plague, 92
Blau, Francine D., 9
Bonaparte, Napoleon, 40, 42
Brandeis, Louis, 115
Brown v. Board of Education, 18, 108
Brown, John, 181
Brown, Michael, 109
Bryan, William Jennings, 32, 142
Burns, Lucy, 112
Bush, George W., 2, 26

C

Calvin, John, 70, 153
Cameron, David, 2
capitalism, 43, 61, 80, 85
Carson, Rachel, 216
Carter, Jimmy, 24
Cartwright, Edmund, 208
Castro, Fidel, 174
Catt, Carrie Chapman, 111
Chernobyl, 206
Chinese Exclusion Act, 114
Christianity, 152, 157
Churchill, Winston, 34
Civil Rights Act of 1964, 108, 109
Civil Rights Movement, 41, 108, 131
Civil War, 115, 211
Cleveland, Grover, 32
Clinton, Bill, 128
Clinton, Hillary, 24, 26
Cold War, 80, 87, 172, 173, 175, 200
Colonial America, 94
Commerce Clause, 17
Commercial Revolution, 81, 154, 196, 202
communism, 43, 44
conservatives, 84, 87
Constitution, 13, 17, 18, 20, 21, 42
Constitutional Convention, 16
Crusades, 152
Cuban Missile Crisis, 174
culture, 138, 139

D

Darrow, Clarence, 142
Defense of Marriage Act, 116
deforestation, 215
Deism, 156
democracy, 38, 39
Democrats, 25, 27, 29, 32
Dewey, John, 5
Diamond, Jared, 56
dictator, 38, 40
Dine, Jonathan, 25
Doctrine of Predestination, 70
Dubner, Stephen J., 127
Duke, David, 23

E

Eastern State Penitentiary, 123
Edict of Nantes, 155
Edison, Thomas, 143, 198
Edwards, Edwin, 23
Eighth Amendment, 125
Einstein, Albert, 199
Eisenhower, Dwight D., 200
Elastic Clause, 17
Electoral College, 16, 28, 29, 34
Enclosure Movement, 56
English Bill of Rights, 155
Enlightenment, 47, 155, 207
Equal Protection Clause, 107
Equal Rights Amendment, 8, 21, 112
Exxon Valdez, 206, 215

F

fascism, 40
Federalism, 15, 17
Federalists, 30, 31
Ferdinand, Franz, 167
feudalism, 196
Fifth Amendment, 18
First Amendment, 19, 156

Ford, Gerald, 24
Ford, Henry, 198
Fourth Amendment, 18, 19
free enterprise, 43, 61
French Revolution, 42
Friedan, Betty, 112

G

Gandhi, Mahatma, 88
Glorious Revolution, 207
Gorbachev, Mikhail, 87, 175
Gore, Al, 26
Great Awakening, 69
Great Britain, 42, 57, 139, 197, 208
Great Compromise, 16
Great Depression, 55
Great Society, 87
gross domestic product, 52, 67
guerilla warriors, 183

H

Hachiya, Michihiko, 166
Hamid, Shadi, 188
Hamilton, Alexander, 31
Hanukkah, 151
Hargreaves, James, 139, 207
Hebrews, 151
Heinlein, Robert, A., 93
Herodotus, 221
Hiroshima, 165, 166, 171, 199, 213
Hitler, Adolph, 38, 40, 169, 199
Holmes, Oliver Wendell, 19
Holocaust, 170, 213
House of Representatives, 28
Hussein, Saddam, 2, 188

I

imperialism, 58

Industrial Revolution, 43, 58, 81, 92, 93, 139, 141, 145, 197, 207, 208, 214, 215
Iran, 159
Iranian Hostage Crisis, 187
Irgun, 186
Irish Republican Army, 180
ISIS, 161, 181, 191
Islam, 152, 157

J

Jackson, Andrew, 31
James Watt, 56
Jefferson, Thomas, 31, 156
Johnson, Gary, 26
Johnson, Lyndon B., 34, 61, 75, 86

K

Kahn, Lawrence M., 9
Kellogg-Briand Pact, 169
Khomeini, Ayatollah Ruhollah, 157
Khrushchev, Nikita, 174
King, Martin Luther, 108, 115
King, Rodney, 109
Know-Nothing Party, 114
Krutch, Joseph Wood, 201
Ku Klux Klan, 115, 142
Kurzweil, Ray, 195

L

laissez faire, 61
League of Nations, 169
Lenin, Vladimir, 82
Levinson, Sanford, 20
Levitt, Steven, 127
liberals, 85, 87
Lincoln, Abraham, 32
Locke, John, 14
Long, Huey P., 63
Love Canal, 206

Loving v. Virginia, 116
Luther, Martin, 153

M

Malthus, Thomas, 92
Mandela, Nelson, 48
Manhattan Project, 199
Manson, Charles, 126
Marbury v. Madison, 20
Marconi, Guglielmo, 143
Marx, Karl, 43, 44, 62, 81, 171
Masada, 152
Mateen, Omar, 181, 191
McCaskill, Claire, 25
Middle Ages, 106, 152, 196
monarchy, 38, 40
Monroe Doctrine, 73
Montgomery Bus Boycott, 108
Morse, Samuel, 194
Mosaddegh, Mohammad, 159
Mott, Lucretia, 111
multi-party system, 26, 27
Mussolini, Benito, 38, 40

N

Nader, Ralph, 26
Nagasaki, 166, 171, 213
National Rifle Association, 127
National Socialist Party v. Skokie, 115
National Women's Party, 112
nationalism, 42, 168, 188
nativism, 113, 114
Neolithic Revolution, 98
New Deal, 86
New Imperialism, 59
New York Stock Exchange, 68
Nixon, Richard, 24
Northern Ireland, 149

O

Occupy Wall Street, 63
Oklahoma Land Rush, 73
oligarchy, 39
Orwell, George, 63, 82
O'Sullivan, John, 71

P

Pahlavi, Mohammad Reza, 159, 187
Palestine Liberation Organization, 180
Parks, Rosa, 108
Paul, Alice, 21, 111
Pax Romana, 183
Persian Gulf War, 188
Plato, 6
Plessy v. Ferguson, 107
population growth, 92
Populist Movement, 86
Populist Party, 32
Progressive Era, 142
Progressive Movement, 32
Progressive Party, 33
Protestant Reformation, 153
Public Facilities Privacy and Security Act, 117
Putin, Vladimir, 176

Q

Quran, 189

R

racism, 130, 131, 132
Reagan, Ronald, 84, 175
Reconstruction, 107, 115
Renaissance, 153, 154, 196
Republicans, 25, 27, 29, 32
Revolutionary War, 42, 183
Roaring Twenties, 142

Roe v. Wade, 13, 15, 18, 127
Roman Catholic Church, 153
Roman Empire, 151, 154
Roosevelt, Franklin D., 86, 114, 199
Roosevelt, Theodore, 33
Rousseau, Jean-Jacques, 6

S

Sagan, Carl, 174
Sanders, Bernie, 63
Schenck v. United States, 19
Schlafly, Phyllis, 112
Scopes, John, 142
Second Amendment, 19, 127
Second Great Awakening, 69, 122
Second World War, 92, 112, 170, 171, 198, 212
Senate, 28
Seneca Falls Convention, 112
Shaw, Anna Howard, 111
Simpson, O.J., 109
Sizer, Theodore, 6
Slater, Samuel, 208
Smith, Adam, 56, 61, 81, 198
socialism, 43, 44, 62
Soviet Union, 53
Spanish Civil War, 212
Spanish-American War, 183
Stalin, Joseph, 82
Stanton, Elizabeth Cady, 111
Stein, Jill, 26
Strategic Defense Initiative, 85
Students for a Democratic Society, 126
Supreme Court, 15, 18, 20, 117, 129

T

Taft, William Howard, 33
terrorism, 180, 181, 182, 185, 188, 190
theocracy, 39

Thirty Years' War, 42, 154, 167
Title IX, 113
Tocqueville, Alexis de, 68, 70
Transcendentalism, 122
Treaty of Westphalia, 42
Truman, Harry, 34, 108, 166
Trump, Donald, 24, 26
Tuchman, Barbara W., 168
Turing, Alan, 199
Turner, Frederick Jackson, 72
two-party system, 24, 25, 27, 34

U

Union Carbide, 205
Unitarianism, 122
United States, 42, 43, 61, 106, 209

V

Versailles Treaty, 169
Violent Crime Control and Law Enforcement Act, 128
Virginia Statute for Religious Freedom, 156
Voting Rights Act of 1965, 108

W

Washington, George, 28, 73
water pollution, 215
Watt, James, 56
Weather Underground, 126
Weber, Max, 70
Whig Party, 31
Whitney, Eli, 209
Wilson, Woodrow, 33, 112, 169
Woodstock, 126
World War One, 167, 170, 212

X

X, Malcolm, 108, 182

Y

Youth Counter Cultural Movement, 126

Z

Zionist Movement, 184
Zionists, 186

www.ingramcontent.com/pod-product-compliance
Lightning Source LLC
Chambersburg PA
CBHW071353290426
44108CB00014B/1524